Companions of the Peace:

Diaries and Letters of Monica Storrs, 1931–1939

In 1929 a cultured English gentlewoman arrived in the barely settled wilderness of northern British Columbia as an Anglican missionary, intending to assuage her sense of duty by staying for one year. She stayed for twenty-one. The years covered by Monica Storrs's journal entries (1931–9) were at times unbearably hard, the depression compounding what was already a demanding existence. She and the group of women she lived with, the Companions of the Peace, were sent out as 'missionaries of empire.' As the journals progress, Storrs's droll British wit persists but her imperialistic attitude softens as her work draws her into the lives around her. Expanding on the initial mandate to start Sunday schools, foster contact with women, and perform church services, she became involved in assembling libraries, lending money for seed grain, financing medical assistance, and organizing theatrical performances and poetry contests. After her death even the non-British inhabitants of the Peace River district described her as 'one of us.'

Helped by the judicious editing of historian Vera Fast, these penetrating journal entries make for an unusually absorbing read, with rare details for scholars of British imperialism, Canadian pioneering, and women's life writing, but with enough story and humour to engage any reader.

VERA FAST is a retired historian/archivist living in Manitoba. She also assisted in the book *God's Galloping Girl: The Peace River Diaries of Monica Storrs, 1929–1931.*

Companions of the Peace

Diaries and Letters
of Monica Storrs, 1931–1939

Edited by Vera K. Fast

With an introduction by Vera K. Fast and Mary Kinnear

UNIVERSITY OF TORONTO PRESS
Toronto Buffalo London

© University of Toronto Press Incorporated 1999
Toronto Buffalo London
Printed in Canada

ISBN 0-8020-4474-3 (cloth)
ISBN 0-8020-8254-8 (paper)

Printed on acid-free paper

Canadian Cataloguing in Publication Data

Storrs, Monica, 1888–1967
    Companions of the Peace : diaries and letters of
    Monica Storrs, 1931–1939

    Includes bibliographical references and index.
    ISBN 0-8020-4474-3 (bound)   ISBN 0-8020-8254-8 (pbk.)

    1. Storrs, Monica, 1888–1967 – Diaries.   2. Storrs, Monica,
    1888–1967 – Correspondence.   3. Companions of the
    Peace.   4. Anglican Church of Canada – Biography.
    5. Peace River (B.C. : Regional district) – History.
    6. Frontier and pioneer life – British Columbia – Peace
    River (Regional district).   I. Fast, Vera K., 1929– .   II. Title

    FC3843.3.S86A3 1999   971.1'8703'092   C98-932865-1
    F1089.P3S86 1999

University of Toronto Press acknowledges the financial assistance to its
publishing program of the Canada Council for the Arts and the Ontario Arts
Council.

CONTENTS

Acknowledgments   vii

Introduction   3
Vera K. Fast and Mary Kinnear

Diaries and Letters, 1931–1939   31

Postscript   199
Vera K. Fast

Notes   203

Photo Credits   237

Index   239

Map   26

Illustrations follow page 120

ACKNOWLEDGMENTS

Grants from the Social Sciences and Humanities Research Council of Canada and from the Anglican Foundation made research for this volume possible, and are gratefully acknowledged.

The staff members at the Church of England Record Centre, London, and especially Dr Hough, were unfailingly helpful, as were those at Lambeth Palace Library, the Fellowship of the Maple Leaf (with Canon Williams going far beyond the call of duty to unpack boxes at an awkward time in the archive's transfer from London to Lichfield), Friends' House Library and Archives, and the U.S.P.G. Archives in Oxford.

In Canada, thanks go to the Fort St John–North Peace Museum, Diocese of Caledonia Archives at Prince Rupert, the Provincial Archives of British Columbia, the University of British Columbia Library and Archives, the University of Alberta Library and Archives, and the Anglican General Synod Archives. Thanks are gladly given to Jane Fredeman, Jean Wilson, and especially to Janice Dickin, all of whom played a part in bringing this manuscript to life; to the late Hope Symons, who not only provided much information but gave permission to use all material supplied to Robert Symons by Monica Storrs; to Hugh Schramm and David Lewinski for sharing their stories, and to Pat and Nora for their warm and generous hospitality. Many individuals granted interviews or supplied valuable written information, among them former Companions of the Peace: the late Elinor Higgenbotham, Kate Earle, Mary Humphries, and Sr Dorothy Warr; also Joyce McKeachie and her sister, Violet Alexander, Tony Flatt, the Rev. Hugh Mortimer, and friends in the Fort St John–Hudson's Hope area. Mary Kinnear's contributions extend far beyond the pleasure it was to collaborate with her on the Introduction, for it was her resourcefulness and encouragement that provided the impetus needed to obtain funding, and then to persevere in spite of disappointments. Peter, my husband, also afforded greatly appreciated support in providing chauffeur services with good humour for thousands of miles to and around the Peace River country, spending hours in archives and libraries, and still refraining from complaint. And then, of course, thanks to the staff of the University of Toronto Press, especially to Gerald Hallowell, the senior editor, and John St James, who saw the book to completion with unfailing politeness and in an incredibly short period of time.

Vera K. Fast
Winnipeg, 1998

Companions of the Peace

INTRODUCTION

Monica Storrs, a cultured English gentlewoman, came to the North Peace River for one year to assuage a sense of duty, and stayed to fulfil an evergrowing love and sense of purpose for the next two decades. She lived and worked in the Fort St John area, serving the Anglican church, together with her community of women – the Companions of the Peace – who lived communally in a log house known as the Abbey. In her journals Storrs's keen eye and sensitive spirit caught the essence of what life in this wilderness of northern British Columbia demanded from its women on a day-to-day basis, and the writings document her ministry during the Depression years. Storrs, who described herself on arrival in Canada as a 'stuffy old cockney – "green English" if ever there was!' has provided an account with visceral appeal, a document of hardship, adventure, and monotonous routine coupled with hilarious descriptions, simple joy, and genuine piety.[1]

Monica Melanie Storrs (1888–1967) was born to the Reverend John Storrs and his wife, Lucy Cust, at St Peter's Vicarage, Grosvenor Gardens, London. She was the fourth child in a family of six: Ronald (1881–1955), who, as Sir Ronald Storrs was governor of Judea, then of Cypress and later of Northern Rhodesia;[2] Francis (1882–1918), a soldier who died in the great influenza epidemic after surviving the First World War; Bernard (1884–1967), whom Monica helped nurse in his final illness upon her own retirement to England; Christopher (1889–1977), later to become Bishop of New South Wales; and her only sister, Petronella (1896–1978), married to Dr Frewin Moor. There was already a Canadian connection in the family: her grandfather had been an Anglican curate in Halifax and a rector in Cornwallis, Nova Scotia, and her father was born in Nova Scotia.

Monica developed tuberculosis of the spine when only two years old and was bedridden until she was nearly twelve. Her brother Christopher, a close companion during these early years, remembers the imaginative stories and games in which they revelled: 'One of our day-dreams together – I almost hesitate to put this on paper – was a plan to assassinate Queen Victoria! I can't remember whether we were ambitious to succeed Her Majesty or simply to win notoriety by this dastardly deed. But I recall that out of a number of schemes which we devised, the most reputable was the presentation to the Queen of a box of poisoned chocolates, which we felt sure would tempt her to her death.'[3]

This sense of adventure and unbounded optimism, coupled with a truly wonderful sense of humour, was to be a hallmark of the older Storrs as well. Adeline Harmer gives us a delightful glimpse of this ebullient and 'effervescent lightness of touch' in the following conversation: '"How can you go off like this and leave your father's Rochester Deanery full of valuable things and nobody in the house?" "Simply turn the key in the door – the Angels will look after it." "No, Monica, they WON'T, they've got more important things to do." "Oh, no," says Monica, "not in AUGUST! They're very glad of it!"'[4]

Still, not everyone appreciated the wit that could at times be sharp. One of her Companions commented that she 'found her sense of fun a little disconcerting,' while some local residents misunderstood it altogether.[5] On the other hand, many felt her humour to be a major attribute of her personality. Dorothy Warr, a Companion, receiving a telegram that read, 'Welcome Warr to the Peace,' felt Storrs's lighter side to be a delight 'beyond price.'[6]

Upon her mother's death in 1923, Storrs became hostess for her father, now Dean of Rochester Cathedral, until his death in 1928. She then attended St Christopher's College, Blackheath, London, to prepare for service in the Church of England. 'The central work of the college,' which tended to be high church, was the training of women to act as organizers, in dioceses or parishes, of the religious training of schoolchildren outside of school hours.[7] In the 1920s many students were middle-aged women who had cared for sick or dying parents and then wanted job-training that built on their religious interest.[8] Notebooks of Frances Wilmot, a student during the 1930s, suggest that St Christopher's curriculum imparted a thorough grounding in biblical and liturgical studies, and also encouraged creative work in the development of sermons and lessons around spiritual themes.[9] Alumnae of the college were active in Australia and South Africa, as well as Canada, but most graduated to work in diocesan or parochial positions in England. St Christopher's was also the recruiting ground for Eva Hasell and her Sunday School Caravan Mission.

Frances Hatton Eva Hasell (1886–1974) and her companion, Iris Eugenie Friend Sayle (1894–1973), were already well known in many rural and remote areas of Western Canada. Eva Hasell was an Englishwoman of independent means who had worked as a fund-raiser in the Diocese of Carlisle, north of the English Lake District, for the Archbishops' Western Canada Fund, an appeal launched in 1910 by the Archbishops of Canterbury and York for men and money to support clergy on the far western rim of the empire. Hasell's volunteer work included the organizing of Sunday schools, and at the age of twenty-eight, in 1914, she studied for a two-year certificate in religious education at St Christopher's College. There she met Aylmer Bosanquet and Nona Clarke, who for four years worked in Saskatchewan as Sunday school teachers, 'raising the standard of public opinion in this young and growing country, not only from the Church point of view, but also from the Imperial standpoint.' Returning to England in 1920, Bosanquet discussed with Hasell a plan of equipping horse-drawn caravans to reach children in isolated areas. Hasell, who had obtained a driver's license and mechanical training during the First World War, was enthusiastic and put her own imprint on the scheme by insisting on a motor caravan, which she herself would purchase, equip, and drive, with a suitable companion. In May 1920, Hasell and Winnifred Ticehurst, also a St Christopher's alumna, took possession in Winnipeg of a customized Ford truck. This was a 'caravan – much like a tradesman's van in appearance. It was painted black, with "Sunday School Mission, Anglican Church" lettered in red and gold on one side. The driving seat could be completely closed in when necessary, for, besides the windscreen, there were half-glass doors on either side, which in hot weather could be taken off and put behind the mattresses.'[10]

Earlier that spring Hasell had written to clergymen and leading laymen in areas she planned to visit to explain her purpose: 'We would like to come and stay a week in [your] locality, living and sleeping in the caravan and doing our own cooking ... but we should be glad to receive invitations and hospitality at times in order to get to know the people. Where there was a Sunday School in existence, we propose to superintend the school and teach, while the teachers watch. Where there was no Sunday School, we should like to have the children gathered together to form one.' At the end of the summer, Hasell donated the van to the Diocese of Qu'Appelle in Saskatchewan, on condition it be used each summer for the same sort of work, and this formula, of van purchase and summer use followed by donation to the local diocese, became her standard procedure. Her work was formally recognized in 1922 by the Canadian primate, Archbishop Matheson, as the 'Canadian Sunday School Caravan Mission.'[11]

So began Eva Hasell's own lifetime mission. She returned to England every winter and raised funds for the enterprise. Every summer she added to her fleet of vans and 'vanners.' By 1929 there were twelve vans and twenty-four workers operating in eight western dioceses. In 1926 two men applied to be vanners, but Hasell, who kept autocratic control, turned them down. 'The van work,' she wrote, 'was started by women for women.'

After 1926 Hasell was accompanied by her friend Iris Sayle, and in the spring of 1928, they arrived in Edmonton, Alberta, to take delivery of a new van. It was not yet ready, and unwilling to wait until July, the two women set off for the Peace River Block. This was beyond the provincial boundary into British Columbia and was rendered accessible for settlers after 1924 by a railway reaching Pouce Coupé. The land was made more attractive by successful wheat harvests in the 1920s, the wheat grown by farmers who were drawn mainly from other Canadian provinces, the United States, and the United Kingdom. Into this new land of opportunity, on the boundaries of empire, Hasell and Sayle hiked after leaving the train. Their kitbags contained 'a light tent, a knapsack, some books and pictures, a saucepan bought at Woolworth's for fifteen cents, two aluminum plates, two spoons, forks, collapsible cups, and pocket knives.' Over that summer they walked 912 miles.[12] Back in England the following winter, they included St Christopher's College in the lecture tour.

Hearing Hasell at the college and meeting her personally, Monica Storrs felt immediately drawn to Peace River. She prepared to sail for Canada in September 1929, aged forty-one, describing herself as 'middle-sized, middle-aged, and fatally English.' She explained why she felt so instantly drawn to this isolated frontier. 'I feel deep roots because of my family connections,' she wrote to Robert Symons, but even more, 'I needed a much greater challenge. In dear, safe old England, one was welcomed and recognized, even respected, far above one's worth. Was this, I used to think, was this going forth with only faith to sustain? [Our Lord] had not where to lay his head; he had to rub out corn between his hands; and there I was with good meals, a soft bed, and a motor car to drive.'[13]

In addition to this need to live her faith, Storrs felt a fierce loyalty to the Crown as well as to the Church of England, a commitment shared not only by Hasell but by many of her compatriots and especially by the Fellowship of the Maple Leaf, from whom many of Storrs's Companions were later to receive their stipend.

The Fellowship counted Storrs as one of their own and she in turn, after retirement, served on its board of directors. The Fellowship of the Maple Leaf, an organization whose support 'enabled British women to seek em-

ployment, adventure and service to others in the Canadian west,' carried
on its magazine cover the acronym KCBC: 'Keep Canada British and Christian.' Its founder, Rev. George Exton Lloyd, had declared: 'The more we
can do to make that great nation of the future Christian according to our
own Anglican form, the more we are helping to keep them British as well.'[14]

The Fellowship, whose guiding light was Lloyd, after 1922 Bishop of
Saskatchewan, supported the emigration of trained teachers for the public school system. They were to be 'missionaries of Empire' who would
provide spiritual leadership for British settlers and promote the assimila-
tion of foreign children and families. Outside school hours the Fellowship
teachers were not to 'imitate the Jesuit. But we can help to make these
schools British in tone and ideal. We can have a Christian atmosphere in
the daily work. We can give plain scripture instruction to the children on
the week day as far as the law allows, and open and close the schools with
daily prayer.' Lloyd originally wanted men to spearhead the Fellowship in
non-English districts of the province, but, in the absence of sufficient applicants, solicited women, justifying this with a ready imperial illustration:
'We are not asking English girls to go into Central Africa or the middle of
China, but into districts where they will always find a certain number of
people of their own view and instincts.' During the 1920s the Fellowship
of the Maple Leaf sent over four hundred British teachers into Western
Canada, 'a group of educated British women and men who otherwise might
never have considered emigrating,' and in the 1930s shifted its sponsor-
ship towards medical and church workers like Monica Storrs.[15]

Storrs was now committed to a religious mission, in company with other
women already at work in northern Alberta and British Columbia. Versatil-
ity marked their origins and activities. 'A woman might come to Athabasca
(the diocese of northern Alberta) as a vanner, volunteering for the Caravan Mission to teach children in isolated places and conduct worship in
remote settlements during the summer. She could then become linked
into the diocesan social service department as the vans distributed [Wom-
en's Auxiliary] bales. Her summer travelling might end with a stint at ...
Sunday School-By-Post headquarters, or she could volunteer to stay through
the winter. In subsequent seasons she might return to the vans, or work at
vacation bible schools, or diocesan summer camps. Alternatively, she might
move into hostel work or become a licensed Bishop's Messenger.'[16]

The reference to 'conducting worship' draws attention to the women's
religious vocation. Many women extended the boundaries of traditional
women's work in a parish setting towards duties that could be interpreted
as more presbyterian in nature. Here, too, many were British who had

graduated from St Christopher's College, although they were joined by Canadian women who had attended the Anglican Women's Training College in Toronto.[17] Marguerita Fowler, like Storrs a sincere Christian in her forties, was 'looking for a challenge in missions after the death of her parents.' Fowler attended St Christopher's and in 1927 met Hasell, who then directed her towards the diocese of Brandon in western Manitoba. Bishop Thomas commissioned her as a Bishop's Messenger, a position that included 'the taking of services, visiting and administering comfort to the isolated and sick ... and in the absence of a priest or deacon to baptize children in danger of death and to bury the dead.'[18] Fowler worked out of Swan River, a town near the boundary between Saskatchewan and Manitoba, and founded a community, St Faith's House, which accommodated up to five women at a time. At St Faith's the women 'took vows of obedience and of regular prayer ... Their primary commitment was to the parishes and the people; St Faith's provided the place of spiritual refreshment and exchange of ideas.'

While Hasell and Sayle wore practical brown uniforms, Fowler's dress resembled the habit of a nun – a blue smock with a cross on the front, and a blue veil. Later Storrs adopted a similar dress, but for several years Companions simply wore smocks over their riding clothes. Not all her workers appreciated this uniform, however. Hope Symons referred to the 'horrible, oh ghastly smocks,' and noted that gradually they were no longer required.[19]

There was one distinction between the two communities of women: although Storrs worked well with her local bishop, jurisdictionally the tie was never as close or direct as Fowler's to the Bishop of Brandon.[20] Distance alone may have accounted for this.

Both communities incorporated social-welfare work into their outreach. Both were empire builders, and both were closely connected with Hasell's regular summer intake of vanners.[21] They were inspired by her, were drawn into her orbit, and agreed with her that as Christians, they wished to 'make God and his world more wonderful.' They were also denominationally loyal: they wished to keep an Anglican, as well as an imperial, flag flying. Whether they acknowledged it or not, their initiative can only be understood in the context of the intellectual and political strategy of the participants, both men and women, in the women's movement of the Church of England.

Women were described as 'the mainstay of every religious assembly of whatever class' by Charles Booth in his sociological analysis of London in the 1880s, and twenty years later, a study showed that twice as many women as men attended services in the Church of England. In England, within the established church, 'the wonderful work accomplished by the mainly volunteer efforts of women' was responsible for 'the immense expansion of activity and of efficiency in ministry to the religious needs of the people,' according to *The Ministry of Women*, a report produced by a committee appointed by the Archbishop of Canterbury in 1919. Much women's work was done under male supervision and direction. However, from the middle of the nineteenth century, some churchwomen, while professing a sincere faith, pushed for greater independence of action and judgment of their own, and some called for equality. The women's movement in the Church of England grew to support the claims of women to more autonomy, explicit official recognition, and eventual equality with men within the church.[22]

By the beginning of the twentieth century, some women worked in the church on a voluntary basis and some were paid, and institutions like St Christopher's were founded specifically to provide both theological and practical training for them. Leadership in the women's movement came not so much from women educated at St Christopher's, however, as from women and men who had attended universities, whose education was on a par with clergymen's.

A focal point of discontent for women in the church crystallized in 1897 and 1898, when parochial church councils were established 'to quicken the life and strengthen the work of the Church' by admitting laymen into church governance. In the Upper House of Convocation, the bishops narrowly defeated a vote to allow women to be members of the new councils. 'This skirmish was responsible for creating Church feminism.'[23] As the male hierarchy continued to develop a firmer hold on all levels of church government, an increasingly sophisticated feminist critque was put forward within and without the church. A major church feminist, both as an intellectual and an exemplar of direct action, was Maude Royden.

In many pamphlets and books Royden analysed the topic of women and Christianity, and women and the church. An Oxford graduate, and former settlement worker, she was thoroughly conversant with the theological and social arguments for women's subordination, and in opposing them drew on her scholarship and down-to-earth knowledge of human nature to promote the idea of women as full spiritual and social human beings. Banned from Church of England pulpits, she nevertheless preached regularly in other buildings. Royden characterized the church's waste of women's spirituality as sacrilege. A charismatic leader, she wanted nothing short of parity for women in the church, and saw no satisfactory reason that could stand in the way of women's ordination.[24]

Besides the spectacular Royden, many women worked within church committees in attempts to make small inroads into the hardening intransigence of the Anglican hierarchy, and could claim some achievements in their attempts to have women's vocations recognized. In 1920 the Lambeth Conference, prime consultative body of the Church of England, gave approval in principle for the establishment of an Order of Deaconesses. A deaconess was allowed to prepare for baptism and confirmation, to assist at, and administer baptism in case of necessity, to pray with and give counsel to women, and, with the approval of the bishop and parish priest, to read morning and evening prayer in church: a list of tasks much like the commission received by Marguerita Fowler at St Faith's. In England, however, the church was still wrangling over the specific significance and applications of the Order of Deaconesses into the 1970s.[25] The personal experience of many women workers was to receive 'a combination of condescending gratitude and tedious warning about the danger of women abandoning their home and family in favour of outside work.' They had 'no definite status,' and received 'no official recognition or authorization' from church leaders.[26]

Had Storrs remained in England, she might have become a deaconess, a settlement worker like Cecilia Goodenough, or a Village Evangelist, working for the organization co-founded by another friend, Evelyn Gedge. All these opportunities for women in the church involved serving under the supervision and authority of male clergy. Women who felt a strong vocation would undoubtedly feel frustrated by the brakes put on their enthusiasm, and the more adventurous set their sights on the empire. 'Overseas missionary activity in the empire was a particularly strong magnet.'[27]

It is no exaggeration to suggest that the vocations of Hasell and Storrs could not have found an outlet in England without ecclesiastical rebuke or even prohibition. Fowler, who always worked closely with diocesan authority, might possibly have been permitted to flourish. The examples of Hasell, Storrs, and Fowler, well known to (if not welcomed by) all the bishops in Western Canada, showed it was possible for women to live lives of effective commitment to the gospel without direct male supervision.

Monica Storrs was no self-conscious feminist. In her accounts of life in Peace River, she sought to divert attention away from herself. Firmly in the tradition of generations of women workers in the church, as much social worker as spiritual leader, she found a useful niche for her talents and interests. In the process she smoothed and enriched the lives of others – women and children in the far-ranging neighbourhood, and her own Companions. Through her letters she imparted spice and excitement to the circle of readers in the old country, where she could always count on the spiritual and moral support of her family, friends, and readers of her diaries.

Storrs was conscious of a burden placed upon her that was not placed upon male clergy. When she felt dispirited because of complaints about 'this objectionable quality of Englishness' levelled against her, she sighed, 'The funny thing is that although Brother Wolfe [the rector, George Wolfendale] is just as English as we are, it doesn't go against him so much. Partly, I think, because he is a man.'[28] Yet Storrs herself consistently deferred to male clergy, even to those younger in years and experience. Hope Symons complained that 'she had this almost reverence for Bruno [the Rev. Russell Brown] or *any* priest or any bishop.'[29] While in actual fact Storrs took orders only from the far distant Bishop of Caledonia, she deliberately placed herself under the authority of the local rector, 'in the interest of Church discipline,' as she wrote in her journal.[30] She was, after all, a product of her time and station in life. She was not Maude Royden.

Storrs's directives from the bishop, remarkably like those given to Fowler, were simple and very general: to conduct Sunday schools, to foster contact with women, and to conduct church services and funerals in the absence of regular clergy. To fulfil this mandate she 'went out on these awful rides,' complained a Companion. 'It was absolutely foolish. We would ride when no Canadian would go out.'[31] Storrs was commissioned by the bishop rather than licensed as a lay reader, as were Hasell's vanners, and was by all reports an excellent preacher who also 'prayed beautifully.'[32] True to her nature, she went far beyond the parameters of her assignment. Among a myriad other things she assembled libraries, lent money for seed grain, distributed used clothing from England, financed emergency medical assistance, and organized theatrical performances and poetry contests.

In spite of her hard work and absolute dedication, her 'Englishness' weighed heavily on Storrs, primarily because it formed a barrier between her and some of those she was hoping to serve. 'It is a difficult quality to shake off or grow out of and what's more, who in their senses would *want* to grow out of it? It's all rather a puzzle to me. If our English speech and manners and way of thinking really hinder the Kingdom of God anywhere, we simply must try to give them up. And yet – well – it's not very easy,' she wrote on one occasion.[33] Some of her English ways of thinking, evidenced also by Hasell and to a lesser extent by Fowler, were unselfconscious expressions of her love of monarchy and empire instilled from birth, such as bringing records of the king's speech to Sunday School for the children to hear. She simply wished to share with others what she herself loved so deeply. Some of her Englishness, however, was defiantly monarchist. For example, she gleefully recorded watching the women's faces as her housewarming shower gift, which included a framed picture of the king, was opened. Hope Symons, herself English, disliked the daily ritual of standing at attention while raising and lowering the flag. 'I couldn't stand it.'[34]

Yet in time Storrs's fierce devotion to imperial emblems was overshadowed by a deep and fervent love for the people among whom she lived and ministered. When interviewed some thirty years later, not one voice from approximately seventy-five was raised to comment on her Englishness, but many spoke of her as 'one of us.' Indeed, when she visited the area in 1958, the *Alaska Highway News* headlined, 'That great old pioneer, Miss Monica Storrs, is in the country again.'[35] And on her death, a memorial service held in Fort St John referred to her as 'the revered Monica Melanie Storrs.' She finally belonged.[36]

One important reason for belonging, aside from her genuine love for and service to the people, was that Storrs no longer had her eyes 'constantly fixed' on the mother country. Albert Memmi observed that '[c]olonials tended to glorify the homeland with its positive values, good climate, harmonious landscape, social discipline, and exquisite liberty, beauty, morality and logic.'[37] As early as 1934 Storrs had moved a long way from such a mindset. When one of her boarders was invited to England to live for a time, she noted, '[R]ather sadly, I think, England has come to be a sort of unattainable Paradise of Prosperity' to the Fort St John community.[38] By 1939, Storrs, as she affirmed in her last diary entry, had *two* homes, and was no longer compelled to romanticize one above the other. Certainly, she longed at times for the creature comforts of England – she came, after all, from the elegant Rochester deanery – but it was her yearning for the services of the cathedral that are most poignant.

The diaries trace her struggle as she began to relinquish her desire to Anglicanize the community: 'Cecilia and I have talked about this a great deal, and sometimes wondered even whether there is any hope that our Church will strike root and flourish in this corner of Canada. The mentality of the people and their whole spiritual aproach are so entirely different from ours,' she wrote. 'And yet we are always brought to the same conviction in the end, that even if this whole block were ultimately to become United Church or Presbyterian, the Anglican contribution would not have been wasted. It has a richness and strength and objectivity which, in so far as we can express them faithfully in our life and teaching, can be used by God to influence the spiritual life of this country, whatever church seems to prevail.'[39] This serene acceptance became even more pronounced as she grew older. Duncan Cran, people's warden at St Martin's, wrote to Robert Symons in 1970 that in one of Storrs's last sermons she declared, 'When Our Lord meets you he won't care what denomination you are and perhaps he won't know!'[40]

While some may have seen this acceptance as a mitigation of her Englishness, Storrs's devotion to the Anglican church and its practices never wavered. For her, prayer remained a joyous and personal encounter with God, a living relationship that shaped her life, gave meaning to her work and enabled her to react with calmness and presence of mind when misery, tragedy, drought, and sudden death intruded upon her little world. Dorothy Warr, who arrived in the Peace later during Storrs's ministry, maintained, 'It was obvious that to Monica the hour soon after 6 a.m. [her time for prayer] was the source from which all strength was drawn.'[41] The cultural patina may have worn thinner, but the core of faith continued to blossom.

Many of those interviewed in 1992 remembered Storrs's church work, her empathy with the women and their difficult lives, and the comfort and help she brought, and, surprisingly, they also spoke of her work with the girl guides and boy scouts, surely very English institutions. Guiding was in Storrs's very blood. Not only was she herself an active participant, but on a visit to her brother, Sir Ronald Storrs, in Jerusalem, she organized the first company in that city. Now throughout the Peace River country she did the same. Storrs did not consider it incongruous to teach camping and survival skills to children who lived their lives in the bush. She saw guiding in quite a different light. In an interview with the *Victoria Times* in January 1936, she commented, 'Breaking the deadly monotony of existence imposed by the isolation and the long, rigorous winters, the Girl Guide movement, adapted to meet the peculiar conditions, is proving a most helpful and healthy influence for the children of the Peace River district.'[42] 'Adapting' provided the key. Storrs did not rigidly implement English guiding practices, but used them as vehicles to provide much needed youth activity for the community. Her 'happy' idea of recruiting both boys and girls into companies that she called 'tribes,' an innovation 'hailed with enthusiasm by the children and their parents as an outlet for youthful spirits,' attested to her success, as did the eagerness of the children, even older teenagers, to participate. 'After all,' she once reflected, 'what else is there for them to do?'[43]

This lack of anything to do except endless, monotonous, back-breaking work was the lot of most pioneer women and even many children. Hardest of all to bear, however, was the isolation. It was more tolerable for those who by temperament enjoyed solitude or for those who had gladly consented to leave their homes for the frontier, but Storrs also encountered and grieved with women who had never adjusted, who came because there was no alternative. They had no close neighbours with whom to share a moment of relaxation, or to give encouragement or comfort; and no refuge from abuse. Storrs noted the vast distances between farms for those on the edge of settlement and visited one woman who had not seen another for almost two years. Hasell had a more extreme story. She told of a former school teacher who had borne nine children, but after resettling had not seen another woman for seventeen years. 'She finally became mental and committed suicide.' Visiting in the Peace River Block, Hasell, and Sayle 'walked twenty miles there and twenty back and never saw another house or family all the way.'[44]

Men had occasion to leave the farm to buy or sell products, or to go to work at harvesting or road-building, but a woman with children rarely left the homestead. The husband's absence might be temporary – a few days for buying, a few weeks for harvesting – but a man who went out on the trap lines or freighting might be away for several months at a time. During his absence the woman was expected to assume responsibility not only for the children and their education, but for the farm and livestock, chopping wood, melting snow, milking cows, and feeding horses, pigs, and chickens.

Women were the primary caregivers in time of illness or accident. There were fevers and childhood illnesses among frontier children, just as anywhere in the world, and occasionally there were serious accidents and life-threatening diseases. Women gave birth without medical assistance of any kind, in both simple and complicated cases, and sometimes they gave birth alone without even a husband present. Dental problems were ignored. There was nothing on which to feed the mind; all culture such as music was non-existent unless provided within the family, for very few could afford even battery-operated radios. For the religious, life from birth to death was lived without benefit of clergy. All this Storrs saw and recorded.

She did more than record, however. She attempted to mitigate the isolation – cultural, spiritual, and physical – by her visits and other means already mentioned. Early in her ministry she built a log home to serve as her base. She herself intended to call it Peace Cottage, but Ken Birley christened it the Abbey and so it remained. When Storrs finally left the Peace she donated the Abbey and its land to the diocese of Caledonia; in 1969 the entire property was expropriated by BC Hydro. But here, from 1931 to 1950, she sheltered those in need for days or sometimes months, hosted lonely teachers, entertained women's groups, and finally used the premises as a hostel for children who could not otherwise have attended school. Not all her co-workers were unreservedly enthusiastic about having the children. Certainly, it meant taking responsibility for the day-to-day activity of lively teenagers and children as young as ten years of age when the Companions already had other duties, often far from home. It entailed a significant invasion of the Companions' privacy and raised the problem of confidentiality when those in trouble came to the door. It also involved extra cooking and Storrs herself was no cook. 'Some of those curds we had to eat! Dreadful! And the ghastly liver, cold or boiled and cut up in macaroni; it was so absolutely revolting,' remembered Hope Symons.[45] Cecilia Goodenough voiced her misgivings right from the start, but Storrs remained firm in her resolve. Some of her Companions said she was 'very obstinate,' and this may well be a case in point. She strongly believed the need of the children outweighed the imposition on her household, and on this belief she acted, with or without the approval of the others.

Storrs may also have reasoned that the Companions were not permanent residents at the Abbey as she herself was. Most stayed for several years, then either returned to responsibilities in England, went on to other work in Canada, or married and raised families. This led to the necessity of periodical recruitment, and here she took a page from Hasell's book: she visited St Christopher's College, speaking in chapel and to students individually. Most, therefore, although not all of her workers were graduates of St Christopher's. Word of mouth, the circulation of her letters, and contact with the Fellowship of the Maple Leaf supplied the other recruits. An interview by Storrs herself if she were in England, or with Adeline Harmer or Evelyn Gedge if she were not, a check of credentials including a reference from the parish, a list of things to bring, and the volunteer was off to Canada. When Storrs was unable to interview the candidate personally, she wrote long letters full of information and advice. In one such missive to a Miss Thomson, Storrs cautioned her to bring warm clothing and strong overalls, not 'feeble fanny slacks such as city people wear on holidays.'[46]

On arrival in Canada the new Companion travelled by train to Edmonton and then to Pouce Coupé, where she was met by Storrs herself or someone delegated to act for her. The moment of truth had arrived; the work was about to begin.

Not all workers for Storrs, Hasell, or Fowler were motivated by a sense of mission or even by an imperial imperative. Muriel Secretan, an associate of Fowler's, admitted freely that she volunteered because of a desire for adventure, and because her family 'didn't know what to do with me.'[47] Isa

McArthur initially came to Canada in rebellion against her father's insistence that she join the family's chiropody practice. 'I couldn't stand the way [he] was trying to control me,' she remembered later.[48] A Moral Rearmament conference in Oxford upon McArthur's return to England significantly altered her attitude, and a subsequent year as a Companion in the Peace River country proved memorable for all concerned because of her leadership and hard work. She did not remain long in Canada, however, but in the end returned to become a chiropodist in partnership with her insistent father. Some workers, such as Jean Ingram, had never considered overseas missions, but expected to serve as parish workers in England until confronted by Hasell, Fowler, or Storrs, or even the principal of St Christopher's.[49] Hasell represented those who felt a vocation for the mission field, but considered themselves too old or too lumpish to learn a new language and therefore chose work in an English-speaking country.[50] And for a few, service as missionaries in a country boasting many more men than women was a stepping-stone to marriage, whereupon they themselves joined the ranks of the homesteaders, only now with a double burden of work, for most elected to give time for ministry as well as for the farm.[51]

The friendships formed between Storrs and her Companions, especially with Adeline Harmer and Cecilia Goodenough, were clearly very close. While the community viewed Goodenough and Storrs as firm friends as well as co-workers, there were, in fact, sharp differences between the two, carefully hidden to preserve an outward façade of unity. Goodenough, considerably younger than Storrs, saw herself as more tactful in personal contacts, and better equipped to deal with the daily grind of pioneer life. Certainly she was a better cook and better on horseback. Harmer wrote of her: 'Cecilia ... was one of those people who could turn her hand to anything. I know Storrs rather envied her the way she was able to sit down and straight away write out her Sunday School lesson or sermon.'[52] Kate Webber, another Companion, saw Goodenough as 'one of those staggeringly clever and efficient women – terrifying in a way.'[53] Storrs's tendency to show amusement rather than annoyance or anger but always picking up on a bungle ('She'd say "coo coo" – she'd never let it go by – it used to drive me absolutely mad'), was an irritant to several other Companions as well as to Goodenough.[54] Read carefully, the diaries reveal a growing tension between the two women, accelerating until Goodenough moved into her own tiny home in Taylor (ostensibly to accommodate a growing need in the Sunday School). It culminated in her rather precipitous return in 1936 to England. This friendship proved to be a friendship of accommodation.

Adeline Harmer's relationship with Storrs, by contrast, began as a family connection when Harmer's father was elected Bishop of Rochester and Storrs's was Dean of the cathedral. When the families became close personal friends, the ready devotion between the two daughters deepened with the years. They worked together at various times, belonged to many of the same organizations, moved together into the lovely cottage, Peacewood, on retirement, and finally were buried together in the same grave. Storrs's Rochester friend, Monica White, referred to their friendship as 'quite outstanding, very noteworthy.'[55] Surely both Storrs and Harmer must have been aware of the assumption in some minds that theirs was a sexual relationship. After all, a change in attitude towards close friendships between women had occurred around the time of the Great War, a change well documented by, among others, Lillian Faderman in *Surpassing the Love of Men*. If so, they were entirely unapologetic and unselfconscious. All evidence in interviews with family, friends, and former Companions, and in their writings, indicates that their relationship was a deeply nurturing and loving friendship. 'Our century has a passion for categorizing love,' writes Faderman, 'as previous centuries did not, which stems from the supposedly liberalized twentieth century view of sex, that, ironically, has created its own rigidity.'[56] There is no evidence that this 'passion for categorizing love' among their contemporaries in any way affected Storrs's relationship with Harmer or, indeed, with any of her other Companions. Nor did the people among whom she worked seem to attribute sexual connotations to the relationships between the single women living at the Abbey, or to their work with other women in the community. It appears that they enjoyed a caring, supportive lifestyle, unsullied by suspicion and innuendo.

Fowler, who 'understood people' according to Claire Adams, a Bishop's Messenger, seems to have been more sensitive to the potential for gossip. In her orientation of new workers she 'explained the difficulties of two women working together, either in being too close or too hateful.'[57] There is no record of Hasell addressing the situation, even though her vanners worked in couples and slept together in their van. What the community thought was also unrecorded. One can project that the isolation and the unmitigating pressure of homesteading tended towards fostering a greater acceptance of many issues, including close friendships between women.

THE PEACE RIVER BLOCK IN BRITISH COLUMBIA, to whose people Storrs devoted herself, consisted of 3.5 million acres of land in the north-east corner of the province, received by the Canadian government from the province in return for the building of the Canadian Pacific Railway, and held by Canada until 1930. Although the Geographical Survey of Canada made observations related to the area in the 1880s and 1890s, it was not until 1904 that actual surveying in the Block began, with most of the work completed by 1912.[58]

This land of Monica's adoption was ruled by the steep-banked, mighty Peace River, which, according to legend, derived its name from a treaty of peace made between warring Native bands. The river has its source in the confluence of the Finlay and the Parsnip Rivers, which amused Monica, who laughed, 'To think that so great a Peace should issue from a "Parsnip"!'[59]

The river flows through mountains and long grass meadows, forests of white spruce and poplar, and parkland similar to that of the northern pairies. Yet it was the plateau lands that were to be the greatest challenge for new settlement, with 'splendid soil for agricultural purposes,' according to the surveyors' reports, but also with late and early frosts that made agriculture uncertain.

As everywhere in North America, however, long before the settlers arrived, the land was inhabited by Native peoples – here, the Beaver, Dene of Athapascan stock, who, along with the Cree and Chipewyans, signed Treaty number 8 with the Canadian government in 1899. In the census of 1931, the year Monica Storrs's diaries in this volume commence, 779 Indians are listed as resident in the areas around Fort St John, with hunting and fishing still their main source of livelihood.[60] They were migrants and rarely entered the village, although several traders in outlying areas dealt with them. Also, the local doctor served as their medical officer. Storrs mentions Native people only in passing, but then with sympathy for their poverty and admiration for their handiwork.

Traders entered the area in search of the coveted beaver, and Fort Vermillion was built by the North West Company in 1788, Fort McLeod in 1792, Fort Dunvegan and Rocky Mountain House (further south) in 1805, and Fort St John in 1806. After the company's amalgamation with the Hudson's Bay Company, Hudson's Hope was added. Later came the small French firm of Revillon Frères, for whom one of Storrs's closest friends in the Peace River, Kenneth Birley, worked for some years.

Missionaries followed hard on the heels of the traders: first the Oblates of Mary Immaculate and then the Church of England, which in Monica's time served the Fort St John area from the Diocese of Caledonia, with the bishop resident in Prince Rupert. The Bishop of the Diocese of Edmonton was also a great friend and supporter.

Although surveying of the land was completed in 1912, settlement before 1914 consisted of a mere handful of farmers, men who tilled the soil
mostly around trading posts or on the flat lands and in the valleys. After
1918 came the soldier settlers, and then, after new strains of wheat en-
sured a crop in the short frost-free seasons, a flood of immigrants from
Great Britain, the United States, Eastern Europe, and from other parts of
Canada. The 1931 census lists a total of 3946 English, Irish, and Scottish
residents, 351 French, 468 German, and lesser numbers of Italian, Polish,
Russian, and other nationalities, for a total population of 7013 in the areas
visited by Storrs.[61] Finally, after 1931, came another great influx, this time
the drought-stricken farmers from Canada's southern prairies. On the
whole, it appears to have been a fairly stable population, with only a small
minority pulling up stakes and leaving for other locations.

During the years encompassed by this volume of Storrs's diaries the world
was edging ever closer to the carnage and destruction of the Second World
War: in 1931 came the invasion of Manchuria by the Japanese and the
international financial crisis, in 1933 Hitler rose to power, in 1934 Germany withdrew from the League of Nations, and in 1935 Mussolini attacked
Abyssinia. Later came the abdication of Edward VIII, the *Anschluss* of Austria
by Germany, and finally, in 1939, the declaration of war. While these and
other world events fundamentally affected Canada as a nation, nothing
changed the face and character of the Peace River country as much as the
Great Depression, in which the international financial and trade crises
played precipitating roles.[62] Exacerbating the desperate financial plight of
the country, years of drought with record-breaking heat descended on the
Prairies from 1931 to 1938. Dust storms turned the southern plains into
arid semi-desert, grasshopper plagues and plant disease devastated the land,
while abysmal prices for the few bushels of grain that were harvested made
destitute the regions' farmers. Many of them saw no recourse but to leave
their homes, and between 1931 and 1941 approximately 250,000 people
moved out of the Prairies.[63] Many of them – the exact number cannot be
ascertained – headed for the Peace River, the promised land beyond the
drought. Storrs frequently described their arrival on wagons, hayracks, or
broken-down, overloaded cars or trucks. Having once arrived at their destination, these settlers, like those before them, sought to begin a new life
as quickly as possible.

To secure a homestead the new arrivals had only to pay a ten-dollar fee
for each quarter-section of land, break thirty acres to the plow, build a
'suitable' house and live on the land six months in each of three years.
While theoretically farm homes could be one mile apart or less because of
the square-mile system of survey, in most areas visited by Storrs the actual

distances varied from one to over a hundred miles. The latter was unusual, but did occur in newly opened regions. This isolation imposed great hardship, especially on women and children.

In addition to distance, the wretched condition of the wagon trails that initially served as roads deepened the isolation and loneliness of many of these early pioneers. Also, until 1939, the year Storrs's diary ended, telephones were a rarity, found at the hospital, stores, and businesses, but in very few homes and on virtually no farms. Even Storrs at this time had neither electricity nor telephone.

Immigrants to the Peace River Block, therefore, did not enter into an immediate utopia, or even experience instantaneous relief from all financial woes. It took several years of incredibly hard work to extract a living from newly opened land, and even then, economic conditions in the 1930s were such that the most hard-working families were frequently forced to apply for government assistance, referred to as 'relief.'[64] Relief in the Peace River consisted of a voucher system that usually provided for food and fuel, but no extras, one reason for the emphasis Storrs and her Companions placed on the distribution of clothing. Taxes could be worked off by labour on the roads, and occasionally married men with dependents were given a few days' paid employment on the newly created highway system that was to link Fort St John with Dawson Creek and other centres. It was humiliating and disagreeable to many independently minded, self-respecting settlers to receive assistance, but for most, there was no alternative.

One source of comfort and social relaxation in these difficult times was to gather with others of like mind, and sometimes this proved to be in the church. The settlers naturally had brought their religious beliefs with them, and in 1931 the census shows 1045 Anglicans, 1960 United Church members, 922 Presbyterians, and 1726 Roman Catholics, among others.[65] Storrs mentions the agreement that existed by mutual consent among some of the denominations not to overlap, so that, for example, where United Church adherents predominated, the Anglicans would not send in church workers, and vice versa. Unfortunately, this arrangement broke down by the mid-thirties and was, in fact, never recognized by the smaller denominations or by the Roman Catholics. Most of the religious services of whatever denomination were originally held in the local schoolhouse rather than in a church, since the latter was generally built after a congregation was established, or when finances would allow.

Schools in any case formed the focal point of a community's social life, providing space for dances, dinners, and meetings of all kinds. Six children were required for the province to provide a teacher and build a school. One-room buildings, usually twenty feet by thirty feet in dimension and constructed of logs, were the norm for schools in the Peace River during this period.[66] The teacher was most often a woman, newly graduated from a one-year course at the normal school in Vancouver, who boarded with a local family. Her salary ranged from approximately $800 to $1200, depending on her qualifications and experience.[67] Frequently, her loneliness in the isolated communities was such that she left after the first year. Her pupils were children between the ages of seven and fourteen, which was the mandatory age for school attendance, although actual attendance varied with the district and the season. Older children, for example, were expected by their parents to assist in the harvest and spring seeding. In 1931, 1068 youngsters were enrolled in the school districts of the Peace River district of British Columbia.[68]

When no school was available, parents were expected to teach children at home with correspondence courses supplied by the Department of Education. This task was extremely difficult for the average homesteader, whose house might well consist of only one room, inhabited by an entire family. Nevertheless, several parents whom Monica visited attempted to teach their children, but many simply waited for the time when a school and teacher would become available. Most children left school at the age of fourteen or after the eighth grade. While boys began working on the farm or as labourers, girls would frequently marry between the ages of fifteen and seventeen, although the average age of marriage for women was between the ages of twenty and twenty-four, as in the rest of the province.[69] Divorce, separation, or desertion occurred also in much the same ratio to marriage as in other rural communities.

These early Peace River pioneers were remarkably involved politically, if their voting patterns are any indication of their interest. In the provincial elections of 1933, for example, 76 per cent of eligible voters cast their ballots; in 1937 this rose to 80 per cent, and in 1941 to 83 per cent.[70] Storrs occasionally mentions 'Bolshevists' in her diaries, and indeed among East European immigrants there was a handful of radical thinkers.[71] These were too few, however, to cause concern to the authorities or even to field a candidate in elections. Yet the Cooperative Commonwealth Federation (CCF, now the New Democratic Party), which was also considered a socialist threat by many, ran a close second to the winning candidates in the three elections under review (1933, 1937, 1941), losing to a Non-Partisan in 1933, and to a Liberal in each of the other two provincial elections.[72] Federally, in the elections of 1935 and 1940, James G. Turgeon, a Liberal, won handily.[73] Storrs's own political sympathies were not specifically expressed, although she indicated deep concern over leftist tendencies among some of those with whom she had interactions.

This, then, was the land of the mighty Peace and these were the people whom Monica Storrs grew to love so deeply and for whom she spent twenty-one years walking on snowshoes, riding on horseback, slogging through mud, and in all ways disciplining 'her patrician, middle-aged body as she went about her Master's work.'[74]

HISTORIANS HAVE ONLY RECENTLY begun to chronicle and conceptualize the experience of women and imperialism.[75] The historiography includes some examinations of Canadian women missionaries, but there have been few books on women who worked in churches throughout the Empire without benefit of titles or prestige.[76] Monica Storrs's diaries therefore are of interest as a source of primary documentation in this area of study.[77]

One may well question why Storrs, at great expenditure of time and energy, wrote these long and detailed letters. Certainly missionary accounts were a time-honoured method of acquainting a supporting constituency with the work in progress and of ensuring sufficient financial support for such work. Yet Storrs herself did not require or request personal monetary aid from anyone. She was self-supporting, as were Goodenough and Harmer, with private, albeit modest, inherited financial resources. As the work grew, however, the Fellowship of the Maple Leaf supplied stipends to some Companions and a small allowance to Storrs for their support. Some friends and family wished to contribute to specific projects and Storrs set up accounts into which such funds could be channelled. But fund-raising was a secondary reason for the diaries. Primarily they were written because of Storrs's need to keep in contact with her large extended family and with her many friends. Her sister, Petronella Moor, remarked on Storrs's 'passionate loyalty to the Family,' extending beyond nieces and nephews to 'cousins of every degree,' and it would be impossible to write to each individual. Hence, the letters were a vehicle of communication, primarily with family members but also beyond them to friends and gradually to more and more well-wishers and interested parties.[78]

For many years Monica Storrs marked her monthly journals or letters 'Not for Publication,' yet as early as 1959, writing to Willard Ireland of the Provincial Archives of British Columbia, she commented that she had considered editing 'suitable portions for a letter book' and publishing this 'somewhere, to be a sort of legacy to my nephews and nieces.'[79] This project did not materialize, however, and when Robert Symons, a close friend and also a writer, approached her in the 1960s about preparing the diaries for publication, she readily agreed. *God's Galloping Girl,* edited by W.L. Morton and published by the University of British Columbia Press in 1979, was based on material supplied by the late Mr Symons and covered the years 1929 to 1931. It was a complete text, without deletions.

In the initial volume Storrs described her arrival in Canada, first impressions of Fort St John and the initiation of her work as a Sunday School teacher and church visitor in the newly opened frontier settlements of the Peace River Block. Her friendships in the Block began to develop and the reader was introduced to her co-workers as one by one they arrived to assist her: Cecilia Goodenough, the Oxford-educated daughter of Admiral Sir William and Lady Goodenough, and Muriel Haslam, one of Eva Hasell's caravan workers. In 1930 Storrs's work meshed with that of the newly organized Fellowship of the West, from whose ranks came the first Anglican rector of the new parish, George Wolfendale. Together with a few resident Anglicans they brought about the organization and building of two new churches, St Martin in Fort St John, and St John's in Baldonnel.

In this volume, too, Storrs shared her excitement on acquiring a piece of land and building her own log residence, the Abbey: 'I really am rather ashamed about it but there is no use in hiding the fact that I am deeply in love with the little estate ... [Y]ou can't quite realize the sort of intoxicating delight in starting a home where there has been literally nothing at all.'[80] The early letters detailed Storrs's interactions with local residents, incoming settlers, and isolated homesteaders in their struggle for survival, and her endless journeys and frequent mishaps on horseback, on foot, and in her ancient car 'Eliza,' in the almost roadless Peace River Block.

Storrs visited England in 1930, but returned to Canada in May 1931, accompanied by Adeline Harmer, who became her first Companion of the Peace. In August 1931 they were joined by Cecilia Goodenough. The volume ended with the departure of Harmer for England in October of that year.

This present edition takes up the story from the time of Harmer's departure, which is how Storrs herself organized the diaries. It is very probable that she recognized Goodenough's arrival and Harmer's withdrawal as a milestone in the development of her mission. No longer was it a personal venture with two close friends as sole arbitrators of the route to be taken. With the coming of a well-educated, superbly organized, energetic, and rather formidable associate, an acquaintance rather than a confidante, the mission was placed on a more formal footing. A few years later, with the arrival of Companions who were no longer completely self-supporting, and with the advent of ordained male clergy, further steps towards formalization occurred. The development of the financial and ecclesiastical structure of Storrs's work is traced in these later letters.

The scope of the mission itself was greatly extended: children came to live in the Abbey as boarders; cultural horizons were expanded by the formation of an amateur theatrical group; new programs such as poetry contests were introduced in the schools; women's groups were organized; the churches grew in number from two to four; and hospital work was added – all in addition to Storrs's primary concern for the physical, emotional, and spiritual well-being of women and children in the area of her influence.

Of even greater personal importance to Storrs, however, was her increasing acceptance by the community, and her own development as a woman. The earlier letters documented her initial impressions; the later ones traced her increasing understanding of the mentality and motivations of the settlers. Her prejudices against perceived moral lapses such as marital irregularities became less judgmental, even as she took stronger steps when physical or mental abuse was evidenced. Her supposed sense of superiority was gradually recognized as rooted in misunderstanding. Possibly the best single illustration of this change in attitude both in herself and in the community is found in her brother Christopher's letter to R.D. Symons in 1972. Storrs was visiting Christopher and his family in Australia where he served as Bishop of Grafton, New South Wales. He wrote, 'She felt estranged from the people, who seemed to suspect, criticize, or even dislike her. At last one evening in the home of May Birley (who later became her dearest friend and supporter) she broke down and cried. Her weakness accomplished what her strength could not ... apparently she had given the impression to the little community that she had come to bring culture and civilization as well as religion to this outlying township. I am sure there was no real superiority complex in Monica; but (as Australians also know!) the English migrant sometimes gives that impression. Anyhow, May's words and Monica's blend of common sense and humility made this conversation a completely new beginning of her twenty-one years work in Canada.'[81] This 'new beginning' was enlarged upon in these later diaries. Janice Dickin remarked that the early Storrs saw as 'her job to judge behaviour and change it.' The later Storrs, like Mary Percy Jackson to whom she is compared, 'is much more free to complain, to joke, and to make honest assessments of people and how they chose to live their lives.'[82]

While the first volume of Storrs's diaries covering the years 1929 to 1931 was a complete text, this present edition, comprising excerpts from the diaries of 1931 to 1939, has been severely pruned because of space restrictions. It represents approximately 25 per cent of the journals of this period. Those wishing to examine an unedited typescript of the complete text may do so at the Provincial Archives of British Columbia, or at the Fort St John–North Peace Museum. The criteria used in the selection and editing involved deleting repetitions of mundane everyday occurrences (such as grooming horses) and descriptions of incidents similar in nature (like Sunday school Christmas programs), and including only those sections considered of most interest or importance. An attempt has been made to include a balance between the mundane and the unusual, the exciting, the annoying, the joyful, and the sober events, for Storrs's life included all of these. To focus only on the humorous or the provocative, for example, or to portray Storrs as a woman without blemish or spot by deleting her sometimes less-than-benevolent observations would be unfaithful to the text. She was very human and therefore became upset, said sharp things, made mistakes. She was also a product of her time and station in life, and her comments are not all necessarily politically correct by today's standards. But that was who she was and this is how she wrote, and she must be allowed to be herself.

It is interesting to consider how accurately Storrs's letters reflect reality in their descriptions. Three Fellowship of the Maple Leaf workers, replacing Storrs and Goodenough during the former's illness in 1933, sent home letters very similar in content, as did Elinor Higgenbotham some years later. Edward Bennett, now a priest, who as a youth in Fort St John knew Storrs, remembered her 'unfailing integrity and straightforward honesty,' which, one may assume, carried over into her writing.[83] Robert Symons, author, artist, and game warden in the Block, knew both Storrs and the community. Later in life he read the original diaries with complete approbation. It would appear, therefore, that Storrs, unlike Hasell, did not generally exaggerate for effect, or keep things back for reasons of seemliness or a sense of propriety, except in the case of personal relationships among the Companions. Even here she hinted at tensions on occasion.

One subject completely absent from the diaries, however, is the use of alcohol. Bradford Angier, who moved into the Hudson's Hope area in the early 1950s, commented with some frequency on the drinking habits of himself and his neighbours.[84] Did the opening of the North Peace River by the Alaska Highway make the difference? Was there simply no money for the earlier settlers to buy liquor? Were there no stills supplying liquor illicitly? Storrs offered no answers, yet why would she withhold such information? She did not belong to the Temperance Society nor did she come from an environment that disapproved of social drinking. With this exception, then, one can safely conclude that Storrs's writings reflect reality the

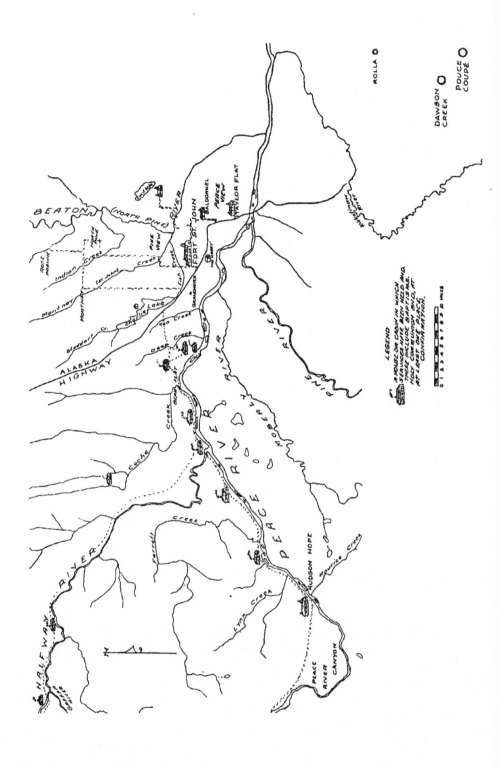

way she saw it, and that the way she saw it closely approximated the way it was.

It was thought at the time of the publication of *God's Galloping Girl*, based on information supplied by Elinor Higginbotham, one of Monica's Companions, that Mabel Causton was solely responsible for circulating the diaries in England.[85] According to Kate Earle, however, also a Companion, the early journals in any case were prepared and distributed by Miss Evelyn Gedge, a friend of Storrs and bursar at Westfield College, London. Earle, a student at the college, became aware of Storrs's work through seeing firsthand the journals in preparation. It may be that Causton and Gedge worked together, or that the arrangement described by Higginbotham came into effect at a later date. Be that as it may, Storrs would almost certainly dismiss such academic conjecture as trivial and urge us to 'get on with it.'

Storrs herself could have expedited the publication of her diaries by identifying persons whose names she initially concealed by the use of capital letters. These identifications have now been made, wherever possible, from full names occurring in later diary entries, from interviews, publications, or directories, or with the assistance of Austin Hadland of Fort St John, whose help was invaluable.

One technical change that occurred in the production of the diaries may be of interest, in that the earlier text was typewritten and multigraphed, while the entries as of June 1935 and thereafter were professionally printed. As Storrs herself commented, 'The first half are typed and clumsy. The second half are neat and portable.'[86]

The diaries end in 1939, when Storrs lost interest in describing her activities to those in England who were facing the threat of the horrors of war. She continued to write occasional letters to the Fellowship of the Maple Leaf that were excerpted in their publications, and she kept brief diaries of her trip to Australia in 1950 and up the Alaska Highway in 1949. These, however, merely chronicle events and places and add nothing to our understanding of either Storrs or her work.

While Storrs's diaries provide a valuable social document, hers is, of course, not the only record. Early-twentieth-century accounts of pioneers and missionaries in northwestern Canada, with few exceptions, were mostly by men about men.[87] Writers of this period seemed disposed to reflect most unsympathetically on local residents, especially Native people, while romanticizing their own roles. Other accounts include Hasell's several books and pamphlets.[88] Hasell tended to write exaggerated but compassionate accounts of the lives of pioneer women and children, laced with large dollops of British nativism and denominational loyalty. Hasell's women, however, were encountered, ministered to as best as possible, then left and, with very few exceptions, were never heard from again. There is virtually no continuity to provide the larger picture.

'I promise to do my best, to do my duty to God and the King' was Storrs's repeated promise as a Girl Guide leader. Like her brothers, she saw in the Empire opportunities for service beyond the borders of England. This volume of her journals testifies to her wider significance beyond the boundaries of a church worker in northern Canada. She and her Companions, like others living in religious communities, 'served their God and their church and in doing so they fulfilled themselves and laid a foundation for all women.'[89] Storrs's was one female voice in an imperial chorus. Her journals show how she gave substance to Christianity and imperial loyalty, and provide a new dimension to the mainly male accounts of imperialism. Like the earlier volume a 'great social document of Peace River Settlement,' *Companions of the Peace* is also a testament to the Christian and imperial understanding of Monica Storrs and her Abbey household.[90]

VERA FAST

MARY KINNEAR (St John's College, University of Manitoba)

Winnipeg, May 1998

Diaries and Letters, 1931–1939

1931

Diary up to November 14th (I hope)

On October 23rd (after Adeline's departure) we [Muriel, Cecilia and I][1] came back in fine style as you remember ... [It] seemed partly exciting and partly melancholy coming home to our empty little house. The boys[2] had both gone home for the week-end, and kind Mrs K[elly][3] had watered and fed the horses ... The two W.A. [Women's Auxiliary] branches are struggling along. They do little but talk so far, but Baldonnel is arranging a grand Chicken Supper and Concert for Church Funds (Horrible Thought), and Fort St John is planning a Tea for the opening of the little Mission House which Brother Wolf[4] has nearly finished building. This is really a combination of Vicarage and Parish Room and measures about 24 by 20. It is quite ambitious having a study, bedroom and kitchen, besides the Parish Room. He hasn't a stick of furniture or any money to buy it with so we shall all have to look round about that soon. We all wonder a little how he will manage when he moves into this large parsonage out of the tiny shack he has camped in so far. There will be so much more to keep clean and it will be occasionally necessary to cook. He is quite capable of doing these things, but never seems to bother, preferring to live like a sort of blend of St Francis and Elijah.[5] I rather think the ravens will have to be largely hens belonging to the sub-species W.A. ...

On Sunday I embarked on a little monthly Sunday School. It is one of those little schools which opened this term and is called Peace View[6] – chiefly, as it appears, because you can see nothing at all all round it but bush. It is a curious new district colonized entirely by members of the enormous clan of A[lexander]s who came two years ago to the Flats. There are six married brothers, one married sister, one mother-in-law, one brother-in-law and *forty-two* children of various ages![7]

The whole area called Peace View is their Promised Land, but so far only three families have moved into it, the remainder still clinging to the flesh-pots of Taylor[8] and the seductions of Cecilia's S.S. [Sunday School]. But there are already two Canaanitish families there in the form of Russians, so the school already has ten children. It's a very inaccessible place, five miles from Taylor up a fearfully steep hill, or five-and-a-half miles from Baldonnel[9] down a narrow trail through the bush ... It was a funny sort of S.S. About eight children came, plus two A-mothers, two Russian mothers and a German-Russian father. We started on hymns, but that was rather uphill work as no-one but the two Mrs A's could sing a note, and the Russian mothers couldn't read a word, either ...

Muriel and I went off on Monday [for a little visit round the district lying north of here], she on Robin and I on Miles[10] with the bed-roll, as usual ... About sundown and after two nice visits, we reached the home of the L[ea]s[11] ... Mr Lea is a hearty Canadian of the jovial, chaffing type. Mrs L. is entirely English – from Essex, I think. She is a refined and handsome, but rather sad-looking woman, who looks especially dignified because she wears what I have not seen in any other house here, a plain dark dress with long sleeves and a broad white apron.

She is one of those people who have not really taken kindly to the home-steader's life. I think it all still feels to her lonely and bare, but her real deep sorrow is the blindness of her little girl. When they first came here nearly two years ago, Muriel, aged seven, pierced her eye with some scizzors. They were just struggling into their house and for some reason, chiefly money, didn't take her away to Pouce Coupé[12] where was the nearest hospital. It was 80 miles off and they had no car and hardly any money, and so they delayed until May[13] heard of it and chartered Tommy[14] to the rescue. Alas, it was too late. The sight of that eye had already gone, and a few weeks later the other went too. Muriel is now at a special school in Vancouver and very happy. But Mrs Lea has never got over it, and I think will never forgive the homesteading life for being the cause of her sorrow.

They gave us a delightful welcome and we had a very nice evening with the two of them besides their little boy, Jimmie, and the teacher of their tiny new school, Miss R[utherford].[15] She was most friendly and warmly invited us to the school next day. Also, she invited one of us to share her bed. So we cast lots for this honour and the lot fell on Muriel. So she had half a real bed but I had the whole of the floor plus blankets for two. Next morning we had Bible reading and Prayers with Mrs Lea, helped her a very little about the house and finished up by going to the Pine View School. There are only six children at present, five boys and a girl ...

After that we had a quick lunch with the Lea's and started off North-ward again for Indian Creek[16] ... We took the wrong trail once or twice ... so we eventually lost about two hours and arrived at last, in the dark and pretty cold, at the house of Mrs J[arvis][17] ... As we rode up to it we met a horseman coming,[18] whom we could hear but not see. I asked him if that was Mrs Jarvis's house just ahead, and he instantly recognized my voice from last year. He is a young man who works for Mrs J., who is a widow, and he instantly went back with us, put the horses to bed, shouldered our bed-roll, pushed open the door and said, 'Here, Mrs Jarvis, here's two visitors for you.'

Instantly, Mrs Jarvis played up just as if she had been watching and wait-ing for us all the evening. Supper was long over, but she quickly produced another, and capped it by even having a spare *bed*, too ...

[Next morning] ... we visited two families and finally reached the school teacher. But we learned from her that a United Church man[19] was already taking S.S. there, so desisted from interference and contented ourselves with Prayer and Bible reading in one or two homes ...

It turned colder that night and we woke on Thursday to a White World ... I will only tell you about one of these next families – the R[obbins][20] – because their house made a more truly mediaeval impression upon us than any other so far.

It is a rather fine, big one-room shack normally occupied by the man and his nice wife and six children. But two or three days before, a new family of settlers had come in driving before them their stock of thirty or forty head of horses and cattle. The weather had turned cold and of course they had no house, so the Robbins just invited them to stay with them until they should be able to build (which may not be till the spring). So there they were living – ELEVEN W[ilson]s[21] of all ages, bringing the house-hold at one bound up to NINETEEN, not to mention the beasts outside and in the barn! And when we walked in out of the snow, there they all were sitting round this fine primitive-looking house. At one end some col-oured blankets were hung across the place where the women and girls slept, while all along another wall were three or four big beds for the boys and men. Then there were tables and stoves and pots and pans and guns and harness and boxes to sit on, and men and boys and children warming among them. Two women were cooking, one or two of the girls were wash-ing up. One man was mending harness and clothes, others were sitting and smoking and making jokes. Another was acting as barber and cutting all their hair in turns, while the children were chasing cats and dogs and adding their bit to the cheerful confusion – except for one little girl, ill in bed. And this was not a picture, but just their ordinary Life! – to go on probably till the Spring! We were gradually introduced to most of the company and talked to the host and hostess, who seemed delighted with their guests, enrolled the Wilson children in the Sunday School by Post,[22] invited everyone to a Christmas Service about December 23rd, and came away. Afterwards I said to Muriel, 'Didn't it look like a mediaeval play?' and she said, 'No, I thought it looked like an old furniture shop.' Yes, and it did look like that, too.

We were fed by a kind R.C. [Roman Catholic] family who entirely approved of our holding the S.S., and so finally got back and held it, taking the same lesson and general plan as before ...

Next morning we visited again, and included Mrs H.M., the charming young Scotch woman whom Price[23] and I found so dreadfully hard up last year. They seemed as poor as ever, in a tiny shack, with the father asleep in a bed in the corner, the children awfully thin and the little fourteen-month baby looking not more than half the size she should be. Mrs H. was as bright as ever, but did look rather pitiful, and we decided to send along some clothes as soon as possible ...

After that we missed the trail for the house we were aiming at and had rather a trying hour in the darkness looking for it in vain. But at last we ... arrived about 8 o'clock at the home of people called W[illiamson][24] ...

My word it was nice to get inside and warm up and we even allowed the men to take the horses away and put them to bed for us, a thing I hardly ever leave to anyone else. Mrs Williamson is a delicate London woman who used to be a Salvation Army Worker and misses her old devout surroundings dreadfully. None of the people round here seem to share her faith, and even her very nice husband is no help to her there. So she is desperately lonely in spirit, and after tea and bread and butter we spent the evening singing with her numbers of slightly terrific hymns. Then we were given the best bed while Mrs W. slept with her little girl and the two men on the floor by the stove. In the night there was a baby blizzard, the wind rose, the snow blew hard, and the temperature dropped to about 15 below zero.

... Luckily we both had moccasins and Muriel had a good thick woolly cap ... Neither of us had a sheepskin because this sudden cold was not expected by anybody. So Muriel put her nightgown under her coat and I my pyjama jacket and after Prayers taken by Muriel, we started off at about 11 ...

We got home soon after four, the horses all silvery, with icicles on their white beards, and ourselves pretty cold but not frozen anywhere, to find the blessed Cecilia more blessed than ever before, waiting with a roasting house and a boiling stew and a delightful welcome home.

Week Ending November 21st (1931)

... Bro. Wolf had gone across the Pine[25] on Saturday and was intending to get back in time for the 3.30 Service, but as he insisted on walking instead of riding, and the snow was pretty heavy, no one expected him to get back in time, and he didn't. I was prepared for this, with a sermonette up my sleeve if required. So at 4.45, as we had amassed about 20 people and the light was going, I began Evensong and had just reached the Third Collect, when he appeared, covered with snow and very cold, but quite ready to carry on at a moment's notice. Of course he had had no dinner, but luckily we are learning to provide extra sandwiches on Sunday, which he devours after Service and before hurrying on to Fort St John.[26] Later I rode over there also, and after Church read him a short Riot Act about: a) walking huge distances when he could ride, b) stupid indifference to meals, c) *never* going to bed.

He had wonderful reasons and excuses for all these crimes, but bore my chastening very well, and in the end we made a mutual compact, i.e., he promised to eat in the middle of the day and go to bed before midnight as long as we for our part keep Monday free from all outside engagements. This may not always be possible, but we are glad enough to do it if we can ...

[Actually] Monday was rather a maddening day. We meant to write letters quite steadily, but a constant flow of people dropping in about one thing and another utterly destroyed it, especially one man who looked in to ask a question at about half past two, and stayed to supper, not finally leaving us until after 8 o'clock. So, after all, I could only manage to finish my Diary by sticking at it till 3.30 a.m. next day.

On Wednesday morning ... we started (Cecilia and I) at about 10 o'clock ... We took Robin and Puck with a little bedroll on each, i.e., the sleeping bag and pyjamas on Robin and three rugs on Puck. Also, of course, the usual two saddle bags with washing things, hymn books, testaments, Guide cards, cord, luncheon, and a big Sunday School picture ...

At 3.30 we reached the school – Crystal Springs[27] – where I was to enroll the first Guides of a new Company[28] that night ... [It] quite wipes out Fort St John as the most Northerly in B.C., and possibly in Canada. They are a group of really big girls (unusual hereabouts) and are so delightfully keen about it ...

Thursday was still about zero, but not blowing or snowing. We revisited

all the families I had been to with Adeline, and had delightful welcomes
everywhere. The C—e family had not yet got their house finished and
were still living in a tent. Such a little tent, too, containing father, mother,
four children and a man helping with the house, also two dogs of course,
and a cat or two. Mrs C—e was wonderfully plucky and bright and begged
us to stay for dinner. Her smallest child, a baby of about 14 months, seemed
dreadfully ill. The tent had a mud floor, of course, and was impossible to
keep clean. In the middle was a big stove making a fierce heat at times, and
all round the edge was the piercing damp cold of the encircling snow. We
didn't stay to dinner because of keeping the horses waiting so long in the
frost, but promised to go again later, when they should be in their house,
and came away longing to bring that poor little baby straight off to
hospital ...

After that, Mrs W[aite][29] again, the sweet Englishwoman from Sussex
with whom Adeline and I had dinner last time. We had purposely gone
after dinner this time because they are so awfully hard up. But this was
another example of the wonderful hospitality of the real poor. The house
was almost bare and bitterly cold, with unfinished walls and roof, and one
window-hole with no glass as yet but only a rough curtain over it. Mrs Waite
was surrounded by five tiny, ill-clad children (two more at school) and told
me their bed had been covered with snow in the morning. And yet she had
heard of our being in the district and killed a chicken and prepared dinner for us in hopes of our coming to her. Last time, you see, she had not
expected Adeline and me and had kept us waiting while everything was
cooked, so this time she was determined to be ready! Cecilia and I were
sorry in a way, and yet glad too, as it left that much more food for them.
She owned that they were very cold, but was full of hope because her husband had at last got a bit of work with another man. From this she hoped
for enough money to buy the missing window, and as soon as it was earned,
she hoped her husband would come home and fix the roof and walls and
put the window in. Meanwhile, she only minded for the children, and only
wanted to make us welcome and as comfortable as possible ...

After that a straight ride North for about seven miles to – the T[urners][30]
... Mr Turner is a bullet-headed, very determined little American, whose
God is Mechanism. He was quite kind to us last year, but not sympathetic,
and we didn't want to trouble him again if we could have helped it. However, it was too dark and cold to be squeamish any longer, so we banged on
the door of his new house and made the usual request – to be allowed to
put our bedroll down on his floor. He let us in without enthusiasm, and
though not at any time a gracious host, he treated us with perfect con-

sideration. Mrs Turner is a very pretty youngish Englishwoman, latterly recovering from a very serious illness. I believe she was glad to see us, but she is entirely dominated by Mr Turner, and it was hard to get into any sort of real conversation with her.

The house is by far the grandest up that Valley – a kitchen leading into a living room, two bedrooms and a pantry, all just finished (except the ceiling) and very smart and clean. But the really amazing thing was ELECTRIC LIGHT AND THE RADIO! Mr Turner has Means and being also scientifically minded and very modern in his tastes, actually makes his own current and charges his batteries and all the rest of it, so we felt for all the world as if we were visiting a log house at Tooting.[31]

In other ways too it was a unique establishment. There were no fewer than two hired girls, besides the hired man, and although one of these is a school-girl, only on duty early and late, and the other a half-breed with a tiny illegitimate son very much in evidence, the whole effect was one of amazing ostentation and luxury. This was the more marked because, though of course the hired man sat down to supper with us, the hired girls did not – which seemed frightfully odd and revolutionary, although I think the real reason was merely that the table was very small and Cecilia and I were occupying their two chairs.

After supper was rather trying ... Luckily Mr Turner had promised to cut his wife's hair, and afterwards graciously consented to cut ours. So although it was pretty frightening (he was so grimly determined about it and snipped and clipped with as much relish as if he were chopping up the Church and the Royal Family), the final effect was not too bad, and was certainly dreadfully needed. All the time I tried to talk to Mrs Turner, but there were so many noises drowning us, and the whole atmosphere was so charged with Mr Turner, that gradually I gave up and fell asleep sitting bolt upright before her ...

Breakfast next morning was full of narrow squeaks because every topic approached seemed to be rushing us to the edge of some frightful controversy – election, Fascism, Religion – it was like steering through a mine field and we were thankful to get away without any fatal collision. Afterwards I tried to get a little more talk with Mrs Turner ... But she was awfully reserved and cautious and he was really there all the time, so at last we had to come away with nothing real said, but I hope a little more friendship. Really, you know, he was very kind, and it's just possible that all his theories are mainly a sort of bluff.

That was a lovely morning, and we visited round the Holdup[32] till one, then fell in to dinner with people called C[allison],[33] whose children go

far to populate the little Holdup school. Mr Callison is rather a strong
Bolshevist as a rule, but that day he was kind and very harmless. Mrs C. is a
good soul with nine large children and all the work of the house, farm and
Post Office on top ... But she gave us a good dinner, and asked incidentally
if we could help the school Christmas Tree with clothes or toys. This is one
of the very poorest districts. They have only been able to raise seven for
everything, and there are about thirty children of all ages, whose only
present in the year comes then or never. We promised to do what we
could ...

Wednesday was the great day of the SUPPER and CONCERT, the first
ever held in Baldonnel, and a great gamble at that ... The men had made
three immense long tables, the length of the Hall, and the women arrived
all the afternoon, bringing endless cooked chickens, a turkey or two, pork,
potatoes, vegetables, pies and jellies, and by five o'clock, out of apparently
complete chaos, there gradually emerged a most marvellous and enormous supper. My modest share was to supply a case of apples for the pies
and all the salt and sugar that was required. And my principal occupation
before the fun began was to help peel an almost infinite number of potatoes ... Cecilia and Mr S[impson]³⁴ held the door and extracted with admirable firmness, 50 cents (2/–) from every grown-up feaster and 25 cents
from every schoolchild, while I wandered round finding people places and
helping generally with the waiting. The supper started at five o'clock, and
consisted of roast chickens, turkeys, cold pork, salad, potatoes, carrots,
cabbages, pies, jellies, bread and butter, tea and coffee – all given in great
abundance.

Of course we had no ideas how many people would come, but hoped for
at least 50 or 60. Well, between five and eight they just *poured* in by families,
sat down, ate a huge supper and moved off to sit round by the walls and
stove. We served and waited and cleared off and washed up, and laid again
and fed again in a glorious turmoil of steadily intensifying heat [and] noise
... Everyone came from Fort St John and Taylor as well as from Baldonnel,
and the final number was well over 200. Everybody (including ourselves in
relays) had as much as they could eat and drink. The tables were crammed
with feasters, the walls and stoves and benches with post-prandial parties,
and all intervening spaces with children, chiefly little girls playing and little boys fighting. Two out of our three loaned lamps burned out, but nobody minded. Everybody was supremely happy and it looked just like a
Wild West picture play.

About 8.30, by colossal efforts the tables were cleared and taken down
(boards and trestles, of course) and gradually the benches were heaved

into rows, and by nine the Concert began. It was the queerest little Concert, collected entirely by Brother Wolf. The Baldonnel boys sang – or
rather recited – two comic songs ... Some other boys did a comic turn,
Brother Wolf sang a very fruity song. Two Fort St John girls did a song and
dance in very remarkable paper ballet dresses. A large German-Canadian
recited a lot of Charles Service poetry, which I think the audience only
really fiercely enjoyed in the rather frequent moments when he forgot his
words ... But the one really good thing was the W.A. play, an excellent skit
on gossiping called 'How the Story Grew.'[35] Brother Wolf had coached
them and they were really very funny. In fact they quite brought the house
down, though certainly that was not very difficult, as it seemed ready enough
to fall. At about eleven, the Concert being over, there was a new turmoil of
benches and everybody prepared to spend the rest of the night dancing.
At this point Cecilia and I felt ourselves at liberty to go home, but before
we went, had to settle plans for the next day.

You see, as Divisional Guide Commissioner for the Block I had promised to spend Thursday and Friday South of the river to meet the local
Association at Pouce Coupé and inspect Guides and Brownies there and at
Dawson Creek. Cecilia was coming too, as Divisional Secretary ... and we
had intended to drive as usual in Eliza. But Eliza is dreadfully on the blink,
having apparently contracted a severe chill on the battery which makes it
apparently quite *impossible* to start her, crank we never so wisely ... So just
before the dance began I approached Bro. Wolf and asked him to ask
publicly whether anybody present was intending to cross the river tomorrow. Upon which he said, 'But I'm going myself to Dawson Creek.' We
were rather surprised as he had never mentioned it before, and his own
car is a mass of fractures and decay. Still, if anyone could drive it over he
could, so we agreed that he should pick us up at ten next morning, and got
off for home at last ...

Thursday morning was colder, for which we were thankful for the sake
of the river. Cecilia and I packed pyjamas and Guide literature and stood
by for Brother Wolf, both in full dress uniform and white shirts. Only we
hid our glory under brown sheepskin coats and caps, and carried our Guide
hats in our hands ceremonially, like Canons in the Cathedral. Also we were
rather like Nebuchadnezzar's image, our feet being displayed in large
moosehide moccasins.[36]

Bro. W. was awfully late, and we began to fear that Lizzie had broken
down at the start. In fact Cecilia was just preparing to saddle Robin and
ride to town to see what had happened when he appeared, having lost his
chains and had to borrow others which didn't quite fit. So instead of at

ten, we got off at about 11.30 and dashed down the 12 miles to the river at a great pace.

At McK[night's] house,[37] which is the nearest to the crossing, we stopped and asked old Jim how the river was. He said, 'Sure, the ice is fine and dandy. There may be a little water but nothing to speak of.' ...

But when we got nearer to it we saw the snag. At the edges there is generally at this time of year on the top of the real ice, a certain amount of water called the overflow. This time, owing to a mild fortnight with strong sun, the overflow on the near side was fairly wide and of course, you couldn't say how deep through, probably it would be about two feet. That wouldn't be much trouble if it really was water, but unluckily last night's frost had just bound it so that it was a question whether we should get over or through. There was nothing for it but to rush it, so Brother W. said, 'All ready?' – and opened the throttle wide. It was lucky he did, for although the top ice broke at once and tried to stop us, his momentum down the hill and full steam ahead just carried us through the foot or so of resistance and water and out on the firm ice beyond. After that there was nearly half a mile of rough but pretty good going ... There was, of course, no definite trail as yet, because so few cars had crossed and none on that day. So we followed what tracks we could and all went well until we neared the other side and saw between us and the bank a far wider overflow also thinly frozen. Bro. W. got out and went and jumped about on the ice, which held him well enough. So he got in again and choosing the narrowest part – about 30 feet with a very steep bank on the other side, he said, 'Here goes then' and charged again.

But this time we were not so lucky. The top ice broke and in a moment the car stuck fast with water just below the doors, and the engine immediately stopped.

Of course it wasn't dangerous because the underneath ice really was sound enough to hold us. But it was rather a puzzle how to get out, as the car appeared to be dead, and the ice was now too much broken to walk over, but not too much broken to make wading very difficult. Bro. W. was perfectly serene as usual, tried everything possible to start up again, and then got out on the running board proposing to wade through the ice and carry us ashore in turns. He would have made a fine modern St Christopher,[38] except that instead of being a giant he is about half our size. Just then Cecilia and I saw a Man on the bank and we *shouted*. He shouted back that he could get one strong horse in about five minutes and would bring a very long rope. So we detained St Christopher and after what seemed about half an hour (and very cold), the horse appeared on the bank and the very long rope was thrown across to us. Brother W. climbed out to the end of the bonnet and made it fast, somehow, and then we had an exciting five minutes. The poor horse plunged and struggled on the shore and the car charged and retreated about a dozen times, till at last it broke its way through, the engine suddenly started again, and we arrived roaring and panting on the top of the bank and on dry land once more. After that we expected the Peace Hill on that side would be child's play because, although steep and winding and about two miles long, it is now quite well graded and we knew that lots of cars had been over the snow. But we forgot the partial thaws of the previous day or two which had started water running down some of the steepest slopes, which the night had frozen into definite ice-slopes. About half-way up the hill we came to the worst of these slopes, and no effort of all of us together could get the poor car up it. About six times Brother Wolf backed down in a most terrifying way and tried to charge up while we rushed at the sides and tried to push. Always we stuck at a point where the wheels rushed round on the ice and the car first stood still and then began to slide down again.

Meanwhile, all the water having long boiled away, Bro. W. kept the cap off and we feverishly fed the radiator with snow. But that was no good either. It soon began to pour forth volumes of steam exactly like a railway engine, and finally caught alight and he only just managed to put it out in time. Of all these exciting manoeuvres Cecilia and I were only more or less useless spectators, as our weight was not wanted in the car, and all we could do to help was an occasional useless shove at the worst moments. But after the car had turned into a pillar of steam and nearly ended in a pillar of fire, we all felt we were beaten, and though Bro. W. was quite prepared to go on trying till it finally blew up, Cecilia and I managed to restrain him and persuaded him to turn homeward again (that wasn't very easy either). Re-crossing the river was not much trouble because we kept carefully to our own tracks and rushed through the overflow on both sides where we had previously broken the ice.

It was pretty sickening, wasn't it to have to come back after all, and we felt very small when we met various Baldonnel people and confessed that the hill had beaten us. But afterwards I learned that no car got out that day, or I believe for two or three days afterwards, so that was a comfort to our wounded pride ...

Late on Friday night when the others were long in bed and I was writing for the Mail, I looked up and saw through the window what appeared to be a *mountain* on the landscape, standing out against the stars. I knew there should be no mountain there, and had a moment's terror that I was suffering from D.T.[39] However just then the mountain shifted and broke in half, and running to the window I discovered it to be three immense horses who had evidently been gorging themselves on our little oat-stack, and were resting under the lee of the house preparatory to another heavy meal. I was filled with rage, put on my coat and rushed out to have half an hour of most exciting manoeuvres with the beggars. They were quite determined not to be driven out of the gate and kept dividing and galloping off into my bush and round and round the dam, while I chased them pretty clumsily through the snow and fell down at intervals. Really and truly it became rather fun, so very lively and warming, and yet queer and silent under the midnight stars, that I was almost sorry when at last the trespassers all bolted out through the gate and I put up the pole behind them. We shouldn't have left it down of course, because there are always stray horses waiting to eat your stack and drink your water (if you have any) but one of us forgot, I suppose.

Before this week closes I do want to thank most tremendously everyone who has sent us any kind of gift for the work. Some of you I have written to and all I mean to ...

With loving Christmas and New Year's Greetings to everyone at Home and from all the Company of the Peace, i.e., from: Muriel, Cecilia, Monica – Companions; Erving, Harvey – Lay Brothers; Robin, Puck – Barn Brothers; Lucifer, Michael – Brother Archangels (Kittens).

Week Ending November 25th

... There are only four or five families [at Peace View] so far, but enough to make a school of 10 or 12, and the teacher[40] is an Anglican and a Ranger but very young indeed – about 19 – and quite inexperienced ... It's pretty hard for these very young teachers ... They find what lodging they can, and are very lucky if they get a room to themselves. In one sense they are very lonely, but on the other hand, being single and young and probably good looking and certainly dressy, they are immensely sought after by the bachelors especially during their first term or two. It's all a difficult life and full of temptations to foolishness, and really I think it is a wonder how well most of them retain their dignity ...

[Monday]: We all love Monday and long for it to last 48 hours at least, instead of which it flies like winking and with nothing done. We promise ourselves that we will read, and discuss Art and play the Gramophone, and be entirely leisured and cultured. But instead of that, what we really do is to spring clean, and scrub floors, mend clothes and melt snow for water and be entirely domestic and lowbrow but happy all the same ...

... On Friday ... we started [across the Pine] about ten o'clock, each complete with bed roll, wall picture, haversack of Guide and S.S. and M.U. [Mothers' Union] books, and [a] sack of toys. It was a pretty parky day, the sort of day when you hate tying things on to the saddle because your hands die at once.

... The horses turned quite white with the frost and we walked faster and faster without speaking until we were nearly halfway up the further side ... We pushed over to the S[pences][41] first, had a hurried cup of tea there while secretly gifting Mrs Spence 22 of Lady Goodenough's delightful toys for her school Christmas Tree (Transpine) ...

After that we had a pretty nippy eight miles back to Mrs Copes[42] ... To our dismay neither she nor her Italian husband was in, but only a very unresponsive Swedish hired man called Olaf[43] who was having his own supper. But we were much too cold to start off again so had to be quite firm with him like this: C. and I: 'Where is Mr Copes?' O: 'He is away.' We: 'Where is Mrs Copes?' O: 'I don't know. She is out.' We: 'Well, we must stop here tonight, and put the horses in the barn.' O: 'The barn is quite full.' We: 'Well, I'm afraid you must squeeze them in somehow and give them a good feed.'

After that we joined him at supper and were in the middle of cold pork and potatoes when our unconscious hostess came home from calling on a neighbour. Like all Canadians, she was excellent about it, and just took our arrival for granted without either resentment or rapture. She put an old mattress on the floor for us, where we slept like logs in no time.

Next morning was quite balmy again, above zero I should say. Cecilia and I ... delivered the second sack of toys to Mrs F[ramst],[44] the Cecil Lake teacher who is a native of St Peter's in Thanet. She was delighted with them too, and altogether we felt awfully happy about that part of the visit, as it will ensure that each of the 40 children North of the Pine gets anyhow one Christmas present ...

Week Ending December 19th
... The Service that [Sunday] was a Toy Service, to offer all the presents given or made by Muriel's Guides, Brownies and Rangers, or paid for by the S.S. collections. Besides these, there were a lovely lot sent to Cecilia by Lady Goodenough ...

We had to get [the Christmas parcels made up the next] night because next morning the Mail went both North and South – South by truck and North by sleigh. And the kind Mail-men took the whole lot as private property and charged us nothing for them, which was indeed a mercy ...

Next morning we had another Celebration here because there was none in either Church on Sunday. Afterwards at breakfast Bro. Wolf developed a new plan, i.e. *a Supper for all the Bachelors in the District!* It is to be in the Mission House on New Year's Day, and he and we are to run it. Of course it is a perfectly reckless plan, as the house is about 20 feet square, and there may be at least 200 bachelors (although of course we shall have no idea how many till they come). A bachelor here doesn't mean any unmarried man, but any man living alone. Of these there are hundreds round here, and lots of them so poor that they will gladly walk many miles for a free meal. How we are to get them all into the house, or how we are to cook all the food in a kitchen about the size of an English cupboard we have no idea at all. Humanly speaking it looks impossible, but that doesn't worry Bro. Wolf at all. So long as we will help him he is sure it will be quite easy. The mere question of the food itself is the least important. Lots of people will give us meat at this time of year, and beans and potatoes are not hard to procure, or pies for that matter ...!

But like all B.W.'s suggestions, it goes much further in generosity and inspiration than anything thought of by us, and that is so delightful that we are ready to back him in anything he proposes because he has the real Franciscan touch and is always ready to do three parts of the work himself ...

One great development of last week I nearly forgot to mention. *The New Room was finished* ... And this has become rather necessary because do you know I am now practically committed to a *Third Boy*! His name is Fred N[ielson],[45] his age is 15, and he passed the High School Entrance higher than any other boy or girl North of the river last year ... He has been on my conscience for a long time and when I last tackled the father, and learned that he could (or would) do nothing for him, I offered to take him on trial if he – the father – would supply plenty of meat and vegetables. He jumped at it, and poor Fred's face took on quite a different look – though he said nothing – as usual.

Muriel and Cecilia are bearing up very bravely, though I sometimes fear they are not so keen on the Lay Brothers as I am. Still the new room will make a lot of difference. It's a good size and will have a stove, so the boys will be able to sit there quite a lot in the evenings. We shall be less congested and our conversations less strictly disciplined all the time ...

Week Ending December 26th
... Muriel and some of the children helped [Brother Wolf] to decorate St Martin's for Christmas while I rode over to St John's for the same purpose, and Cecilia most nobly stayed at home to clear up our pretty filthy house ...

When it was too dark to do any more (though not finished) I paid one visit near by and then went on to Peace View as promised. Mrs Sam Alexander[46] gave me supper and the show began at about eight. The school was jam-packed full as they always are – people coming in sleighs from miles around. Then followed the Christmas Tree as usual as far as I know, but having been dead asleep for much of the time I couldn't really tell you much about it ... and after midnight I escaped, and started on my nearly 12 mile ride home ...

Muriel prepared generally for Christmas, and our little guest Phyllis M[oon], the Peace View teacher arrived. She is only 19, very small and quiet, and this is her first school ...

Christmas Day was wonderful compared with two years ago. We had no early Celebration, but at nine Muriel and I rode over to St Martin's for a Children's Service, followed by Holy Communion, which alas only four besides ourselves attended ...

We got back to supper at six ... We had a marvellous dinner cooked by Muriel – Bro. W's turkey, Mrs Haslam's pudding, fruits and sweets and biscuits from the Harmers and Lady Goodenough, and heavenly tiny trees and candles for the table also from Lady Goodenough. Cecilia and Moon had decorated the house most beautifully, and put a real little tree in the Chapel, so we felt as festive as possible, and Bro. Wolf seemed to be in a state of complete enchantment with everything, especially with the dinner, for he had practically no food all day ...

Later we put [out] all the light but the candles on Lady Goodenough's tiny Christmas tree, and in the hands of my little Rothenburg angels, and by these lovely little lights we sat and listened to some carols on the gramophone in the next room ...

Saturday was our second and I hope our last late morning, breakfast instead of 7.30 being at 9! The morning was chiefly spent in catching up the time lost over chores, etc., but at one o'clock Cecilia and I rode over to Baldonnel once more for the Annual Public Meeting. About 20 people came – not many, but enough for the purpose – ... and [afterward] we went home full of deep thankfulness and tremendous hope for the life of the Church and Hall this coming year.

1932

Week Ending January 2nd, 1932

... We have no thermometer, but can roughly gauge how cold it is by various signs and symptoms, such as ... the degree to which all the food in the pantry [freezes]. Of course it's awfully convenient for the food to freeze, that is, meat and cooked vegetables and butter. But rather a bore when it's milk, potatoes or eggs, because these, when thawed out, seem to have lost a good deal of their first fine careless rapture.

I'm afraid we look more like Cossacks than holy Spinsters, but that can't very well be avoided, and anyway we are all three practically identical as Church Cossacks. We wear fur caps with ear-flaps (mine is Cyprus lamb), short brown canvas coats lined with sheepskin, two pairs of mitts – the inside wool and the outside horse or moose hide – brown corduroy breeches, two pairs of woollen stockings fastened with thongs of the same undressed hide which crosses round and round the ankles and twist in anywhere – rather like the shepherds in a mystery play at Home ...

On Wednesday the plans for the Bachelors' Supper became dominant. The supper was to be on Friday for an unknown number of men. Brother W. was taking Services in the Montney and Cecilia and I were responsible for raising provisions. So we divided the district between us and each spent the whole day riding in different directions and obtaining promises of meat, vegetables, bread, milk, or pies at every home. It was a very successful enterprise on the whole, and when we finally met again for supper we had secured between us the promise of five cooked turkeys, various joints of beef and pork, potatoes and turnips, and nearly 60 pies! Also May undertook to cook at least 25 lbs. of beans, and Mr Birley to bring them round on Friday, so apart from the gift of a joint of deer and a piece of moose on sale or return so to speak, there was nothing more required of us except manual labour.

On Thursday therefore we loaded up the horses with necessary pots and pans (Bro. W. having almost nothing in his house), extra loaves, and the moose and deer ... and rode over to the Mission House to cook potatoes chiefly, and to see what else would be required. Bro. Wolf had just returned from a very happy Christmas round-up of the Montney, and was in great spirits working at the house. I must say we could hardly appreciate his optimism about it. The walls and roof were up, it's true, and rough partitions between the three tiny rooms and what he gloriously calls 'the Hall,' i.e., the parish room which is about 16 by 10 feet. But the floor was only half finished, the walls were still rough lumber waiting to be covered with ship-lap, there was no cooking stove and every inch of space was full of lumber and junk!

We said, 'Where can we peel half a sack of potatoes?' He said, 'You can't. It's too uncomfortable here. I'll peel them.' 'When?' 'Tonight.' 'Nonsense; we'll peel them in your study at once.'

The Study is the one completed room in the house. It is about six by eight feet (Cecilia says not so big) and is almost entirely filled by a large iron heater which when in action turns the room into a very fierce oven. It is also the bedroom at present as nowhere else is finished. So besides the fiery furnace, it contains two tables, a tiny bed, and all his books, clothes, letters, Christmas cards, spare stoles, offertory bags, photographs of bishops and football teams – in fact all the normal possessions of a parson in high compression and sublime confusion.

The potatoes took us from one o'clock till 5.30 with one short interval connected with a water barrel. Usually Bro. Wolf melts snow like the rest of us, but in view of an indefinite number of guests he had borrowed a barrel, and Jim[1] was to fill it with water. When the barrel arrived it was found to be nearly full of frozen creosote (a deadly poison). So first Cecilia stood on her head breaking it up with a hammer, and afterwards I stood on my head trying to scrub the blessed barrel clean. As a matter of fact we both found that from crouching in Nebuchadnezzar's furnace[2] to burrowing in a frozen barrel outside was quite an ideal change of air and attitude.

At about six we came away leaving Bro. W. still putting up the ceiling and lining the walls by the light of a lantern ... We remarked encouragingly, 'You can't *possibly* get the house finished.' 'Oh yes I can.' 'Why it would take two days more at least.' 'Well, we have got tomorrow till five, and I shall stick at it all tonight till it's time to come to you tomorrow.' And so he did ...

New Year's Day, 1932

This year came in clear and cold and still ... I did a very little house work, and stood by for Muriel's departure [for a brief holiday] ...

She has been working here without a day off that I know of for fourteen months and is pretty tired, for I never knew anyone more conscientious and thorough, or more capable of concentrated intensive sort of work for a long time without flagging. Every Sunday in heavy rain or heat, or deep snow, she walks the 11 miles for her two Sunday Schools, and on five days in the week she plods round again for Brownies, Cubs, Guides, Rangers, and Bible Class, besides cooking all our food that is cooked, except breakfast ...

Both [Mr Birley] and May thought the Bachelors' Supper never could be ready, and when we reached the house I thought so too. Bro. Wolf was *still* carpentering, all the rooms were still full of lumber, sawdust and shavings and hired plates and cups, *plus* a welter of turkeys, joints, turnips, beans, and *60* pies all lying about in sweet confusion – especially in Nebuchadnezzar's furnace ... It was one o'clock and the supper was to begin at five, and nobody had any idea how many guests to prepare for.

Meanwhile there were no tables or benches, and the little parish room was completely blocked by junk. I commented mildly on this to the host, who was happily finishing off the ceiling with his mouth full of nails. But all the satisfaction I got was: 'That's all right. I'll make the table and benches directly I'm through with this. You arrange the food where you like. Yes, make a table – that's fine. Don't worry, we'll be ready.'

Of course neither of us believed him, but we plugged on – Cecilia at the turnips and potatoes, with Alice [Hunter],[3] a red-haired Brownie of ten, and I at making a long food counter and washing up tables with Thelma [Howe],[4] a little black-haired Brownie of eight.

About 2.30 Brother W. made us sit in a row on the pile of lumber while he produced tea and served us.

After that, things went with a rush; the tables and benches were made, the room cleared and swept, the dusty hired dishes all washed, the food all cooked and heated, and being kept hot in masses everywhere ...

Before five, the bachelors rolled up, all sorts of them, elderly and youths, old-timers and new-comers, familiar to us and unknown. But to our surprise the total number was only thirty, instead of twice or even three times that number, for which we had prepared. Apparently, as we learned afterwards a great many men who might have come thought there was some trap in the invitation and that it would inevitably lead on to either a Service or a Soaking (for money) ...

Poor Bro. Wolf was a little daunted at first by their heaviness, and ran out during the Pie Act with, for the first time, rather a harassed look. 'What on earth shall I do to get them going?'

'Go back and sing them a song,' said Cecilia and I, cynically enjoying the fact that it was his party and we were only irresponsible scullions.

So he went back and started in with a little speech of New Year welcome, to which a bachelor replied. After that, several of them were induced to give personal reminiscences, and then gradually they worked up an endless series of songs and comic stories, getting more feeble and giving more and more pleasure as the night wore on, just like men all over the world.

We washed up, piled and protected the vast quantities of remaining food, and wrapped an extra pie in paper for each man to take home. Finally between nine and ten when all possible jobs were finished, and there seemed to be no possible reason why the fun should ever cease, Cecilia and I slunk away, leaving B[owes]⁵ the Garage man and N[eal]⁶ the Schoolmaster to collect another supper, if required – *which it was.* For at midnight Tommy arrived back from Dawson with three other men, and sure enough, they all started all over again.

How Bro. W. stood it we couldn't think, considering he had been working for 36 hours at a stretch and hadn't gone to bed at all the previous night.

But when we went back next morning to clear up, we found him quite fresh and lively, with the same two Brownies clearing and washing up the hideous mess and confusion left by the second supper.

Cecilia and I looked rather faintly at the piles of food still left over, and rashly asked, 'What about all this food?'

'Oh,' said Bro. Wolf brightly, 'We'll have another supper on Monday and invite all the children. And you shall tell them tomorrow in Sunday School.'

'Oh – Yes.'

Week Ending January 16th

... On Wednesday, after Guides, we had the first meeting of the new [Baldonnel] Hall Trustees, and we decided to have a worthy book-case made for the really first rate library which Cecilia is getting together there. The nucleus of it is the consignment of books sent out to me by the Victorian League,⁷ and to that have gradually been added gifts from the Imperial Order of the Daughters of the Empire [*sic*]⁸ and the Fellowship of the West,⁹ while a lot more have been collected and are being sent out by Sir William Goodenough. Altogether we shall have about 300 really decent books both children's and grown-ups, and the Baldonnel Library will be the only one worthy of the name North of the Peace ...

Diary Ending January 30th

About 2.30 [Wednesday] we started off Northward on a good trail and a pleasant mild winter afternoon ... I visited the Russian family which supplies the two girls to the school. Poor Mrs S[olorenko][10] suffers from asthma, pretty badly, I'm afraid, so the eldest daughter Nellie has been obliged to leave school and run the home. Mr Solorenko, who certainly looks a typical Trotsky, was as usual busily occupied in sitting with a long pipe by the stove and burning up the logs which his daughters saw and split for most of the day.

Cecilia joined me after having been nearly blown away by a fearfully boisterous but not very cold West wind. Then we rode on eight miles to the S[pences] whom we decided to honour with our bedroll that night. We arrived pretty cold at about six, and were just standing inside the house discussing where to put the horses as the Spences have not yet built a barn, when suddenly there was a shout from the kitchen where little Marjorie was lighting the gas-lamp. Mrs Spence and Cecilia and I ran in to find the room apparently a mass of flames ...

Mrs Spence and Cecilia grabbed together at the only blanket within reach and threw it over the flames, which however took very little notice of that. I herded the *seven* children ranging downwards from 12 to two into the outer room where the younger ones all started sobbing and the dog barking – rather a good stirring accompaniment to the brisk battle in the kitchen. The flames jumped and ran so quickly that there was no time to look for more blankets, or even to unfasten our bedrolls, so we hurled them on just as they were – two large sausages, each enclosed in a rubber ground sheet. That wasn't much good but gained one moment's grace while we both tore off our heavy sheep-skin coats and hurled them on to the fire. I think these just saved the game, for the gas had practically burnt itself out, and the coats just smothered the burning cupboard and saved the roof until the whole of the water barrel had been thrown all over the room.

Altogether I suppose it lasted 15 minutes but it was quite exciting, and without the two coats I don't believe the house would have been saved. Poor Mrs Spence was rather shattered afterwards and no wonder, with all that family, and deep winter snow outside. If the house had been destroyed it would have been a bad business for them.

The next little job was to mop up the kitchen which was full of water, charred wood and knocked down pots and pans, and of course quite dark now that the fire was extinguished, and by 10 o'clock the excitement had died down and we all went thankfully to bed ...

I found [the Binnells][11] in a small one-room shack with three little children, all very clean and happy and pleased with themselves. They came in late last autumn, and Mrs Binnell described to me how first she and the children stayed in someone else's shack while her husband cut a trail into his land. Then they lived in a tent on the land while he hauled logs and put up the shack. And finally they moved in and lived inside on the mud floor while he hewed logs flat enough and laid them down to make a real floor of which they were very proud. All this with three tiny children and no neighbours except Mrs P. three miles away, no milk, and no store nearer than Fort St John 20 miles away across the unbridged North Pine River. Pretty wonderful these people are, and make me pretty well ashamed of our urban helplessness ...

Fred Neilson [came on Wednesday]. He is 16 years old and nearly six feet tall ... He certainly isn't foolish, but by far the most intelligent boy or girl I have met out here – deeply interested in every sort of fact and topic and with a real thirst for knowledge. He gets on splendidly with Harvey which is a great credit to both, and they are both living blissfully in the new room of which they are immensely and rightly proud ...

Fortnight February 13th

[Sunday] I went to Peace View on Robin, and had to break trail or plow and flounder for the last three miles. But it was worthwhile as there were 16 people – ten children and six grown-ups chiefly of Russian or German stock. I took a supply of the Mirfield Mission Hymnbooks[12] sent us by Messenger Maud,[13] and left them there to be the Peace View Hymnal ... There seems to be nothing in the Mirfield book which could rouse the suspicions even of the United Church of Canada.[14] We have no instrument there, none of the children seem to be able to sing, half the adults being Russian can't read, and the other half couldn't sing a hymn they actually knew, but in spite of that we ... had a very hearty if not strictly 1662 Service[15] ...

Brother Wolf is away till Holy Week. That gives me five Sundays in St John's Church and I am trying with great trepidation to speak on some of the fundamental questions about Religion, i.e., Human Needs; the Reality of God; Suffering; The Cross; Discipleship. I fear it may bore some of them desperately, but feel it may meet a real need for one or two ...

In the morning ... we had a little warning [of the intense cold] in the way our fingers froze when trying to fasten the bedrolls, but the real fun began when we got right out of the shelter of the bush and started going North up the valley to the Holdup. Then we discovered it to be a far colder day than yesterday, a much harder frost and a strong biting wind which drove the snow into our eyes where it froze on our eyelids and blocked them very neatly. After about three miles of this (which poor Puck and Robin disliked intensely) through not seeing properly I suddenly ran into a deep drift where Puck first floundered and then stuck quite fast. I rolled off and pulled him out, only to find that in his efforts he had corked (spiked) one foot with the other shoe and it was bleeding ...

So we led the injured Puck and walked on another mile to Mr T[urner]'s house, to ask his advice and help. He was awfully kind, examined Puck carefully, said the cut was not deep and only needed to be filled with turpentine to save it from the frost, and told us to go into the house for dinner. We went in and found poor Mrs Turner lying in the living-room in full flu with a temperature of nearly 102, with the one year old boy playing round her and two strange men waiting for dinner ...

Friday morning ... [we] started off for home at 10.30 ... We argued a lot to keep warm, alternately trotted hard till too cold, then adjusted the slipping bedrolls and walked, then rode again, and got home at last just before five with every limb intact ...

Week Ending February 20th

Last week was rather harassing and not at all according to plan ... I met Cecilia coming home from Sunrise[16] and looking very perturbed, and no wonder. She had only been 15 minutes in the Sunrise School with the five or six children who come to Sunday School there when suddenly they discovered that the roof of the school was on fire and blazing merrily. There was no ladder, no means of reaching the place and of course no water, and it was too high to smother it with snow. So Cecilia sent one boy flying to the nearest house half-a-mile from the school for help, while she and the other children, knowing they could not save the building, set to work to save as much as they could from the inside. Presently a man arrived to help, and amongst them they got out every single thing that could be moved, i.e., the desks, the books, the maps, the blackboards and finally even the stove, while the helping man with an axe cut out and saved the windows. But only a short time after that the poor little school was burnt to the ground. It was the newest of all the schools up here, only finished in October, a log building like all the rest but very well finished. It was really no one's fault, except that there should have been a ladder by which someone *might* have reached the roof and done something before the fire took too firm a hold. But the cause was just the strong West wind which happened to blow some sparks down on to the wooden shingles (tiles), a thing that can happen to any house, but oddly enough very seldom does, as almost always the chimney carries them clear.

Cecilia was very much agitated by it all, though as no one was hurt and everything moveable had been saved, I think there was much to be thankful for, and certainly she had been the means of saving most of the things herself ...

[Monday] About five I rode into town to post the mail and find out what I could about trails for tomorrow. But in the Post Office two men came up and asked me to take a funeral. One was a nice middle aged man called Johnny B[rown][17] whose father had just died in hospital. I never knew the old man ... but during Brother Wolf's absence I am a 'Temporary Incumbent' responsible for such emergencies. So we arranged for the funeral to be on Wednesday at three, and for the body to be immediately taken from the hospital to the Church – there to rest while the coffin was made and afterwards until the Service. The alternative was to leave it in an iron shack where machinery was stored, and this seemed so unseemly a mortuary, that I felt sure Bro. Wolf would approve of my offering the Church instead.

So Muriel and I altered our plans once more and both spent Tuesday in long overdue visits ... Most of these people can produce their own essential food (meat, wheat, vegetables, and usually bread and butter) but for twelve months or more hardly any of them have had any money, so they just have to do without everything which they can't either produce themselves or obtain by barter in kind. The result is that almost everybody is desperately hard up for clothes, and every garment is patched and patched till it's practically all patchwork.

This was not quite so much the case last year, and I didn't then realize how horribly my new and varied clothing was ill-according with our profession here. We are gradually working down to a uniform and discarding everything that doesn't accord with it. It's a curious uniform for a Sisterhood and not *very* ecclesiastical, i.e. brown corduroy breeks and moosehide moccasins, a heavy brown or blue jersey for hacking about, plus a plain blue smock for Service and Sunday School. And out of doors a short brown canvas sheep-skin-lined coat, such as the farmers wear when they can afford it. In summer of course this and the jersey will go into dock, and we shall probably wear buff smocks for every day (because they don't fade) and the same blue for Sunday School and Church ...

Fancy all that about *our* clothes, when I was really talking about necessitous families ...

In the afternoon I went on to Fort St John to see that all was in order for the funeral ... They were still digging the grave, or rather blasting it with gun-powder, as the frost makes the ground into solid rock just now. And I was a little disconcerted to find the poor body still lying along a bench in the Church, waiting for the coffin which was not yet ready ...

The Church was quite full as it always is for funerals, and Muriel joined me there to play the hymns. In accordance with the extraordinary custom of these parts, the coffin was still open, but knowing Brother Wolf's mind about this, I insisted that it should be finally closed before the Service began – quite expecting a protest, and thankful that the revolution was accepted so meekly ... Another curious custom is that the congregation, however reverent and attentive, firmly refuses to take any part either in responses, psalm or even hymns. It seems to be considered disrespectful to the dead; so much so that the mourners even refuse to stand or kneel for any part of the Service, but sit like statues throughout. So Muriel and I had to respond and sing together like parson and clerk, which was altogether more exhausting than inspiring ...

The next day we made a sad and dreadful discovery about our little Harvey. I wouldn't tell you, except that we do so need your prayers for him.

During several weeks we have been losing things in the house. But being always on the run we all thought we had just been stupid and mislaid them and should find them directly we could really make time to look. But on Wednesday my little flashlight disappeared, and I knew I hadn't lost it. We wondered and we thought – and at last very reluctantly Muriel and I went to the boys' room and found it in the pocket of a coat someone had given Harvey. Then Muriel found a little notebook of hers and some pictures.

After supper I sent Fred out on a chore, and then had it out with Harvey. I asked him whether he had seen my flashlight. 'No.' Then would he mind if I searched his pockets (we had left it there)? I have never hated doing anything so much, but there was no choice, was there.

Then I asked him for (other things) and he denied all knowledge of them. I tried and tried every form of appeal to make him own up, because by that time we knew beyond any doubt that he had taken them. But still he denied. I sent him to bed and gave him till the morning to choose between owning up and being given another chance, or refusing and be-ing taken home to his father. It was a perfectly miserable night because I do love Harvey and his mother deserted him when he was two. After break-fast he denied again, and I had to do a vile thing, search him.

After that there was nothing for it but to take him to school (to find a fountain pen) and then straight home. It was the first ride I have ever had with Harvey and a pretty wretched one for us both ... The only moment when he showed any feeling was just before we left the house. He suddenly offered to give me back an old woollen scarf I gave him before Christmas. He said, 'This is yours.' I said, 'No, that's your own. I gave it to you.' And then for a moment the poor kid cried a little. We went West first to school, where I had to ask Petter[18] to let me look in his desk, and there was Cecilia's pen together with a box of clips of mine. She was awfully nice and really understanding about the poor child's hopeless background. But she agreed that the only thing was to banish him from school for a bit, and then to give him another chance.

So Harvey and I mounted again and set off for his home ... I hated dreadfully telling his father the whole story with the lies and everything. Mr Cheverton is a shabby little oldish man, about as inexpressive as his son, but he was clearly awfully upset about it. He kept saying, 'I can't understand it at all. He always used to be a straight boy. I can't understand it any.'

Harvey said nothing. He sat on the bench beside us (we were all three crouching by the little stove) trying to look entirely unconcerned. I told Mr Cheverton that I should have to leave him there until more things were found – Muriel's purse and my knife. Then if they were not stolen (as Harvey swore before God they were not) I would have him back and give him another chance.

'I want to believe you Harvey. Indeed I do. But if I'd told you as many lies as you've told me, would you believe me?'

'No,' said Harvey quite definitely.

He went back part of the way with me to help haul the horses through the drifts. Then before we parted, I made one desperate appeal to him to turn over a new leaf ... [He] stood looking at me very fixedly and adding something else under his breath which, as usual, I couldn't hear. But I thought it might be sort of regret or penitence or new resolve, so asked again, 'What did you say, Harvey?'

'Yer noseisfroze' ...

I've told you all about him, not as an idle tale, but that some of you anyway may understand enough to care for him and pray for him now. He's only 12, and has had practically *no* chance hitherto. Besides, who could resist

'Yernoseisfroze'

We'll get him honest somehow.

Up to the end of February

On Sunday ... Fred and I walked to Fort St John together at ten, discussing at some length the momentous problem of his Career. His dream is to go to sea as a wireless operator and I believe he would be quite good for this job if only I knew how to get him into it. The only danger at present is that being 16 and never having seen *any* society so far, he is at present dazzled by the glamour of city life – *as enjoyed in Fort St John!* There is a group of boys and girls there – chiefly the High School boys and girls – who go to all the dances, and often spend Sunday in sleigh outings and altogether live a gay life according to the possibilities here. It's perfectly innocent and not expensive, because no one has any money. They only feast on one another's pork and turnips (no: I should say potatoes, as the turnips are all finished up for this year) ... It's difficult to know how to draw him for a bit, and to keep his mind on the work and study for which he came here, and for which he really has quite real capacity, without seeming to be a dreary old kill-joy. Still, I've got to try ...

By the way, did I tell you about Cecilia's *NEW FRIEND?* His name is Ginger. Quite between you and me he is not good looking, but apparently bores through the deepest drift 'as easy as nothing' and to judge by this characteristic, combined with his appearance, I should say that his pedigree may have been

By Guinea-Pig out of Snow-Plough.

But Cecilia is a little sensitive about this.

On Tuesday morning ... who should walk in but Harvey. He looked awfully cold and exhausted and brought a note from his father asking if he might take back some more bedding as they hadn't enough for two ... So of course we fed him and warmed him, and after luncheon made up the bedding and some extra clothes in two sacks, and I decided to let him carry them back on Puck and to ride with him.

To tell the truth I longed to repent of all my sternness and keep him at once, but having determined to banish him for a fortnight, managed to be very judicial and cold ...

Poor Harvey! It seemed beastly to return him to stock like that. But I can't think how less than a fortnight's banishment can make him realize the real sin of lies and stealing, can you?

End of February till March 5th

... I spent most of Thursday with Miss Claxton[19] who was still in bed and had been suffering a great deal from her poor torn and dislocated knee. On the way home I called on the Sister Superior of the Providence (R.C.) Hospital,[20] and had such a nice welcome and pleasant half hour of real French conversation. They are delightful Sisters, from Quebec of course ...

On Friday I visited in Baldonnel, and especially plugged up to Mr Cheverton again, and after a suitable pow-wow, agreed to give Harvey another chance and let him come back on Sunday. The poor child was evidently longing to come, so we had a short earnest talk about the New Beginning, and I came away full of joy ...

Week Ending March 12th

... The ice on Charlie Lake[21] is at its very best now: 33 inches thick and splendidly hard. Directly the spring thaw begins it will soften gradually, and that process *might* begin any day now. So we agreed that Mr Colpitts[22] should haul me 28 blocks (two loads) from the lake, each one measuring 22 by 22 by 33 inches and weighing approximately 4½ cwt. These he will cover all over with saw dust, separately hauled from the lumber mill, and then he will haul enough poplar logs from his own land to build a nice little log house round them measuring about 10 by 12. So our drinking water for all the snowless part of the year – roughly seven months – will cost 40 dollars (roughly £10) the first time, but very much less another year after the ice house has been built ...

Our little Prodigal (Harvey) had arrived before us – by appointment – and was preparing for our return by lighting the heater, a little incongruous, but a comfort all the same. It seemed so natural to find him there that I could hardly believe the trying scenes we had been through the fortnight before were anything but a dream. We simply said 'Hullo Harvey' and he said 'Hullo.' Then we warmed up the soup and sat down together as usual. But after supper I took him into the Chapel and had as straight a talk as possible, and then we had some Prayers. Harvey is far from expressive. In fact he very seldom says anything – that you can hear – but I do believe he means to keep straight now ...

Next day [Muriel and I] separated and visited until 3.30 when we each took a short Sunday School ...

[I found a] young and lively [woman], very self-complete. She told me quite frankly that she had no use for any kind of Religion as Science had disproved it all. That led to a marvellous conversation, during which she told me as a well known fact that Scientists had already created perfectly good living organisms, but the Church by the Power of the Purse was keeping it as dark as possible. Of course lots of the men are like this, especially the Americans, but this was the first woman I had so far met out here. She did admit the necessity of some Supreme Cause behind the universe, and thought It was probably Electricity. So I said, 'Is Electricity your idea of God, then?' 'Yes, if you like to call it that. Electricity is the greatest power we know and accounts for everything.' 'Does Electricity account for Love and Beauty and Courage and Self-sacrifice?' 'Well – Yes – Anyway (triumphantly) you couldn't have any of them *without* Electricity!' ...

[Next day] in passing the store a man ran out to me with very sad news indeed. 'I've just come across the Pine. Mr Framst was killed this afternoon by a falling tree. I left him in the bush and came straight off to tell the Policeman.[23] Yes, it's sure too bad isn't it? Will you be able to come and see Mrs Framst soon?'

'Yes, of course, I'll come tomorrow.' It was already nine o'clock and Puck was pretty well spent after his 25 miles of heavy trail, otherwise I would have gone at once. But Mr Framst, wasn't that dreadful. Such a nice quiet Swede, almost the first man to settle across the Pine, and with his English wife and four little children the only family I found when I went over there last September year ...

Poor, poor Mrs Framst ... First thing next morning I went of course ... It took me three hours to reach the quiet little log house surrounded by deep bush ... Inside I found George T[eather][24] the English bachelor who was a sort of partner to Framst, and a woman neighbour and the two younger children having dinner. No fuss and no sign of anything different except that neither Mr nor Mrs Framst were there. I found her in the little bedroom sitting on the bed in stony silence, and on the other bed the elder girl and boy (12 and 10) were lying, silent too.

I only stayed an hour, and arranged the funeral with George Teather. Mrs Framst was too stunned to discuss any details. Only she asked that he might be buried on his own land and not taken across the Pine to Fort St John ... So we arranged to hold the funeral on Monday, starting from the school-house at two o'clock. Meanwhile Teather was to make the coffin and the neighbouring bachelors to dig the grave which is a long job at this time of year. They have to make big fires on the ground and thaw it foot by foot until they get right down below the level of the frost ...

Next morning at 9.30 the faithful Cecilia called for me with Puck to go together across the Pine for Mr Framst's funeral ... We arrived before one and went straight to the Framst's house ... They fed us very quickly and then I had a few words with Mrs Framst who was still sitting quite quietly on the bed exactly as she had been last Friday.

Then Cecilia and I said we must go on to the school to get ready ... We took the Sunday School cross and cloth with us, and tried to arrange the teacher's desk to look as much like a Church as possible ... The school soon got packed full and at last the coffin arrived from the house, a home-made one of course, of rough boards covered with cheap black cloth. But on top were a few paper flowers, beautifully made. I had previously asked Teather *not* to open the coffin, as it seemed to be too painful, and as Mrs Framst really is English, she would not expect it ... I gave the little address first and then we had the most beautiful Service of the kind that you can imagine.

The school was quite crammed, I suppose 40 or 50 people, nearly all men, and only a dozen sitting. We sang the hymns unaccompanied of course, they sang wonderfully well; and instead of the usual display of grief, there was perfect restraint and dignity all through. Mrs Framst was quiet and dignified, with Muriel and little Ellison looking after her very tenderly (the two smallest girls were left at home). In spite of the rough bare school-room, it reminded me of a Service at Home more than any other I have yet taken part in up here. There was such a real feel of quiet and reverence and controlled sorrow ...

The grave had been dug on the Framst's homestead, about a mile from the school. We drove to it in 12 or more sleighs going at a foot's pace and looking very beautiful as they turned a corner of the trail; plain rough waggon-sleighs of course, and chiefly drawn by heavy farm horses, the drivers standing up in their fur caps and sheep-skins and the snow still falling thick as cotton wool.

We drove into a patch of deep bush, and there was the grave all carefully lined with spruce boughs. There was hardly a sound. The bearers' footsteps were silent in the snow, and even the occasional soft jingle of a sleigh bell seemed muffled by the thickly falling flakes. Mrs Framst stood still and steady with her two children. It seemed an irreverence to break into such a deep quiet even with the words of Committal. And so we laid the body of this simple gentle pioneer in the soil of his own homestead, and all among the trees which had killed him ...

Next morning Cecilia and I ... went right through to the Holdup in five hours and slept with Mrs Slyman,[25] the French-Canadian whose husband is a Mahommedan-Syrian-Canadian storekeeper. He is constantly away freighting and she gets very lonely especially as she has never learned to read, *or* had a child. So she welcomed us, and actually had a spare bedstead, so we slept in luxury off the floor. As a matter of fact a cousin of Mr Slyman's was staying there too, to do the chores for her, another Moslem called Frank N[asser].[26] After supper we all talked a bit about Religion; and finally we had rather strange evening Prayers together – Cecilia and I, a Roman Catholic and a Mohammedan.

Next morning we went on to the Blueberry River ... After about 12 miles the forest thinned out into coulee and open spaces, giving us a delightful

feeling of having discovered a new world. Then after another mile or two
we found the first house and visited a lady called Mrs S[mith].[27] She was
young and really French-Canadian; and about 200 yards away lived her
mother-in-law, another Mrs S[mith] whom we also went to see. Both houses
were of course one-room shacks, very rough and poor and with no sort of
floor as yet. One Mrs Smith fed us most generously on bacon and potatoes, and then we discussed with the other the problem of her little child
of three who has a terribly deformed leg. We are trying to get her out to an
Orthopaedic hospital at Winnipeg, but my goodness the cost of it! When
you see these people in their remote little floorless home, you wonder
what can be done about it. However there are the Daughters of the Empire, and the Red Cross might help – and possibly Muriel could take the
poor little girl so far with her when she goes Home in May ...

Holy Week and Easter
... [Phyllis Moon] had borrowed and brought with her a tall grey colt called
Battleaxe, under four years old and quite untrained. We put him in the
stable with the rest, but decided that we couldn't possibly take the responsibility of letting her ride him while staying here ...

[Easter Day] Muriel, Phyllis Moon and I went into Fort St John for the
9 o'clock Celebration ... There were only six of us at the Service there, but
it was marvellous to have one all the same, and to feel at one with all of you
everywhere ...

[Later] I saddled Battleaxe and mounting Phyllis on the more fool-proof
Puck took her off to Evensong at Fort St John ... Afterwards we started
home carefully in the dark, Muriel ahead on Robin. Suddenly in the heavi-
est part of the trail Muriel called out, '*Dog team coming!*'

It's a very strange thing that horses, who of course don't mind loose
dogs at all, are absolutely terrified of teams harnessed to sleighs. We heard
bells jingling, and about 50 yards ahead could just make out something
low down coming swiftly towards us over the snow.

Instantly all the horses lost their heads. Robin and Puck leaped sideways
and fell over into deep drifts, but I had no time to see what happened then
because Battleaxe swung round and started a war dance all his own. After
three or four minutes I managed to get him on all fours again, and was just
recovering my breath and stirrups when the other two flashed past me,
riderless, and that was the last straw for Battleaxe. He shot me over the
horn on to his neck and went off like a rocket, and so, after a short ten
seconds, did I.

Beaten after all – wasn't it sickening!

We all crawled out of our respective drifts and looked for each other in some anxiety. I was really anxious about Phyllis, but she was all right, thank Goodness; so then we tried to find the horses. There was simply no sign of Robin or Puck, and no hope of finding them in the dark. But oddly enough I came upon Battleaxe and caught him without much difficulty. So we agreed that I should ride him straight home lest Cecilia should be worried by long delay, and the other two should walk the remaining mile ...

And so eventually we all got home, not a bit worse apart from a bruised cheek which I think I had acquired from contact with the saddle horn or Battleaxe's head – or something, I don't know what. We left the gate-bar down in hopes that our little prodigal ponies would eventually come home too.

And so we came to the end of a perfect Easter Day. Next morning was below zero again, but fine and bright. I ran to the stable – but no Robin or Puck was there. So after Prayers and chores Cecilia and I went off on the other two to look for them ... We told Mr Pickell[28] at the Post Office, and the stores, and the restaurant and were just starting off to explore another road – when over the brow of the hill we saw two riders coming; and as they got nearer we recognized with joy the familiar black and brown. The men had found them about six miles North of Fort St John, and as they were walking to town themselves, they each took a lift, and as Robin and Puck are known to everybody, they knew well enough where to bring them back.

You can think how delighted we were, especially as they were both quite unhurt, and Muriel's haversack full of S.S. properties was still safe on Robin's horn.

We started home in triumph, Cecilia leading Robin to Ginger. Battleaxe wouldn't lead or be lead. So I rode him and let Puck follow loose. And we had just come half way home when – would you believe it – that blessed dog-team turned the corner again!

They were still a hundred yards away, but we were on a fenced trail so bound to meet, and I knew we couldn't hold four against them so soon after last night. So I shouted to Cecilia to dismount and tie up, but before she could do it, Robin had broken away and Puck was off like a flash.

However we did secure the other two, and then started to give chase on foot. After a mile of uphill running we found them caught and tied up by some unknown Samaritan. We waited cautiously till the dog-team had really gone by and was out of sight, then collected our quartette once more and got them all home at last, feeling we had spent an ideal Church Workers' Easter Monday ...

April 9–15, 1932

... Our last news is very sad indeed. Harvey was caught during the Easter holidays catching and killing a neighbour's chickens – goodness knows why, but he had killed a turkey too – so they complained to the Policeman and before I even knew about it a charge was filed against him. Of course I went at once to the Policeman, and went into every detail of the wretched business. Apparently there is some kind of kink in the lad, due I am sure, to all the neglect of his life.

Anyway he is alas, convicted, and the law of this country allows no alternative but to send him away to an Industrial School[29] for two years. I had a huge talk with him, and tried to get it all straightened out. He seems really sorry for the grief he has caused his father and the disappointment to me. And he has promised to take his punishment like a man and ask God's help to make a new start.

Perhaps it's the best thing for him in the end, but we are all terribly sad and shall miss his slow silent companionship in the house. Of course I shall write to the authorities and keep in touch with him, and May is going to write to him too if we are allowed to do so ... It may be the making of him yet; but it's a great sorrow to let him go.

Week Ending April 16th
... On Tuesday Muriel and I started for Rose Prairie[30] – what might be called the East Montney Circuit ... One woman called Mrs T[hompson] has two tiny boys and a baby girl,[31] and the early history of each one was pretty agitating. The eldest boy, Buddy, was the one I told you about 18 months ago when he was *lost in the bush for two days*. He was two and three-quarters years old and wandered off after a puppy when she wasn't looking. They searched everywhere for 52 hours and were just giving up all hope when he was suddenly found in deep bush about two and a half miles from home. He had been out for two nights and nearly three days with no food or shelter, in fairly hard frost at night. He was wet through, had lost his shoes and socks and his feet were all swollen and full of thorns. But otherwise he was none the worse for it, and after a good meal and sleep quickly recovered – a good example of what a Guardian Angel can do.

Then two or three months before the birth of the second boy she was out riding somewhere when the horse threw her, trod on her and broke her ankle. She crawled homeward several miles and then mercifully met her husband who carried her the rest of the way. The little girl was born two months prematurely, when Mrs Thompson was *entirely alone* in the house – except for the two tiny boys. They were too young to do anything but cry, which they did steadily all the time. The baby was born at 11.15 in the morning, and it was not till 2.30 that another woman happened to look in and see her ... But she and the baby are both thriving ...

[Next day] after Prayers we started Southward again, Muriel going round by three or four families towards Indian Creek, and I taking most of the day to find and visit Mrs Kelly (our late neighbour) in her new home ...

All the way to the Kelly's I was rather nervous, because you see, I am in Mr Kelly's blackest books, and it was quite on the cards that he would refuse to let me into the house. The reason of this is a rather pathetic little row I had with him – or rather he with me – as long ago as February. He is a very selfish and bad-tempered husband, and treats Mrs K. rather like a black slave, so that she is terrified of him. One day after I had seen her crying through fear of him, I couldn't bear it, and told him it was a shame and he ought to treat his wife with more consideration and not wear her out with work and chores. From that moment Mr Kelly stopped all inter-course between the two houses, forbade Mrs K. to do our washing or to sell us bread (rather a clever reprisal that!), refused to let them come to a farewell supper or have any dealings with us at all.

This went on for their remaining two months as our neighbours, and then they went North. So you can understand why I rather funked this visit. But on the other hand I knew her to be miles from any other woman, and probably pretty lonely, so it seemed obviously right to go. Only I couldn't help feeling a little like Jacob going to meet Esau,[32] and wishing that I could send on two hundred she-goats and 60 milch-camels with their colts by way of peace offering.

The homestead seems a good one, and the buildings, though still unfin-ished, very good. Georgie Kelly knew Robin a long way off, and ran out to meet us. But he tied him outside the door and not in the barn. Mrs K. was alone in the house and greeted me with marked nervousness and restraint. Mr K. was out hauling firewood from the bush, but would be in soon. She showed me over the house (which of course didn't take more than three minutes and most of *that* was the cellar). And then I sat and made conver-sation while she got the dinner and both of us kept one eye cocked on the door, outside which poor Robin stood as a kind of shock absorber.

At last Georgie came in and said, 'You're to put your horse in the barn.' 'Did Daddy say so?' 'Sure.' ... So I followed Georgie to the barn and found him [Mr K.] there putting in his own team. We looked at each other in dead silence for a moment; then I said something stupid and hearty and held out my hand – and after what seemed like hours he took it.

We walked back together talking about how he had chopped his toe with the axe, and directly we got inside the house Mrs Kelly became a completely different person – all her constraint vanished and she beamed all over. We had a very cheerful dinner and I stayed a long time afterwards, finally getting some Reading and Prayer alone with Mrs K. It really does seem as if the hatchet is buried and I am *so* thankful.

It seemed a long way from there to Indian Creek. It was raining and cold and the trail was all deep water or slush, so that Robin was tacking all the while and could only trot or rather flounder a few steps at a time. Suddenly I felt dog tired and found myself thinking of drawing rooms at Home! And of reading a book on a sofa! Luckily these unhealthy meditations were interrupted by a visit or two of no particular interest; and at last just about six I got to Mrs Jarvis ...

[Next day] On the way home we went to the Police Barracks to find out about Harvey, whose pitiful little trial had been the day before. I would have stayed for it had I been able to help him in any way; but the Policeman, with whom I had discussed it all beforehand, said that there was nothing I could do. So now as we had expected, he told us that Harvey was found guilty and had to go away to an Industrial School for two years next Monday. I asked leave to go and see him. He was just in bed in a little attic upstairs.

I said 'Hullo, Harvey,' and he said 'Hullo' and after that there seemed no more to say. You see we had talked it all out in the Chapel a week before. So I sat by his side for a little while and then said a Prayer and promised to come and see him tomorrow. But downstairs I got bolder and asked the Policeman whether Harvey might come back to us for his last Sunday. It seemed so dreadful for him to be kept there where all the school children go by.

To Muriel's and my delight he said 'Yes,' if I would take personal responsibility and bring him back by 9.30 on Monday morning. So it was arranged that we should fetch him next day, and we got home at 10.30 pretty tired but thankful for lots of things ...

Cecilia brought Harvey in the afternoon [Saturday], more silent than ever, but quite natural and at home. He went about the usual chores, helped me to wash up supper, and seemed quite happy. None of us can make out whether he minds going away for two years or not. But I know I mind him going. He seems to be part of the house.

Week Ending April 23rd

... [Next morning] we had short Prayers and Harvey chose the hymn 'Holy Father Hear Me.' Then he said Goodbye to the others and I rode with him to the town. He wasn't allowed to take any clothes beyond what he had on, so he had no luggage of any kind; and all I could give him had to be in his pockets. So I gave him a New Testament, two kittens made of soap to remind him of Lucifer and Michael, four stamped envelopes, a packet of sandwiches and three chocolate bars. We parted at the door of the Police Barracks, and a little later when I was in the town I saw the Mail-truck go by rocking and skidding through the deep mud. In the cab, beside the driver sat Mr S[mith] the Policeman, dressed, as they all [say] here, exactly like a Scoutmaster. And behind, swaying in the Mail bags, sat Harvey. It will take them anything up to twenty-four hours to get to Dawson Creek, then another twenty-four to Edmonton, then two days or so to Coquitlan where the Industrial School is. He has promised to write me a line on arrival if allowed by the authorities, and to his father also. That's what the envelopes are for ...

... [Wednesday] I rode Southward again across the broad featureless and quite trail-less plain to join Cecilia at the Callisons. They are the Old Family of the Montney, having been there three whole years, and their house, apart from ours, is I should think, the largest North of the Peace. It has *four* bedrooms and a living room and kitchen; so as their own family only numbers nine children plus the Schoolmaster you can understand that they are always ready to welcome visitors. Cecilia and I slept very happily in the living room, as there were already two or three extra upstairs. Breakfast time was a fine sight, very like a Dutch picture – no, a Teniers[33] perhaps. It's quite a long room with a long deal table down the middle of it, and a stove and a washing basin at the end. There were 14 people of all ages, all trickling in and gradually accumulating, first at the communal washing basin, some washing and some combing their hair; then at the stove, some bringing in snow, some fetching water, and others filling bowls of porridge, and finally all the benches and boxes round the table. All these things happening at once in a fairly small space, and with a great deal of talk made a fine picture, framed by guns and horns and bearskins hanging on the rough wooden walls ...

Week Ending April 30th
... Thursday I spent in Fort St John, writing for the Mail, doing commissions for the family, and visiting the Society Leaders of the City. This is where we are all the least happy. It is this objectionable quality of *English-ness* which in this tiny community of Americans or born Westerners is so unpardonable. It is a difficult quality to shake off or grow out of it and what's more – who in their senses would *want* to grow out of it? It's all rather a puzzle to me. If our English speech and manners and way of thinking really hinder the Kingdom of God anywhere, we simply must try to give them up. And yet – well – it's not very easy. Cecilia even thinks it's not very easy at 26; but that's absurd of course.

I don't think any of this difficulty exists among the real homesteaders. It's only the rather smart ladies of the little City. The others are much too scattered and struggling to criticize that sort of thing; and besides many of them are from the British Isles or Europe, and all seem to take us for granted as women and therefore friends.

The funny thing is that although Brother Wolf is just as English as we are, it doesn't go against him so much. Partly I think because he is a man, and partly because he really is so amazingly all things to all men, that I believe he would willingly turn black in the company of a negro if that would be *any* help.

On Friday Cecilia and I suddenly discovered that we had a day in hand. So what do you think we did? NOTHING.

We turned the horses out in the pasture, and after the morning chores, we took two chairs outside the house and read aloud and mended for two whole hours. It certainly was a unique occasion and we enjoyed it awfully, though feeling rather guilty all the time. We read the Hibbert Journal[34] first, and might have gone on to something even more sparkling had not Mr Simpson arrived to look at our still-born well ...

Week Ending May 14th
This diary is so fearfully self-centred that I'm sure you must think us utterly parochial and absorbed in our own absurd little narrow life with no consciousness of the world outside, but I can only just achieve the time and energy to record our own tedious little adventures which will certainly never be recorded anywhere else. Honestly we aren't ostriches, but we do follow events as well as we can in weekly papers always three weeks old. The Boat-race was a great excitement because you see Cecilia is *fatally* Oxford.[35] But Muriel is mysteriously neutral, and Fred had no idea what it was all about; so we had great fun telling him the whole theory and practice of Putney to Mortlake with fierce wrangles, which surprised him very much at first!

We didn't hear the result till Wednesday of Holy Week, when it came through on one of the few radios in the town. But all through the interval I had Puck's bridle beautifully decorated with strips off an old blue night-gown, so he was all right anyway – while Cecilia lacked the courage or was *too wise* to risk any colour on Ginger. I congratulated her afterwards on her good sense, which enraged her very nicely ...

Next morning Muriel and I started off for the Holdup ... We took the old trail across the Reserve[36] ... and finally about nine o'clock, fetched up with Mrs Cyril T[omlinson], the lady whom you remember with nine dogs in a one-room shack ... Mrs T. was most welcoming ... so we tied Robin and

Puck under trees to nibble at the baby grass for an hour or so before putting them in the little chicken house which at present acts as a stable.

After that it was rather strenuous, because Muriel and I having ridden all day against a strong wind were dropping with sleep, while Mrs T., having been alone for two days, was bursting with talk. We carried on brightly enough till about eleven, when I suggested Reading and Prayers and she agreed very willingly ... After Prayers and a longish talk, she allowed us to get ready for bed and showed us a fine big couch to spread our bedding on. We were just undressed and tucking in when the nine dogs started barking louder than ever and Mrs T. shouted, 'There he is coming up the trail.' Muriel and I were just dropping off when the door burst open and in he came – 'Miss Storrs, Miss Haslam,' cried Mrs T., 'You don't want to go to sleep now that Cyril's come!' We pulled ourselves together and were introduced to Cyril, feeling rather funny as we were both recumbent in sleeping bags. But he thought nothing of that of course, and the bright talk started again for another hour. After that, it being after one o'clock, I deliberately and firmly went to sleep, and left our host and hostess to finish their supper and get into the neighbouring bed ...

The Nicely's[37] [whom we visited later] are poor like everyone else. The children barefooted and wearing dresses made out of an old sheet. Having no cow, they had no milk or butter, also no meat or porridge and of course no jam. But they've got chickens so we breakfasted off fried eggs and potatoes. There were cups for us three grown-ups, but the children drank their weak milkless tea out of saucers, and we all washed in a very old dinted cooking pot.

Yet the house was as clean as a pin and there was no trace of squalor or depression. The whole family were as bright and jolly as possible, and after breakfast insisted on another Sunday School! ... It was quite hard to leave this family; it was so appealing. You see they are quite out of reach of any school and yet very bright intelligent children, loving everything and *very* well brought up ...

Finally [Friday] Muriel and I [visited] ... the one Store-keeper's wife, Mrs T[itus],[38] who is a very great lady with padded arm-chairs, thin China and a piano. She was most friendly but rather too classy and rich for us after our bare-legged and milkless friends. Still I'm sure she is nice and must get to know her better.

At 4.15 we started for the last 21 miles home ... We found Cecilia full of good works, with supper waiting, bread made, a clean house, a lot of garden dug and all the district visited. She really is a marvel, and so delightful to come home to.

Week Ending May 21st

... On Tuesday, after a hurried early lunch, Muriel and I started off again ... [At Rose Prairie] I twice went to the house of the Scientific Materialist lady to whom I had sent a book, and wanted to find out if she had read it, but the wretch was out all day.

... I had lunch with a grey-haired Anglican Irish woman named Mrs M[urphy].[39] She is pretty spirited for an old bird. For when things went wrong in Ireland and her husband wouldn't move, she left him with the eldest son to carry on and came out herself with the younger children to make a new home for all of them. So far the husband hasn't joined them, but she hopes that, as he is a good Loyalist and lives in County Cork, the repudiation of the Oath[40] will stir him at last to action. Besides that, she is a tremendously keen Churchwoman and longs for our Services, and wants the two youngest children to be confirmed like the rest. And most remarkable of all, when I began the preliminaries of leaving, said, 'You'll sure not go without a word of Scripture and Prayer.'

This is the first person actually to ask for it, and she an Anglican.

One of the new mothers we came across, gave me some more out-grown baby clothes, and I found a mother further South most thankful for them. Everywhere the clothing problem is the toughest ... Dozens of children are bare-legged, and the women make up underclothes and dresses out of flour sacks, or old sheets, while the nicest and most respectable men are in rags ... I am mentioning this now in case you know of any working-parties or clothes collections who would like to start soon preparing to send us things in the autumn, ... but please don't forget the men. They have to work out of doors in all weathers and are often in rags which are far beyond all patching.

If you know Any Men, and you probably know Some, please ask them for an old vest or flannel shirt. It would make something to talk about at dinner parties anyway ...

Do you know we found in the Montney some families can't even afford to buy vegetable seeds, which produce the staple food of the country. However, I believe Brother Wolf has some to give away.

Also, instead of tea or coffee, they are using wonderful home-made brews. In one house we had coffee made of roast wheat, and in another we drank 'Pea tea!' Both seem to us a little dreary, but they are distinctly harmless and don't require cash, so I suppose you can get to like them. Certainly these people teach us much about adaptability, as none of them seem to mind in the least what they go without, and never grouse about any physical hardships ...

Week Ending May 28th, 1932

Trinity Sunday was observed here, not under that name, but as an Empire Festival in anticipation of the 24th. So instead of the ordinary Sunday programme we all mustered at a 'United Service' in Fort St John in the afternoon ...

For once, having no Sunday School to go to first, I was very leisurely and grand, and *walked* into town, in full Commissioner's Uniform, cords, SKIRT and all. You see I have the honour to be Commissioner for the Peace River Block; and although nobody here has the faintest idea of what a Commissioner is or does, I wear the uniform very occasionally – chiefly to subdue Cecilia.

The Service was shared between Brother Wolf and Mr Birch,[41] the newly arrived Presbyterian Minister. He is a very tall, thin, dark young man, who seems to be delicate and rather helpless. There are hardly any Presbyterians up here, so he rides about on Ping, the slow and lame but very gentlemanly horse that I had for a short time the year before last. Brother Wolf is typically kind and brotherly to him, had him stay when he first arrived, told him about all the different districts, and tries hard to co-operate and not compete. But we can't help being a little sad about it, especially as a United Church student has now arrived in the Montney, so now all our Divisions are getting fully established ...

Next morning Brother Wolf came over at eight and celebrated for us in the Chapel, Muriel's last Service with us ... I shall miss her enormously, and do so wonder whether she will come back again ...

So now we are two only, and waiting for Sister Tertia,[42] whoever she may be.

Week Ending June 4th, 1932

... The children [at Fish Creek][43] are delightful, quite unspoilt and really keen ... The chief family there consists of seven children, the M[iddletons].[44] They range from Billy aged 14, to Gordon aged three. After School Billy gave me a note asking me to go back to supper with his mother, and as she is a special protégée of Muriel's I agreed at once of course ... Before supper they all washed in turns without being told, waited for grace, passed the food round spontaneously, talked politely, and asked to be excused before rising from the table – and Oh My! you would hardly understand how this nearly took my breath away ... Poor Mrs Middleton. Her husband doesn't care a rap about her or his family. He lives a mile or two away and never comes near them or takes the smallest interest in his children. She feels it all very bitterly, and I am afraid it is affecting her health ...

Week Ending June 4th

... On Friday ... after lunch we went to the *Stampede,* a sort of Cowboy Meet in the town in honour of the King's birthday. Everybody was there and it was rather fun for an hour or so, wandering round the field on Ginger and Puck and greeting our friends on their Gingers and Pucks. There were bucking competitions and steer-roping and races, and most of the men looked very delightful in their immense hats, and big hide or bear-skin shaps on their legs. There were the usual excitements. One horse jumped a fence into the spectators and knocked out an innocent old man, another fell down dead during a race, while the mare that Cecilia was asked to ride in a race (and would have but for her [sore] thumb) ran right off the course and bucked her rider over her head. Altogether it was a typical Western show, and as such, I suppose, not wasted time ...

Week Ending June 11th

... [Tuesday] we went on to the Blueberry ... At last we got out to the Smiths, and had a long visit arranging for their little crippled girl to come down to Fort St John and be taken out by Miss M—e to the Victoria Solarium.[45] It took a lot of discussion, during which they kindly fed us with fried eggs, and promised to start in lots of time for their 30 to 40 mile waggon drive, and to bring a tent and camp outside Fort St John on arrival. We offered to put them up for the night before the child's going, but they preferred to be independent, and I rather admired them for that. We prayed with them for the little girl – she is only three and has a dreadfully malformed and shortened leg ...

[Then] we went on to the Morrows[46] for the night. Mrs Morrow is much happier than she used to be on account of a new and quite unexpected addition to the family. An Indian Squaw a few miles North of them died in giving birth to a baby boy sometime in April. The Indians had no cow and couldn't feed the baby. So they packed it tightly in moss and bark and the father brought it down to Mrs Morrow and begged her to keep it for him. So when we got there we found this little papoose, now nearly two months old, looking rather sweet, just like an Indian doll. She said it was almost starved to death when it arrived and she had an awful job peeling off the moss and bark from its poor little body. Anyway the new interest has done her a lot of good. She loves the baby and wants Brother Wolf to christen him; but when I inquired by what name – thinking of something like Hiawatha – she gave me rather a shock by saying – 'Frank'!

After supper and Sunday School by Post and Guide talk with the two girls, I suggested rather nervously a Bible reading; and just what I dreaded took place. The Morrows welcomed the idea, but after a few verses *Mr* Morrow launched out into a flood of cranks and heresies which continued far into the night. In fact Cecilia and Mrs M. discreetly retired to bed and I was left grappling with the beasts of Ephesus[47] till one o'clock, and even then could only hack my way out of the conversation and leave him still exposing the wickedness of the Churches. However ... Mrs Morrow told me in the morning that he had greatly enjoyed the evening as he simply *loved* arguing and up there no one existed to argue with him except herself and Myrtle who had long ceased provide any sport ...

Diary Ending June 25th

... Having provided for the dependents [Cecilia and I] took Ginger and Robin and of course Kristin, and started off at about 11 o'clock [on Monday] for the river pack trail ...

The first of [my visits] was a delightful elderly Durham miner and his wife – pure Durham and pure miner and openly ignorant of farming but most happy in their attempts to learn. They said it took them *ages* to milk their cow, and the pigs were still full of mysteries for them; but they took me with immense pride to see the sow and her nine little pigs. This happy mother's name is Phyllis! ...

The last seven miles were very dense bush, and the mosquitoes thicker than ever. But we reached the A[rdills][48] in time for supper and had a delightful evening with them. Mr Ardill is a son of an Irish Canon, and Mrs Ardill is a highly educated Dutch lady full of humour and very charming, and they have four of the most delightful children you can imagine ...

[The next] morning my first visit was to the two sisters of two young men called A[llen][49] ... You can't think how exciting it was to find *two grown-up Spinsters and one of them as old as me – yes, I really mean it.*

They were *so* nice, at least one was, and I'm sure the other is too, but unfortunately she seemed too shy to speak. The elder talked enough for several, and told me all their history as usual ...

... (Thursday) I received two telegrams, one from Ruth Spooner[50] announcing her arrival on July 13th, which is most delightful; and the other from a complete stranger called Margaret Harris,[51] asking whether she and a brother could visit us on Saturday, i.e., the day after tomorrow. She said they would arrive in the Mail-truck, so we knew they might be up by noon, i.e., before we could reasonably hope to be at home. So I sent a night letter telling them either to wait at the Mission House or if they preferred to find their way to my house which is of course always open ...

On Friday we started off for home at eight o'clock ... As we rode we wondered and wondered who the mysterious Margaret Harris *could* be. The telegram said Bishop Rix[52] had told her to come here, so we assumed at last that she must be a Church Worker travelling for some Society, and had rather fun putting her together. We decided that her brother would be a dark silent Clergyman probably recovering from a break-down. We wondered how long they meant to stay, and what on earth we would do with them if they couldn't ride ...

But what do you think? Our elderly Church Worker and broken-down parson brother turned out to be a most delightful girl and boy, aged 21 and 19, having a tour of Canada before the boy (whose name is Ronald) goes on from Harrow to Oxford. They had come over for three months, and had visited almost every part of the country, including a long trip up the West Coast in the Mission Boat 'Columbia' ...

Well anyway, in about five minutes they were completely at home, sat by and told us where they had been while we hastily ate cake and cheese, and afterwards joined us in all the chores that were waiting to be done – cleaning out the water barrel and filling it from the dam, splitting fire wood, fetching the milk and generally starting up life again ...

Week Ending July 2nd
... On Monday the Harrises departed ... I was really very sorry indeed to see them go, and am tempted to hope that one day Margaret might come back and join the sisterhood as a fellow-worker ...

... [Next week] we prepared for camp in good earnest ... All this time *no rain* and bitter complaints, so we felt that our little camp was destined to be the required Jonah.[53] And sure enough, Tuesday opened grey and heavy with a stiff West wind and steady drizzle. Poor Cecilia, it was just exactly what she expected. We got up at 6.15 ... and then, while Cecilia was loading the car, I took the horses to their new lodging. While I was doing this, the Heavens opened and the rain descended in floods. In about five minutes I was soaked to the skin, and realized that if this went on we simply should have to postpone for a day anyway, as of course the site is miles from any sort of building. This I broke to Cecilia, who thought it poor-spirited, I think ... Of course having done all this it *did* begin to improve. The torrent turned to a shower, and then to a drizzle, and then gradually stopped, but the sky was still heavier than lead. Still it was soon clear that we *could* [leave], and we decided that we would ...

The site is very delightful, a spit of land clear of bush, looking down to and across and up and down the lake ... The water was very good until Friday afternoon, when it rained heavily and a stiff wind blew across the lake from the East – since when a green scum produced by some weed has collected, and the water has turned to pea soup. At first they wouldn't bathe in it, but we have got over that. And for drinking we strain it three times which changes it from a bright green purée to a palish blue green consomme, which, however, we refrain from drinking neat ...

One difference from English camps is that you require no artificial screening for anything ... Another difference is that when not in Uniform we *all* wear the Universal Uniform – Overalls (i.e., trousers with a breast piece in front and braces all in one) – and if you saw the roughness of the ground and the bush, you would know the reason why. Anyhow, they are strong and protective without being hampering, and you can't think how nice all the children look in them, with different coloured shirts or sweaters underneath the braces. Cecilia and I wear the same of course, and we all have bare feet as far as thorns and snags permit. Most of the children go barefoot during the summer and their feet are splendidly hard ...

All Wednesday night it seemed to be pouring, and I had an anxious hour wandering round the tents, throwing ground sheets over their larger holes and securing pegs and guy lines. In the morning it was still pouring; so having no means of drying, should the children's only clothes get wet through ... we kept them in the tents till after breakfast. Cecilia heroically got the fire going in torrential rain and we took round the porridge and tea. After breakfast to our great joy the rain stopped, and the rest of the day was cloudy but fine. Neither cold nor rain nor green scum could check the passion for bathing ...

After supper [on Friday] they all played the fool gloriously by the lake side, especially two born comedian sisters called Iva and Iowne.[54] These two girls aged 14 and 13 are not Guides yet, but want to be. They come from Indian Creek, and have been deserted by their mother who sounds like a regular bad lot. They in turn got tired of living with their father (who all the neighbours say is perfectly harmless and kind) and once last fall and once this spring, they ran away from him and tried to get out of the country alone to seek their fortune. Both times they were caught and taken home; but you can imagine the whole thing is a bit unsatisfactory. Now they have taken a fancy to us and want to be Guides ... They are both good-looking, very athletic and *tremendously* vivacious and lively – more like gifted Cockneys bred for the Music Halls than normal settlers' children of Canadian stock ... These two gave immense pleasure by their really skilled acrobatics on floating logs, until finally Iva crowned a successful performance by falling backwards into the lake and crawling out wet to the skin. Then came the immense fun of all pulling off her soaking dress, trousers and petticoat (!) and wringing them out, while an immediate collection was made to re-clothe her for the walk home ...

The last girl to arrive was Dorothy St[evenson],[55] who rode with her father from Indian Creek and arrived on Saturday at about 11 o'clock ... We collected some breakfast for them, and as they sat eating in front of the store-tent, Mr Stevenson blurted out to us the most terrible news.

Do you remember my mentioning Mr Hoffstrom,[56] who built the Church Hall at Baldonnel? He is a hearty cheerful Swede with a mouthful of solid gold teeth, and he owns the lumber mill down on the Peace River at Taylor Flats. We knew him chiefly as the devoted father of four fair-haired little girls aged from five to thirteen, whom he took with him everywhere he went in his car (he being one of the very few men who can still afford a car). All the time the Church at Baldonnel was building we used to see the four little daughters playing round. Mrs Hoffstrom is a stout placid Swedish lady. They had the sorrow of losing their fifth child, also a little girl, a year ago. Mr Hoffstrom's central care was for his children, and he was very friendly to us for their sake.

They were at Taylor School of course, and therefore in Cecilia's S.S. and the two eldest were a Guide and a Brownie. These two she had expected would come to camp, but at the last moment Mr Hoffstrom wouldn't let them come, because he was afraid of the lake.

Well, on Thursday he had taken all four of them for a great treat to the Dawson Creek Sports ... Coming off the ferry [at night] on the North side, as he had come a thousand times before, Mr Hoffstrom by some inexplicable mistake started up the car *in reverse*. It ran straight back and plunged into the river, and all his little girls were caught ... and drowned.

Somehow he himself got swept out of the car and carried by the current half a mile down the river. Then he was washed up on the bank and rushed back, only to find that the car had completely disappeared in the swirl of mud and the darkness. It was not till morning came that it was found and pulled out of the river.

The news fell upon us all like a thunder bolt, especially upon the girls from Taylor who knew the little Hoffstroms so well ... After dinner Mr Neilson (Fred's father) suddenly arrived with notes from their parents, saying that the funeral was to be at Taylor at 11 a.m. on Sunday and that all the Taylor girls were to go and not come back to camp. So he took four and left four for Cecilia; but not until we had a little talk with them all to try and give them the right thoughts about it all, and brace them to act as true Guides the next day.

After that it was rather difficult to revive the camp. Cecilia and I were both staggered, she because she knew the children so well, and I on account of the father and mother. And the rest of the Guides, even though they didn't know the Hoffstroms, felt the cloud, and to them as to us, the camp seemed like turning to dust and ashes.

But we couldn't allow that. So with a fearful effort we pulled it round, and ended the day with a good strong camp fire once more. Only at the finish I spoke to them a little about their comrades and we sang 'Abide with Me' ...

In the late afternoon Cecilia came back. The funeral had been held in the open air at Taylor as the school was far too small. She said, thanks to Brother Wolf and the steadiness of the Guides, it had been very beautiful and dignified, though very heartbreaking ... We had a campfire Service that night, and next day a final ceremony with torches. The children quite recovered their spirits of course, and the camp ended most happily. In fact, it was one of the best and happiest camps I can ever remember ...

On Tuesday ... we got back to the town filthy but happy soon after midday ...

At last [on Wednesday] Ruth arrived ... I dragged her out of the Mail-truck and transhipped her joyously into Eliza. You know I haven't seen Ruth since 1924, so it was a pretty great event. But she hasn't changed one bit, and it was enchanting to see her again ...

After luncheon [on Thursday] we all drove down in Eliza ... and crossed the river to [Hoffstrom's] mill. They are living there because for the present they can't bear their house a mile North with all the children's clothes and possessions lying about. At least that's what we were told.

I went into the mill kitchen first, and found Mrs Hoffstrom with a sister-in-law come from Rolla[57] to be with her. She was very self-possessed and quiet, and pleased with a bunch of flowers I took her which were the very first picked from our own garden. I made way after a few minutes for Cecilia, because of her much closer connection with the children ... Presently I came upon Mr Hoffstrom, looking pitifully worn and haggard. We sat down together on a pile of lumber quite quietly, and for a long time there was nothing to say.

Then at last I said, 'You are sawing a great lot of lumber.' 'Yes,' he answered very quietly, 'A man must work hard now to keep sane.' After a bit he added, 'I've been thinking. If I gave the lumber and a bit of land, do you think the others would help to build a little Church in Taylor Flats?' 'Do you mean in Memory?' 'Yes. In Memory. Not a dance hall – just a little building for straight Church and Sunday School. I would sure like to do that. They loved Sunday School. As we came down the hill to the river they were singing the hymns. It seemed like they were ready.'

I said I was sure people would help him, poor though they all are on the Flats, and promised to mention it to Br. Wolf. Soon after that I joined Cecilia, and we came away ...

Week Ending July 23rd

... We have just finished the first week of our famous HOLIDAY, and it has been one of the most blissful weeks I have ever enjoyed ... Our daily programme is a delicious blend of Carmelite Cell with L'Après Midi d'une Faune; that is to say, we have our regular Prayers and Religious reading, morning and night, and spend the rest of each day in complete sloth, bathing or eating or sleeping in the sun. Our maximum dress is a smock and shorts. For bathing three times a day we dress as the nymphs do, and our feet are rapidly becoming as hard as satyrs' hoofs.

All this sounds rather silly, I'm afraid; but you don't think what a blissful rest and change it is, or how absurdly we are enjoying it. We read aloud quite a lot – Taylor's *Faith of a Moralist*[58] for heavy (and it's heavy all right. Unluckily both Cecilia and I fell into a deep sleep while Ruth was reading to us this morning!); *The Life of Janet Erskine Stuart*, who, I'm afraid, wouldn't altogether approve of ours, and the 'Week-end Book.'[59] Also we have lots of music, especially Brahms First Symphony and two of Beethoven. But our prime recreation and delight is Ruth Spooner who dropped straight from Heaven to be the making of this holiday for us ...

Diary of the Second Part of our Holiday
July 24th – August 13th

... Directly we arrived [at home] we discovered a disaster. *Eleven* stray horses had jumped the pole which is my front gate, and having almost entirely demolished my little stack of oat sheaves, were now busy with the crop! The whole eleven months that the fence has been up, no horses have jumped that pole. They just waited till the house was empty. Aren't they fiends! ... It's lucky I'm not a homesteader, as there is no legal redress, and such a loss would be desperately hard on them ...

The following day being Wednesday was fixed for the start of a tour up the Peace to Hudson's Hope and Carbon River ...

We found our way to [a] shack where we were to spend the night. It belongs to a man at Hudson's Hope called G[ething],[60] who lets anybody use it freely. His instructions to me were very simple: 'You'll find all the pots and dishes you want, and a bit of food I always leave handy. Just make use of anything you want. And by the way, you may find an old guy staying there called Jim McN[amee]. If you do, just tell him you're to have the shack and he can sleep in the cache – unless of course you'd rather sleep in the cache yourselves; there are fewer mice there.'

Sure enough we found the shack on a lovely slope by the river just above where it goes into the canyon, and there was Mr McNamee in possession ...

Before we were ready to be off next morning another old man turned up, riding of course and leading a packhorse. He is a queer old wandering trapper and adventurer called 'Racehorse Ed,'[61] whom I have met from time to time when on the trail and struck up a vague sort of acquaintance. Racehorse Ed had heard from the gold washers that we were there, and as he was temporarily living further up the river, he hurried along to offer to escort us on our way to the Beatties[62] ...

... [T]he trail was lovely, and R.H.E.'s life story was rather fun, being so very different from our own ... All his life he has wandered about this continent, on ranches and farms, in mines and lumber camps, sometimes trading, sometimes trapping, sometimes gold washing, sometimes gambling, never settling anywhere, never attempting to make a home or lay up for the future. There's a kind of unworldliness and detachment about it that is rather wonderful in contrast with so much of our Christian Carefulness; and I couldn't help feeling he had one side of a splendid friar. But alas the other side is completely missing; as like old McNamee he stands outside all Religious practice.

About 5.30 we came in sight of Jim Beattie's farm ... Jim Beattie is an Englishman from Norfolk, and a man whose sufferings are only equalled by his pluck. Through some accident or disease (I'm not sure which) he has had years of continuous illness and pain, destroying his work, eating his savings and eventually costing him his leg which had to be amputated after a year in hospital. Mercifully he has a calm and tremendously hardworking German wife and perfectly splendid children. The two eldest girls, Louise and Mary, can do any work on the farm. Louise, at the age of 14, could break and plough and drill, and reap and everything else just like a man.

... We all had supper during which Mr Beattie came in. He's an interesting looking man; and his wooden leg and crutch combined with a great big floppy hat pinned up on one side give him the appearance of a wounded Anzac. Unluckily we know that he doesn't want any Religion for his children. Apparently some bad mistake in his own childhood's training put him off all Sunday Schools and Religious teaching. He allows us to send the Sunday School by Post, but doesn't want a Sunday School in the house, and up to the present has refused to have the children baptized. Apart from that, he was very friendly and welcoming to us, and very full of talk and fun. He is building a new and much bigger house, and took each of us all over its skeleton in turns while the others admired the vegetables with Mrs Beattie and the girls ...

At about ten [next morning] we started on the last stage, only 12 miles to the Joneses[63] at Carbon River. There was no more waggon trail now (that only goes as far as the Beatties and is kept open by them) but an unfrequented pack trail ... After what seemed like hours of in and out [among the trees], we emerged upon a lovely broad slope thinly covered with Jack Pines and there on a shingle bar at the other side of the river we saw A BOAT.

This was a marvellous sight because it meant we must be there. You see all we knew about the Joneses house was: that it was on the opposite side of the river; that it was completely hidden by bush so that you couldn't see a sign of it ...; that the Joneses had a boat and would fetch you over if you could make them hear; that the river being a quarter of a mile wide and Charlie Jones being very deaf, the only sure way to attract attention was to *fire a gun!*

We hadn't got a gun so we fell to shouting and shouted in chorus for about a quarter of an hour ... [At last someone paddled us across] in a rather dicky canoe, and so shortly before six o'clock we arrived at the home of Mrs Jones.

We got the most delightful welcome you can possibly imagine from a real *London-born* lady and her much older, deaf, active, friendly, little Canadian husband ...

Mrs Jones was originally a school-teacher, who came to Canada in the days when English ones were wanted here. Then she drifted in to secretarial work, and finally met Charlie Jones.

Last year she came into a little money, and went Home to England for the first time after 20 years ... She had a whole year at Home and enjoyed it immensely, but said the most thrilling moment of all was when she got back again to Carbon River. She has no children and must have had pretty lonely times in the past. Charlie used to go off trapping in the winter and be away for a week or two at a stretch, leaving her with her only neighbours 12 miles away by a rough pack trail on the opposite side of the river. On her own side (the South) her nearest neighbour is 100 miles away with no trail of any kind. I asked her whether she minded and she said she sometimes got a bit anxious about Charlie lest he should have any sort of accident and not be able to let her know. Otherwise she was happy enough.

My Word! Think of that! They are both educated people with lots of books, and luckily her little fortune makes it unnecessary for him to go off trapping any more. On the contrary, they have a radio and a *pump* connected with the Carbon which runs close to the house – and a LONG BATH – without taps of course, but with a waste pipe. This was so exciting that we all three had a bath, and cast lots for the order of getting in. I won the toss and started off. My first long bath for 15 months. You needn't be shocked. I'm perfectly clean. You don't need a bath to keep you clean. A dish pan varied by a lake and a river are just as good.

... On Tuesday morning when we had to start [back] they got us breakfast at six and Mrs Jones came across in the boat to see the last of us. She kissed us all at parting, and made us promise to come for at *least* a week next year, which we most certainly shall ...

This time we kept the trail nearly all the way and got to the Beatties in time for dinner ... From there it was another 20 miles back to the Portage Landing ... There was only one intermediate house, and we stopped there a few minutes to make friends with the two well-off English brothers who lived there. They are called Henry and Tommy S[64] ..., and apparently they live there just for fun and do nothing but hunt (big game) trap and fish.

Tommy was out, but Henry was at home, and took us into their delightful one-room shack, full of books and guns and fishing tackle ... Henry S. is an Oxford graduate, and it was so funny to hear him explain all these treasures in the most pure and scholarly English, as if they were exhibits in a museum. He was up at Oxford the same time as Cecilia, but they never met ...

Nevertheless, what do you think is his real intellectual interest? ASTROL-OGY! He has heaps of books, and little note books, full of calculations for horoscopes. He shewed them to us, and we discussed them very seriously, and I believe poor Cecilia longed to give him the date and hour of her birth – but desisted – for fear of me!

I told her afterwards it was a fearful give-away for Oxford – and she rose accordingly ...

Diary from August 2nd to 13th

... On Wednesday we only had the 17 miles back to the Hope to cover. But halfway through the bush, Cecilia and I left Ruth to rest herself while we took a trail at right angles in search of two outlying ladies called Mrs M[urphy] and Mrs B[arkley].[65] We tossed up as to who should go look for which and then separated. After another four miles of rather desolate bush and badly burnt forest, I came upon both ladies together gathering blueberries, and I knew that poor Cecilia had drawn a blank ...

Mrs Murphy turned out to be an R.C. [Roman Catholic], but her little girl, Marvelee Anne, gets the S.S.P. and likes it. So she said to me in a tone of great awe, 'Do you know *Mrs Story* who sends them to me?' 'Well, yes, I suppose that's me.' Marvelee Anne's jaw dropped at first with wonder, and then lower, I think with disappointment. Alas I am always most impressive as a Myth ...

We got back to Hudson's Hope for supper and stayed that night ... The weather was glorious, and every time the trail ran down to the river Ruth and I bathed in great bliss; but alas Cecilia couldn't because of [an injured] foot ...

After one of these dips we had dressed again and were eating our luncheon on a little flat down by the Peace, with the trail just behind us running up along a steep hill to the top of the 7–800 feet bank. The horses were grazing loose as usual ... We lay on our backs gazing at the green hills and the clouds. Presently Ruth remarked dreamily, 'How picturesque those horses look on the distant sky-line.'

'Yes,' I said. 'Lucky they're not ours.' Then suddenly in completely different voices we all shouted at once, 'THEY *ARE* OURS'!

The little beggars had stolen away while we were bathing and Cecilia dozing, had run quietly up the trail and were heading straight for home, when mercifully Ruth saw them just before they vanished over the edge. Poor Cecilia couldn't give chase; but Ruth and I pounded up the hill, and then separated to stalk them. By another mercy there was excellent grazing on the plateau above, so instead of running on they had all three started grazing, and thanks to their terrific greed, it didn't take us long to catch them all again ...

Between 10 and 11 that night we got home, ... after ten most delightful days on the trail, and 230 miles ...

On Friday to our deep regret and loss Ruth left us ... It was horrid seeing her go, but what an ungrateful thought. It was enchanting having her ...

Monica Storrs's Diary to August 30

... The [next] two weeks were devoted to preparing in various ways for the Bishop's visit, due on the 27th, and of course our great Annual Event, as it was also to be the Anniversary of both the Churches and to see the Consecration of a third. Oh, but I haven't told you about that one, have I? Well, you remember our visit to the poor Hoffstroms a week after the tragic death of all their children in the river, and you remember Mr Hoffstrom thought about building a Church to their memory? I told Brother Wolf just before we went for our holiday trip up the Pack trail. And just last

Sunday (August 7th) he said to me after Church: 'It's all settled about Taylor; we're going to lay the first log on Tuesday and have it ready for Consecration on the 27th.'

'Eighteen days, less three Sundays – 15 working days! Brother, can you do it?'

'Certainly we'll do it. All the men will help. We'll have a shingling bee, and Miss Goodenough will collect the women to help in that, and furnish the Sanctuary.' And it was so. But I'll tell you more about it presently.

Meanwhile there was also the Baldonnel Church to get ready, and Brother Wolf had decided that it must be painted outside and in, besides a lot of clearing and re-fencing of the ground ...

So he set to work collecting the men and we women for all these mighty works, because everything was to be done by what is called in this country 'donated' labour ... Meanwhile [he] designed the Taylor Church, mixed the Baldonnel paints, went on collecting and using the casual helpers and flashing backwards and forwards along the 12 miles separating his three centres like a melting streak of relativity ...

In the second week we had the two Bees, the Shingling Bee at Taylor and the Painting Bee at Baldonnel. Do we have Bees in England? I can't remember. But they are the regular plan here for getting anything of a public nature finished ... The men bring tools and the women bring food, and the children swarm round; also the babies and the dogs. It's the most marvellous form of democratic free co-operation you can imagine, and everybody seems to love it ...

Friday was the Baldonnel Bee, and on the whole a rather great success ... Whenever there was nothing else to talk about, [we] criticized Brother Wolf's scheme of colours. He and I quarreled about that, because I wanted it all one colour, plain cream for preference. But he insisted on a second colour to border the windows and Chancel arch ...

The final result of the controversy (which the ladies breathlessly enjoyed) was that I left it *entirely* to him and he, to please me, reduced his trimming colour to a mild dove-grey, which is no great shakes as an artistic conception, but as an Anglican Compromise is perfect!

We painted and cleaned up till dark and then if you please, we had a Parish Social ... We put away the paints and tools, swept up the mess, rearranged the benches and from 9.30 to 11 o'clock had a concert. Then lunch (as it is called, even at midnight) and a little speech or two in honour of the first anniversary of the Hall, and at last, when the dancing began, Cecilia and I slipped away and rode thankfully home, getting to bed about one o'clock. But not so Brother Wolf. He stayed to the end of the Social and then went straight on to Taylor and continued building the Church for the rest of the night and all next day ... It made Cecilia and me rather sick to think of, but once in bed it didn't prevent us from sleeping like logs ourselves.

... Sunday, August 28th, was ... my first sight of the [Taylor] Church, which is a remarkable little building, much more ambitious than I expected ... It has a porch, a nave, a sanctuary, a tiny vestry and even a little newborn spire at the West end. But the distinguishing feature inside is the height, which is about 16 feet, and *vaulted* – not a flat ceiling like St Martin's and St John's. Altogether, when finished completely, it will be rather a gem of its kind ...

The Bishop and Mrs Rix had already arrived with the Proctors when I got there and he was waiting, robed, in the little vestry ... I had to play the faithful little portable harmonium, which is still all we have for every purpose, and we began by singing 'We love thy Place O God.' The Bishop was dignified and gentle, as always, and the Service was very moving. He consecrated the Church by the name of the *Good Shepherd*, which was Brother Wolf's admirable suggestion, as it was built in memory of children, and chiefly for children. Then the boys and girls sang 'When He cometh, when He cometh to make up His Jewels,' as a very simple little anthem in memory of the four little Hoffstrom girls who had loved the Sunday School and had been singing that hymn on the night that they were drowned ...

Then followed the Confirmation of Lillian and Willie K[ehler],[66] a big boy and girl of Russian parentage from Peace View. They had come forward after some of our Services there and Brother Wolf had prepared them somehow, I can't think when. It was the very first confirmation in the parish and caused quite a stir of excitement ...

Week Ending September 3rd, 1932

... For the next four days [the Bishop] was billed to go up the river to Hudson's Hope[67] and hold Services there and on the way. This is the trip which ended so badly two years ago, do you remember, when the boat broke down and he was stuck in mid-stream for two days and nights and finally got nowhere? Last year his programme was too big and there was no time for Hudson's Hope; so *this* was to be the First Visit. From the start it was rooted in controversy because Canon Proctor[68] and all the rest of us said he must go by boat ... as it is without doubt the safest, surest and most comfortable way, in fact the way everybody goes, except those who ride. But Brother Wolf *insisted* that he must go by car, so as to visit all the houses which could not be reached from a boat, and to hold Services in some of them.

As you know, there is still no road to the Hope but only a very rough and frightfully hilly trail. Only three or four cars have ever been over it, and none this year on account of the unusual depth of the Halfway River. So you can imagine the searchings of heart that had already been going on for some weeks. In fact, since Arius[69] the Church can hardly have been more torn – well no, I was going to say that, but realize it can hardly be true because in this matter there were no two *parties*, only Brother Wolf like Athanasius 'Contra Mundum'[70] and like Athanasius he won, that is he persuaded the Bishop in the teeth of all our Better Judgments to let him drive him and Canon Proctor and Mrs Rix and Mrs Proctor via all the houses to the Hope ...

At last about two they started – five of them – the Bishop and Brother Wolf in front, Canon Proctor and the two wives behind together with their personal luggage for three days, as well as Episcopal and Clerical robes, heavy coats for the open boat, Prayer books, hymn books and food. It was too full to shake much anyway. I saw them off and longed to go too, but that was out of the question, clearly! ...

Next morning I had to go to the Blueberry River on a mission for Miss Claxton. You remember little Irene S[mith] with the deformed short leg? After various visits and much negotiation during the summer, we arranged for her to go to the Solarium at Victoria, to which Miss Claxton herself took her when she went for her own holiday in July. But since then the doctor has written to say that amputation and an artificial leg are the only remedy, and asked us to go and see the parents about it. Miss Claxton has lately dislocated her knee and cannot ride much, so we agreed that I should go for her, and save time by taking the car to the Holdup and then borrowing a horse ...

Just before reaching the abode of the Smiths I met both Mrs Smiths on the trail together with their four little children. They gave me such a welcome, and said they'd been looking out for Cecilia and me for weeks ... We wandered along all together to visit Mrs Mann[71] and her new baby and as we went we discussed Irene's leg. The mother was marvellously sensible about it, and entirely agreed to amputation and a false one, as the poor little girl's best chance both for appearance and walking ...

We found Mrs Mann as usual baking bread and as usual, in a gentle friendly muddle ... Only two children were in, so I corrected their Sunday School books, and then one of the women remarked that they had never had a Service there. I asked if they would like one at once, upon which they all agreed and we began ... It was a very curious Service in the low, dark ... little one-room shack ... After each hymn there was a moment's pause for the bread to be inspected in the oven, and two or three times we were also interrupted by another very little Mann running in triumphantly with a new-laid egg. I read and spoke about Martha and Mary;[72] we sang very heartily and prayed very simply, chiefly about the children. I'm afraid the Prayers had no place in either 1662 or 1928.[73]

When it was over [it was] obvious ... that one Mrs S. had the tooth ache. I discussed this with her and she said she had suffered badly for a long time and was getting worse, but had no means of getting into the dentist[74] at Fort St John. So I suggested she should borrow a horse and come back with me tomorrow morning, when I could take her all the way from the Tuckers[75] in Eliza.

This produced immediate discussion. The children? Oh yes, the other Mrs S. (her mother-in-law but exact contemporary of 22) would look after them. Money for the dentist? I thought he would be kind, anyway I'd see that he was. How would she get back? Cecilia or I or Miss Claxton would drive her back to the Tuckers [where] she could borrow a horse as I had done ... But then – fatal stumbling block – what horse could she ride to-morrow? ... [However] we soon made a splendid plan.

Mrs S. took Jimmy [the borrowed horse] and rode a mile, tied him to a tree and walked on. I walked after her, picked up Jimmy, rode on, overtook her and changed places again. By this means, Jimmy got a rest every mile and we had lots of variety and no chance to get tired of each other's company. As a result we got through the 14 miles of bush and swamp in four hours and both reached the Tuckers as fresh as paint. I can't too strongly commend this method to all of you at Home who may have to share a horse in crossing St John's Wood or Shepherd's Bush[76] ...

Next day, being Thursday, the Bishop and Co. were due to return from the Hope and have supper with us, and then the Bishop and Mrs Rix to sleep ... I did a good deal of changing sheets between us and the Rectory and collecting two young chickens from a neighbouring farm for Cecilia to roast. We also cleaned the house terrifically, [and] made the upstairs bedroom as episcopal as possible ...

Cecilia prepared a wonderful supper of chickens and vegetable marrow (present from May) and peas and potatoes and pies (our own). At 5.30 it was ready and we were washed and changed out of overalls into skirts. Lots of rain, but no Bishop.

At 6 ditto. We fed Mr D.[77] but not on the chickens.

At 7 ditto. We fed ourselves, but not on the chickens.

At 8 ditto. The chickens were getting a little tired.

At 9. A knock. We rushed to the door and found Miss M. and Miss H.[78] the caravan workers! They had come by our invitation for the big W.A. meeting next day ... At midnight we decided that they must have slept somewhere and went to bed horribly disappointed.

At two we were awakened by H. shouting, 'They've come.' We jumped out of bed, ran straight out into the rain and found the car, the Proctors, Brother Wolf, Mrs Rix, but no Bishop. Being only half awake and dazed by the car lights in the streaming rain, I was for a moment quite frightened, till Brother Wolf explained that he was coming down by boat in the morning and Mrs Rix had come to stay with us.

The car went off and we brought Mrs Rix into the house, lit the fire and gave her tea and cake while she talked. She was very tired but still more excited ... Apparently the whole journey was a saga of pains and perils ('a bit rough in places' admitted Brother Wolf); the brakes were faulty so they got full benefit of the steep hills and when they reached the Halfway they found it too swollen and swift to be forded.

Then Brother Wolf collected the Halfway men and spent all day building a huge raft on which, at six o'clock, he crossed the river with the car, empty of course, the Bishop and Proctors having crossed in a boat. Apparently the raft drifted down stream and striking a gravel bar, got tilted so that the car started to slide off – great excitement and everyone quite confident that Brother Wolf would be swept away and drowned. Of course he wasn't, but readjusted the weight somehow, got her ashore, and they went on their way rejoicing. He swears there never was the slightest danger and certainly he has cone down from Hudson's Hope on a little raft lots of times ... Still, this with the car was rather a good show and I did long so to have been there. But then it never is my lot to be where anything happens ...

Next day, September 2nd, was sacred to the First W.A. *Deanery* Meeting to be held at Baldonnel. It was billed to start at 1.30 with a cold luncheon supplied by the Baldonnel and Fort St John branches, to as many ladies of the South of the River as might come. Then there was to be the usual meeting with Mrs Rix in the Chair,[79] and then tea and what remained of the lunch to eat.

Cecilia and I rode early to help in the preparations while Mrs Rix rested until Canon Proctor should call for her at one o'clock. Meanwhile Brother Wolf drove down to Taylor Flats to meet the Bishop, and the Fort St John ladies were to bring along eight quarts of salads to be the grand plum of the banquet.

Well, 1.30 came together with car loads of Southern ladies, all beautifully dressed like an English drawing-room meeting. But no Mrs Rix arrived and no Proctors, and although we had seen Brother Wolf go down to the river, he never came back. No Bishop, and worst of all, no Fort St John ladies with salads. It was all rather harrowing. We talked feverishly to the fair Southerners about the beauty of the Hall and the dryness of the summer, with one eye cocked on the door in an agony of longing for either Prelate, President or Salads.

At last Brother Wolf appeared with an empty car and signed to me. I went out and he told me that the Bishop was too tired to come to the meeting ... and I was to carry on while he went back in search of Mrs Rix. So we carried on with 50 feasters and while we were feeding them on bread and butter and ham and tea, suddenly the salads arrived (they'd had a flat tyre) and a few minutes later Mrs Rix and the Proctors (they'd had a damaged axle).

So in the end the luncheon was a great success and I think the meeting was too ...

Month of September, 1932
This is a terrible Business. This diary is exactly a month behind; and that for no special reason except that I have rather feebly abandoned the habit of staying up till three to write it ...

... [This] week was all visiting, and included a tremendous heart-searcher with Mrs B[rown][80] who helps me in the Sunday School. She is a great friend and keen supporter on the whole. But she is also a Presbyterian, and every now and then is subject to sharp attacks of anxiety about our Anglican ways. Just now these came to a head, and I found her very worried indeed. So we had a strenuous afternoon grappling chiefly with Fundamentalism and Fonts. Each of us clung to one of these (I won't say which) and looked askance at the other, and by the end of the afternoon neither had budged an inch. Only, through the mercy of God, we had somehow become better friends than ever before ...

Cecilia and I have talked about this a great deal, and sometimes wondered even whether there is any hope that our Church will strike root and flourish in this corner of Canada ... You see, tradition means nothing, continuity with the past, common Prayer and Praise, Mystical Union in Christ, the heritage of the Saints, the meaning of Worship itself ... And yet we are always brought to the same conviction in the end – that even if this whole Block were ultimately to become United Church or Presbyterian, the Anglican contribution would not have been wasted ... And although, of course, we long and try to plant something like the Church life that we know, it *may* be that the seed will grow up quite differently in this new soil – and yet be God's crop none the less ...

Do you know Mrs Armstrong?[81] I forget. She is very large and stout and Methodist and warm-hearted. She lives in a little shack about 12 feet by 9 feet with her little son of nine called Loris; and in that space they sleep and cook and eat and live, and she takes in washing for a livelihood. That was all plain sailing enough; but when I looked in on Saturday I found *six* more children established there. They are the little half-breeds called B.[82] whose mother I buried last February during Brother Wolf's absence. She died in giving birth to the baby, and their father has been trying both to support and look after them, which of course is impossible. So the heroic Mrs Armstrong has taken in the whole bunch while he tries to earn something somewhere (*very* doubtful), and I found her washing and patching endless little pairs of torn and filthy overalls, and trying to make underwear out of flour and sugar sacks, while the whole little tribe swarmed all over her ... They all sleep in two bunks, one above the other, and Mrs Armstrong works harder than ever to wash and mend and clothe and feed them, and at the same time [wash] our sheets and smocks to earn enough money to add another room to the shack ...

Month of October, 1932
... On Sunday the 9th, Brother Wolf returned, bringing with him in triumph – A Bride.[83] She is young, small, dark, and very gentle and quiet. At present she is awfully shy and very grave, except for a ready and charming smile; but of course we don't know her yet, and in fact none of us have seen her alone without the proud and delighted but completely dominating presence of Brother Wolf to cramp her style ...

On Friday the 11th, Adeline arrived. I borrowed Eliza ... and set off in the morning to meet her at Dawson ... We greeted each other as emotionally as if she had been to Grande Prairie for a week-end, and then recovered her luggage and piled it into the car as fast as possible.

... We jeered at [Adeline] a lot about her huge lot of luggage, but when it turned out to be composed almost entirely of presents for us, we felt rather foolish! ...

I slept [the next night] with the Bell's,[84] one of the oldest families of the Montney ... Mrs Bell is elderly, grave and spiritually minded, and very affectionate ...

It's a district full of rather special difficulties because of a bad drink influence which has got in among the young ... Mrs Bell is very worried about it, especially at the dances, which take place about once a fortnight in the winter ..., and to which every girl goes as a matter of course, from 12 years [old] and upwards. There was a dance that night to which Mildred and her three brothers went, so Mr and Mrs and I had a long talk, and ended with Bible reading and Prayers together. They are a United Church family, but tremendously responsive and appreciative towards Anglican work ...

I slept in Mildred's bed, where she joined me toward 5.30 a.m., and at eight I emerged from the little bedroom and nearly trod upon six young men sleeping in a row on the living room floor. While the older B's and I were having breakfast, these woke up one by one and joined in the conversation ... all equally happy and natural! ...

The following week was across the Pine again ... I slept two nights with the P[hillips's][85] ... They were more affectionate than ever, and Mr P., of whom we used to be rather afraid, as a formidable and apparently hard man with a tendency to Bolshevism and materialistic dogmatics, said he hoped that none of us would sleep anywhere else in that district unless we had to, and that we should *never think of a bedroll again*. He used to be a pretty successful big contractor in Vancouver, and also a speculating builder. He twice had a big boom and became very prosperous indeed, and then was twice broke, by the war first, and then by the present slump. So they pulled right out and came up here to this remote corner in the bush across the Pine, and settled in the tiny poplar shack. I think Mrs P., who is in the fifties and mature at that, has felt it all pretty badly, especially the lack of women friends ...

Monica Storrs's Diary for November, 1932
... Next day was the Baldonnel Chicken Supper, a repeat of last year's grand W.A. effort, which had been so successful, and produced $80 for the Church ...

But just before starting [for Baldonnel] I received, via a passing man, a pencilled note from Cecilia, who was down at Taylor; it said, 'Would you bring to Baldonnel my reel of blue cotton for finishing the Good Shepherd Frontal, and also the little pig that May has promised me for the Fosters?' So I went to May expecting the usual gift of pork for a destitute family, and took a small sack in which to hang it on the saddle horn. I said, 'Can I take Cecilia's little pig, please?' 'Yes,' said May, 'if you can catch it – but I warn you the mother is dangerous – she has had 13, and we've taken away all but two, and now we hardly dare go near the sty.' Lovely news for a semi-invalid Cockney like me! ...

She came with me to the sty and brought a fork to defend me against the outraged mother. I took a pail of boiled wheat and tried to separate her from the little ones. But it had all been done too often, and she knew better than that. Until in a moment of great luck I got the pail inside the house part, and she ran in after it. There was just time to slam the door on her before the babies followed – it didn't quite shut, and there was no proper fastening, but it gave me a minute or two before she could force it open, and May stood on guard with the fork! ...

Being so very much alive, I didn't dare try to carry [the little pig] on Robin, so decided to walk and pack him like a baby. But the snow was pretty deep and the trail very rough, and he weighed about 50 pounds, and was fearfully active inside the sack; so after half a mile I wondered how long I should take over three [miles]. Just then Mr Birley came along in his car, going to Fort St John. He called out, 'What the — have you got there?' And then like a brick he turned round and carried us both all the rest of the way to Baldonnel. I had to park the poor little pig in its sack at the Eastern end of the Hall (but not in the Church part) where the sun shone on it, and it would not freeze, until its new owner should arrive.

The supper was billed for 5.30, and I got there at about two to find nothing and nobody there, no cooking stove in yet (we have to borrow one from the N's across the way) and the table-tops and trestles still lying outside buried in the snow ... It seemed pretty hopeless by three with still no progress to speak of; and just then the tide began to come in. First Mr and Mrs Colpitts and their three small children arrived in their 'stone boat,' i.e., home-made sleigh made of about a dozen boards nailed across two birchwood runners ... Then came the Hadlands[86] and the Ohlands[87] and the Kirkpatricks[88] ... and after that half a dozen more stoneboats or sleighs, each containing a parent or two, several children, largely infants in arms, and food of all sorts.

I helped to unload mothers and babies and parcels, and they all staggered in, covered with snow, and parked themselves all over the place and seemed like wild confusion. And yet, do you know, out of that chaos came the most perfect example of evolution I have ever seen. There was no one in command, no visible organization or plan, only a welter of people and things, a bleak hall with bare trestled tables, and a *tiny* little kitchen with as yet no stove. And yet there was an invisible controlling purpose which held everyone together and kept everything going without any real confusion and certainly no clash. One or two of the men went to fetch the stove in a stoneboat, others brought in water and wood, while the women simply buzzed round like bees, no one giving directions, all on equal terms, each doing what seemed right in her own eyes. The place swarmed with children. At every step you nearly trod on a baby or knocked down a toddler or ran into a group of boys fighting or fell over the numerous dogs (including Kristin) who were wandering round in search of windfalls; and yet by five o'clock the process of evolution was complete, and everything ready. From then on the guests began to trickle in, and soon we had quite a crowd ...

Everyone paid 50 cents and had as much chicken or turkey, or pork, cabbage salad, gravy, potatoes, bread and butter, jelly, pie, and cake as they could eat, with tea or coffee. And to our great delight, at least 150 feasters came, and the food held out perfectly. No one was kept waiting (except for room at the tables) and everyone seemed well satisfied ...

I forgot to tell you that in the middle of the preparations before supper, the cry went up that the pig had escaped; sure enough, some cunning person had let it out of the sack, and it had run off into the bush! I tried to organize a search party, but the grown-ups had no time and the children were too excited to stick to it. Cecilia and I were dreadfully disgusted, as you can imagine ... However, we learned afterwards that about two in the morning, while the dance was still going on, the little pig got lured back by the sound of the revels and was caught after all ...

[Coming home from Charlie Lake next day] we had a flat tyre, and were just battling with the jack in the snow when Mr S[oman],[89] the Roman Catholic storekeeper, appeared to help us. He facetiously remarked to Miss Claxton, who was thanking him, 'And don't you wish at times like these that you'd got a man always?' 'Yes,' said Miss Claxton immediately, 'I'd love to have one always under the seat, so that I could say to Miss Storrs, 'Just look under the back seat and get out the jack and the wrench and the man!' Mr Soman was very resentful! ...

For the rest of the week I was pledged to cross the river and visit the Southern Guides as Divisional Commissioner ... All the time I had been trying to find a means of getting home before Sunday ... On Friday therefore, after supper, I ... left Babylon (Pouce Coupé) and walked to Nineveh (Dawson Creek), from whence the Mail should start. The road was fearfully drifted and heavy and I was rather tired ... when, to my great thankfulness, I was picked up by Mr McL.,[90] the School Inspector of the Block, who came out after me on purpose with his car ... It took about an hour to make the seven miles. And I was grateful to him for so much help on such a road. But of course Dawson was only the very beginning; the real job was to find and board the Mail ...

So I slept in the little hotel, and before 8 a.m., made back to the Post Office. I found a small rough sleigh piled quite ten feet high with sacks, to which were already being added a man and wife and two children bound for the Montney. Gumbo Slim[91] looked at me dubiously and said, 'It's going to be kind of hard. These folks must sit on the feed at the back, and you'll just have to hang on where you can.' 'Can't I climb up on the Mail-sacks?' 'Well, it's not exactly legal, but I guess you can, as there's no way else to travel except standing on the runner.' As the journey was going to last two days to the river and beyond, I was not very keen about standing on the runner, and instantly climbed to the top of the sacks. It was like riding on an immense nobbly elephant, pretty cold because below zero most of the time. But there was very little wind, and so it was quite pleasant.

So we set off from Dawson Creek at the reckless speed of three miles an hour and 60 miles to go ... But the weather was fine, my fellow-passengers were nice people, and Gumbo Slim was delightful ... Mr S. was nice too, very quiet and respectable but friendly too. He was just recovering from a leg broken in Saskatchewan, and was still a little lame, but most active and unselfish all the time. Mrs S. (pure Scotch) is young and pretty, tremendously reserved, and fearfully strict with their adorable little boy of five called Norman. You can't think how sweet Norman is. He has fair hair and brown eyes and the most perfect courtesy and sociability I have ever met in a child ... He reminded me all the time of a little lost Prince. But evidently his mother had no such illusions ... I taught him 'Comin' Through the Rye,' and part of 'Little Orphant Annie,' which he simply loved. On the second morning he puzzled me by saying, 'I want the Turkey Song, please.' 'The Turkey Song?' Then I realized – the last line of 'Little Orphant Annie' is: 'The *Goblins*'ll get yer if yer don't watch out.' Norman thought Goblins were Gobblers, and was revelling in the delicious horror at the thought of persistent sinners eaten by *Turkeys*!

Well, we crawled along from 8 a.m. till 6 p.m., just too fast to walk behind on account of the deep snow, but dropping off every hour or so to run behind for a bit when numb with cold ... [and that night] slept with a Danish family at the Cutbank River[92] ... At sunset [the next day] we reached the top of the long Peace Hill, and at dusk came down to the river. Ed G[roate] the Mail-carrier met us. He had just made the crossing , but said it was not safe to attempt to get the Mail over that night, so we must all stop with Howard F[eenie],[93] the second ferryman. It was nice to be so near the end of our journey (only 15 miles), but I was sorry to say Goodbye to Gumbo Slim, who seemed like an old friend.

... Directly after breakfast we set to work to get the Mail across. It was a cold dark morning, snowing again rather steadily, and Ed Groate said he wanted all the help available, so there was old Herbie Taylor and Howard

Feenie and Mr S. and me to start with. But almost at once poor Mr S. slipped and fell heavily on the ice and hurt his broken leg again, so that he had to retire from the conflict; horrible bad luck for him. The river at this point is about 700 yards wide as the crow flies, but the way you have to cross it is over half a mile ...

First the horses drew the Mail-sleigh right down onto the ice at the river's edge. Then they had to be taken out lest it shouldn't bear them, and the rest of us had great fun hauling and shoving the sleigh out to the middle, i.e. as far as was safe. Even so, the last few yards were rather exciting, as the sleigh got on a bank of snow and began to sink through into soft ice. Herbie Taylor shouted, 'Throw off the Mail bags quick.' So we piped all hands, and threw them off, just in time to haul the sleigh back on to solid ground. From that point the Mail bags had to be dragged by ones and twos, straight over the thinner ice. For the first trip you may be sure I followed Herbie Taylor with the devoted attachment of a dog, as he chose a path, avoiding the deepest snow and stepping on the naked ice whenever possible. I felt rather like King Wenceslas' page – 'In his master's steps he trod' – only for quite a different reason.

We all went the same way, dragging two, three, or four bags at a time, and keeping at a respectable distance from one another. We each made about ten trips and the whole game took about two hours and was perfectly delightful ...

Finally we went back and collected the S. family. Poor Mr S. was still in pain from his leg, and had to be hauled over on a tiny hand-sleigh ... Then the sacks were piled on to another sleigh, and we set off on the last lap. Eventually I reached home at supper time, having taken exactly three days from Dawson Creek. I rather expected cries of welcome and relief from Cecilia and Adeline, instead of which all they said was 'Hullo! We didn't expect you till Wednesday!' ...

My last trip of the month was with Cecilia across the Pine ... to the newest settled part, which for want of any name we call at present Northern Transpine ... There is at present no school, but a store run by a very keen and enterprizing middle-aged English couple called A[kister][94] ... The Akisters were planning a Christmas Tree for the children of their district on December 20, and asked us to come to it and hold a Christmas Service too. They could only afford fruit and candies for the Tree, so I promised to send toys for the children, and yarn and flannelette for the parents, and to ask Brother Wolf to go if he possibly could. They were thrilled at this, as he hasn't been able to get there yet. The flannelette and yarn all come out of *YOUR FUND* (Trust N.2).[95] I have got nearly 400 yards of one and 30 pounds of the other for Christmas presents to all the mothers with young children. It sounds prosy enough, doesn't it? *Grey* flannelette too; but for shirts and knickers and general underwear it's just what they most need, and has been received everywhere with unbounded delight.

And here endth November – At Last

Month of December 1932

December 10th was Charlie Lake day ... I had a nice suppertime at the Red Cross and a talk with the two patients, both rather pathetic cases. One ... was a girl of one month under 16 who had just given birth to still-born twins. She was married last year in the face, of course, of all our disapproval and distress, to a man of about 35. They miscalculated her time and one twin was born before he came for Miss Claxton, leaving the poor little wife alone in the shack ... Both babies died at once but the husband seemed so incapable of looking after the little wife that Miss Claxton wrapped her up and took her straight back to the Red Cross, and there I found her recovering. These child marriages are dreadful and we try hard to prevent them, but girls are few, bachelors are many[96] and alas, many mothers seem to be driven by poverty to allow their girls to marry anyone who will give them a home. But gradually we hope that the increase of families and therefore of daughters, combined with some return of prosperity, will allow a better public opinion to grow up, and then this bad pioneer custom may fade away ... The earlier part of the following week was entirely full of toys, yarn and flannelette [for Christmas distribution] ...

Then some of the children arrived with the ingredients for the Christmas pudding which they are sending to the Indians up at the Squaw Creek. They were to bring not less than one cupfull of anything they could – so one brought seven cupfulls of flour, another a cup of raisins, another of sugar, another seven eggs, and so on. Sister Wolf let us mix it in her dishpan, the miller gave us a flour sack to boil it in and Mrs K. took on the actual boiling.

The Squaw Creek is about 15 miles North of the Blueberry and is just a small permanent Indian camp ... I wanted awfully to go there myself and take the pudding but it would take at least three days each way. None of us can speak the Beaver Indian[97] and scarcely any of them English, and we simply couldn't abandon the whole inside of a week just before Christmas for a speechless visit. So we entrusted the pudding together with a number of suitable sacred pictures framed in passe-partout by the Guides, to one of the freighters going up to Fort Nelson and hope he wont get too hungry on the way. Later I mean to go up to Squaw Creek to learn more of the actual conditions and find out whether something could not be done in the way of education, both religious and at least industrial. Meanwhile the pudding and pictures go ahead as ambassadors of good will ...

[Sunday] I went to the house of Kansas Pete.[98] He is a middle-aged bachelor with one eye who drove up here ten years ago from Kansas in a small 'caboose' (covered waggon) ... He is housing for the winter a family called M[orrison],[99] who have at present no home. They consist of Mr and Mrs and six children. I do think it speaks wonders for Pete's real goodness that after ten years of solitary possession he can live quite peaceably with eight newcomers swarming over his small bachelor shack. I found the nine of them having supper. The house seemed to be completely solid with table, people and beds, but there was a curtain behind which I suppose the Morrison ladies sleep. Pete was delighted. He really is a Godly man and said of course he would come [to a Service] and some of the Morrisons ...

Next day I stayed a bit and only came back as far as Mrs Titus with whom I stayed the night. Titus' house has for me the interest of being a sort of stopping house, where you may meet odd trappers and Indians journeying North or South. That night three Indians came in with dog teams, snow shoes, and moose meat, all very picturesque. They came and sat with us, silent and inscrutable, all evening. The relations with them are entirely friendly and I have never heard a white man or woman speak other than sympathetically about them. They really are good to them and often feel real compunction about their rather pitiful condition ...

Before seven o'clock [Christmas morning] in the frosty starlight darkness, May arrived, having walked from home to join us and walk on to Church. She walked ten miles through snow before breakfast. The Service was all we could desire ... We might easily have been at Rochester or St Peter's.[100] There was no near or far or anywhere ...

Then Puck and I stole two dozen hymn books and pounded over to Charlie Lake for the first Christmas Day Service ever held there. Only five adults and four children came, but there again they told me that the whole district is laid out with flu ... Of course they dribbled in late and then we had to ride like the man who brought the good news from Ghent to Aix[101] in order to bring back the stolen hymn books before five o'clock Evensong at St Martin's. As it was ... the congregation had assembled and Brother Wolf and the verger were both standing anxiously in the porch when I galloped up very dramatically and cast my trophies at their feet, i.e., 24 Canadian hymnals.

This, you realize, was the first big Christmas Service ever held at Fort St John ... and we had a full festal Evensong with lots of hymns and carols and quite hearty singing ...

I left [Brother and Sister Wolf] to their dinner and rode home to mine. The others were already in and after dinner we piled all our own mail and personal presents on the table and sat round in bliss until we went to bed ...

So the Old Year froze to death at 25 below – a hard anxious year for many million people, and for us in this house a year of many failures and a good many disappointments but far more interest and happiness, and thanksgivings without number. With love to you all for the year that's begun, and boundless thanks for all your prayers and gifts, from Monica, Cecilia, Adeline ... Companions of the Peace.

1933

OUR EPITAPH: 'They wandered in sheep-skin.'[1]

The New Year opened pretty keen at 18 below and no hint of this 'soft winter after Christmas' which the Indians had promised ... The next day Fred came back, travelling in a caboose or covered waggon, with his little brother Gordon and another little boy who lives with them, called Leslie.[2] They had been to Cache Creek with freight for their father – 25 miles of an awfully steep and heavy trail, and were nearly frozen when they got to us. The horses were unhitched of course, and put in, and the boys spent the night with us. They are both 12 and Cecilia's Scouts at Taylor ... In the morning early, pitch dark and 21 below zero, they ran out in their almost threadbare coats to hitch up the team and departed like middle-aged freighters who had been on the job for years ...

I nearly forgot our second Epiphany innovation – another Boy. His name is Tony F[latt][3] and we first met him last summer when we went up that pack trail. His father and mother are entirely English. Mr Flatt was in a Bank in Cairo before the War and remembers Ronald. Then he served through the War as an officer in some line regiment and Tony was born in Egypt nearly 11 years ago. They have lived about 12 miles West of Fort St John for the last ten years I think, and are extraordinarily nice people and great friends of Brother Wolf's. They asked him if he could take Tony so that he might go to school, but Brother Wolf's house is not ready yet for a permanent boarder, so he referred them to me, and Mr Flatt brought Tony over on the 8th with much gratitude and the promise of butter and vegetables and anything else we need from time to time towards his keep ...

Tony is 11 in March. He is middle-sized and sturdy with a round red face, round blue eyes and a large square mouth. He has a strong clear and ludicrously English voice, and is completely at home with everybody and every situation from the first moment of confronting them. He has hardly ever been away from his family for a night before and never been to any school, but he loved school from the first day, and learned all the ways of this house in about ten minutes. He is completely unselfconscious and has marvellous manners ...

He and Fred have struck up a great friendship and are a delightful contrast – Fred a big charming Dane, 17 years old, six feet tall – very slow and quiet, intellectual about the Universe and forgetful about the chores; Tony not 11 yet, about four feet high, wide awake, quick and full of talk – quite obliging to the Universe but dead nuts on the chores ... He loves school, loves Sunday School, adores the animals, is eager to help everyone and scrumptuously obedient and polite. In fact, the only thing he doesn't seem to love is washing. On Monday I saw him gliding off to bed after less than 15 seconds at the public washing-stand. 'Hullo Tony, what about washing?' 'Er, well, Miss Storrs, I thought I'd wash on Tuesday's.' 'Tuesday's only?' 'Er, well, perhaps Thursday's too.' 'Well, but what has Monday done anyway?' Pause – then with noble resignation: 'Yes, all right, Miss Storrs, I'll wash on Monday too' ...

On Friday of that week Mr Simpson came to us for a night in order to build a sorely needed rabbit fence. I haven't told you about our specific pest this winter – the RABBITS. They are everywhere in swarms and swarms – pure white of course, and with long fluffy fur. At first we thought them so pretty, but now they have become a public menace owing to the fearful havoc they make in the slender feed-stacks everywhere. No amount of dogs or snares can keep them down, and in the evening when we went to the barn, the stack would be quite white with them, like a moving snow drift in the Mid-winter Night's Dream ... There is only one thing to keep them out – a solid lumber fence, shoulder high and close-fitting, and this Mr Simpson built for me, in time, I hope, to save the new sheaves anyway. It is very ugly and rather awkward for climbing in and out, but I can't afford $75 to feed tame rodents ...

After Sunday School [at Charlie Lake] Miss Claxton and I have immense fun because our horses are great friends and get tremendously excited when together. So we say goodbye to the children and gather up our hymn sheets and pictures and Testaments as sweet saintly spinsters and the next moment are steeple-chasing away across ditches and through deep drifts in a reckless Point 8 Point;[4] hardly Sabbatarian, but Robin and Major know nothing of that ...

[On Tuesday] I hit the Highway for Indian Creek, where I was to take the monthly Guide meeting directly after school. I found Mrs Williamson waiting and four of the six Guides very smart in home-made uniforms and the mauve and green ties we had given them. But alas, Iva was absent with no satisfactory reason and Iowne was out of uniform for the absurd reason that she had 'grown out of it' after three months' possession ... Mrs Williamson has been marvellously good to them, having them to stay in turns and trying in every way to make up for their defaulting mother. But I found her awfully anxious about them; apparently the wild streak has broken out again. Guiding has lost its novelty and she doesn't know what is to hold them now. No more do I.

February, 1933
... Some effects of the cold are rather comic. For instance, we fetch our milk half a mile away – a quart carried in a three pound lard pail (the universal container here), and four or five nights a week when it arrives, the milk has to be cut out with a knife ... All meat has to be thawed out for hours before cooking. So two or three days a week we have a joint hanging above the living-room stove, looking very like a medieval roast ... The stove is always being surrounded by things to be thawed out – the axe after chopping open the water hole, the horses' bits, the water pail which every day or two grows into a deformed and monstrously heavy lump of ice. But I think the nastiest thing to look at were the eggs we had preserved last summer in water glass. The liquid froze and broke the crock. Then somehow the eggs froze too, and broke their shells and emerged all hard as rocks and looking very disgusting. However, they also were eventually thawed out and did all right for cooking, though I don't think anyone could persuade them ever to boil or poach again.

... On Wednesday I visited round Charlie Lake ... On the way home I fell in with McLeod,[5] a half-breed freighter to the North. These freighters are marvels of endurance. They load up big sleighs and start off in mid-winter for the Indian trading posts and for Fort Nelson, which is over 300 miles North of us, with no white settlement and scarcely a shack in between. They camp in the deep snow and face incredible weather – all for two dollars a day. The last trip had been one of the worst he had known. For two days and nights they had to keep going without any longer stop than half an hour, for fear of the horses freezing to death, and didn't dare go to sleep themselves for the same reason ...

Next day Adeline and I went across the Pine and slept with the Phillips' as usual. They were all feeling rather disheartened about Mr Phillips' health which isn't very good ... So they had reached the point of deciding that he and she should pull out when the spring comes ...

It was only about two miles away that we found the [Costello's]⁶ shack all surrounded by bush – rather like a fairy story. Mr Costello was away working; but Mrs C. gave us a great welcome and said she had been expecting us for some time. She had no feed to spare, but luckily we had each brought a good-sized bag of oats (we always do now) and she was delighted for us to stay the night. Later in the evening Mr C. got home, having walked the 17 miles from Fort St John in heavy snow all the way, so you can imagine he was tired. She told us how they had lived for years in Saskatchewan, South of Regina, in a prosperous farm. Then the bad years began, about 1927. They hung on always hoping for a good crop to make up for the loss on the last. But every year the summer got drier and drier, till at last there was no moisture at all; the seed was blown straight out of the ground after sowing, and even the weeds ceased to grow. The snowfall failed as well as the rain; and the sand and dust drifted and blew in black clouds, covering the fences and filling the houses, till the only difference between summer and winter was hot dust storms and cold dust storms. Last summer they could bear it no longer, so collected their three waggons and remaining horses and cows, loaded up the most necessary furniture, and just pulled out and abandoned their home to its fate. They travelled for three months, living in the waggons, picking up other travellers on the way, and finally reached Fort St John with just enough money to file on a homestead and *no more* ... They could get no Relief because you have to live six months on your land first; but having saved and brought with them enough flour to make bread, lived on that plus any prairie chicken, partridge and rabbits they could *snare* – not shoot, because their cartridges soon ran out and they couldn't buy any more ...

In the late fall, however, Mr C. built a good shack and now appears to be living on Relief, like most of the other new-comers. This is a small monthly allowance graded according to number in family, and earned by road work of different kinds, as and when demanded by the authorities. Of course there are endless difficulties about all this, but I think it works better and is *far* less demoralizing than a straight unearned dole. The allowance takes the form of an order on stores for the most necessary groceries, such as sugar, coffee, baking powder, soap, but is not allowed to be spent on luxuries like sweets or tobacco. Of course every family is supposed to raise its own meat, milk, butter, eggs and vegetables and to pick and preserve its own wild fruit. If they can't produce these they go without. So now you will see again why the main problem is *clothes*. The Relief does not cover clothing, and you know how it wears out, but most of all in a rough life like this. So I really can't think what would have happened up here this winter without the magnificent supply from Home ...

On Wednesday the.22nd Cecilia and I rode North together ... We took sandwiches and ate them at the Kinneys, who are the first family beyond the Indian Reserve. Mr Kinney is an Englishman and she comes from South Wales and still talks like that too ... They have no horses, but a cow and two nice red pigs, all, alas, terribly thin already, and with no apparent future beyond six sheaves and the nourishment to be extracted from snow drifts ...

As a matter of fact, horses can survive most winters like that, although they come through pitifully thin and have to be fed up very carefully in the spring before they can be worked. But this winter is much longer and the snow far deeper than the average, so that horses are already dying of starvation. One man I know has lost six horses, another seven, and all round it seems to be regarded as a matter of weeks only for most of them, *unless* the spring comes suddenly and stays. Some men are shooting the horses they can't feed, and of course there is wholesale slaughter of pigs and steers. But they keep the cows in, and feed them as long as possible, because they are much scarcer than horses and can't rustle for themselves ...

All this has worried me very much and I tried and tried to think whether the Church couldn't buy up available supplies for free distribution to those most in need. But there are two drawbacks to that scheme: 1) The shortage is so colossal that we could never find funds to meet it; 2) Everybody says the available supplies are simply not worth considering ...

I pushed on the nine miles to the Williamsons and had a hasty talk with Janet (Mrs Williamson) before we went together to the Guides. Alas, the two Sandry girls are causing anxiety again ... It is, of course, that very frequent problem of whether the Guides can save them – or they spoil the Guides. If we turn them out they have nothing else to help them because there is now no regular Sunday School and only a three-weekly Service there, which influences them precious little, I'm afraid.

The actual Guide meeting was a great success ... Of course the Sandrys played up splendidly and were excellent leaders. In fact, if we have to depose them it will be (outwardly at least) a fearful loss to the little Company ...

[Back in Fort St John] there was time to go and see Mr Pickell the Postmaster about the feed problem. (He is sub-Government Agent for this district) ...

While there I learned of a new crisis – starvation among a group of Indians 150 miles North of Hudson Hope. A white trapper had come in on snow shoes and reported two adults and three children already dead. It would take eight days at least to get supplies to them by team and sleigh through the untrodden snow of the bush. Mr Smith, the Policeman, was rung in for consultation. He wired to the Indian Agent[7] at Drift Pile, a place about 300 miles from here and asked whether an aeroplane could come.

Well, to shorten all that, we learned that the Agent himself should come in a Government aeroplane next day, and load up a ton of flour and all necessary supplies for three months. I hastily fetched the Sunday School pudding (which hadn't *yet* got off to Squaw Creek) and 50 yards of Church flannelette, and gave them to Mr Smith to add to the collection. Then we had quite a talk about the whole Indian problem round here, which always seems to me rather disgraceful. These tribes of Beaver and Cree Indians who live all round us on the North are steadily losing their best hunting and trapping grounds through competition with whites. They have learned *nothing* in return but drink, and live nomadic lives in almost incredible poverty and ignorance. I asked whether he thought we could induce the Government to aid the Church in opening a boarding school on the Reserve, and he said he thought it would be the best thing possible. So I decided to come in next day and try to get a few preliminary words with the Agent (Brother Wolf being away at the Hope). And after that I went home ...

Will you pray that we may be shown God's Will, and how to help the Indians in some way, if not that one ? ...

March, 1933

... [The Phillips] had had the luck to kill three moose this winter, and as it is illegal for a family to kill more than one, and the game-warden[8] was expected to cross the Pine, they had a double motive for generosity [in bringing some to us] ...

As a matter of fact the game laws are horribly hard on people up here in these abnormal times. Farming doesn't pay at all, and hunting and trapping, by which many needs can be supplied, are so restricted and the licences so expensive, that lots of people have practically to break the law or starve. Of course no one shoots moose or bear or anything else for fun. They can't afford a cartridge for that. On the contrary, the head and horns, and all that a 'Sportsman' would value, they leave in the bush to rot, but not a bit of the meat or hide is wasted. The hides are precious for the toughest kinds of clothing – especially mitts and mocassins. It is home-tanned, chiefly by the Indians, looks like very coarse heavy chamois leather and smells like tremendously strong kippers ...

I'm glad to say that the Government, in the form of the Postmaster, did at last make a move about the feed problem. He put up a notice asking anyone who had any sheaves or thrashed oats to sell to report to him, and another authorizing feed-orders to a value not exceeding $14 to every farmer with horses or cattle in danger of starvation. This brought a long procession of sleighs drawn by poor emaciated horses – all rather like the Children of Israel coming into Egypt.[9] Each man had to state his case at the Post Office, and if satisfactory, was given an order for a free grant from one or two or three who still held reserve stocks.

These latter were paid by the Government at a controlled rate, and the receivers undertook to pay back by road work whenever called upon to do so. It sounds [like] good old Socialism, doesn't it? ... The sad part is that there wasn't *nearly* enough to go round, and dozens of men who drove their tired teams through many miles of heavy snow were too late and had to go home empty. If it had been merely a question of money I would gladly have supplemented with my own savings and even some of the Trust money, for a man's beasts are quite as important in the end as his clothes. But money can't produce any more feed. There simply is no more in the country...

The following week Miss Claxton and I had our first expedition [to Indian Creek] together ... That forest is quite untamed, and inhabited by no one but occasional Indians or wandering white hunters. It's all rather like a picture of life and death – this slow climb and quick descent, the sudden drop out of sight, and the immense unknown beyond.

On arrival at Indian Creek, which has just started to call itself North Pine, Claxton went off to investigate her case, and I went off to the Guide meeting ... Then Miss Claxton rejoined us and we had the usual happy night with the Williamsons.

[Mr W.] is a delightful man, full of real gaiety and badinage, and a really devoted husband ready to back his wife in anything and put up with any inconvenience that her outside interests may entail. They are one of the few couples who seem obviously in love, and not only yoke-fellows but play-fellows too ...

On Saturday morning I had a long interview with Brother Wolf, chiefly on the subject of our visit to Hudson's Hope the following week ... Adeline and I didn't at all want to go with the Mail, which would mean starting on Saturday instead of Monday (and so missing a Sunday here) and not being our own masters for a moment either way. However, Church discipline demands submission in these matters so we were very much relieved when he said the night frosts had been holding well and the river was still safe, in spite of a good deal of rather unpleasant overflow ...

The Beginning of Spring (April, 1933)

... Adeline and I got home from the Hope on the last day of March, which happened to be Tony's eleventh birthday, but we kept it the following day, being Saturday and therefore a whole holiday. His father sent us a turkey for the occasion, so we gave Tony a ceremonial birthday dinner, to which he invited two school friends ...

He certainly [is] the dearest little boy you can think of – terrifically talkative and self-possessed ... And he is almost ludicrously self-supporting in the sort of ways where most boys are so helpless. For instance, he will sit quietly on his bed in the evening darning his sweater and patching his breeches, and is quite prepared to wash his clothes or cook the supper at any time ...

The final rapture of the birthday was late in the afternoon when May looked in, and she and I tore ourselves from higher duties for half an hour's snow-folly with Tony ... [We] crawled into [his snow] cave and pushed each other out and slid down the steep slope to the drift at the bottom and crawled up again to storm the cave – a very perfect recreation for elderly Church Workers.

On Sunday morning (Passion Sunday) I had the silliest little accident, which actually put me out of action for over a week. I was riding most innocently to School on Robin, who was for once quite innocent too, when we met a bunch of loose horses galloping hard towards us ... Robin and I held peaceably to our side of the trail, hoping that they would do the same. But instead of that, they charged down upon us four abreast, and [one] colt clashed with his great bony hip straight into my left shin. It hurt quite a lot at the time, but I didn't think much of it, because a barked shin always does ...

The next day I got up of course but [my leg] was all black and blue and rather bloated; so May, who happened to drop in, took another high line and forced me into BED where I remained in humiliation all Tuesday ... Saturday Dr. Brown actually looked in and said I must abandon all idea of Sunday and not expect to go across the Pine on Tuesday ...

Sunday seemed so odd, a sort of enforced Retreat, with no companion but Fred, who having accidentally *burnt* his second pair of underwear and most of his socks to cinders the day before, was obliged to stay in all day while washing and drying his only other! Poor old Fred, it was so like him to hang his precious garments immediately *over* a hot stove and then go out to do the chores. When I commented on the tragedy, all he said was, 'Well, they were very old ones, practically worn out.' I pointed out that if he had meant to burn them, it was hardly necessary to wash them first – to which, as usual, he mildly agreed. This conversation took place on Sunday afternoon with me in bed and Fred standing in the doorway.

From that we passed to Religion, and had a long and very frank discussion. He has an interesting mind, the mind of a really intellectual adolescent, full of pseudo-scientific difficulties, and terribly dominated by the atheism and complete moral indifference of his father. 'You see, my father doesn't believe in anything, and he always seemed to know everything – though I sometimes wonder now whether he's always right' ...

The hopeful part of Fred is his frankness and complete sincerity. But of course we can never talk like that unless we are quite alone, so up to that point I knew what the bumped shin was for ...

Yesterday was Good Friday, the greatest day in the year as it seems to me, not the most joyful of course, but the most truly wonderful – the day when you really reach the heart of things and see God face to Face ... Now we must all go to bed, and be up before six tomorrow to meet the Risen Lord ...

May, 1933
[This week I] fetched up at the Williamsons' for supper. Poor Mrs Williamson is having a bad crisis with her little Patrol, because Iva and Iowne, the two leaders, ... have been showing the cloven hoof again – apparently drinking, swearing and I don't know what else besides ... But for the last two months or so I had had to warn them; and now alas! they seem to have gone right off the deep end again. However, there was only Mrs Williamson's statement plus vague rumours to go upon. So I spent a rather miserable Thursday investigating these and trying to get to the bottom of each. It seemed quite clear in the end that they were no longer attempting to keep the Guide Law;[10] so I finished up with a long disheartening interview with the two of them on a wood pile outside a tiny shack. Their defence was simply that everything said about them is untrue, but that as everyone always believes it, it doesn't matter what they do and they have no further interest in trying to keep straight ... So as they no longer even *profess* to keep the Promise they can no longer be called Guides, which is tragic both ways because there is nothing else for them to join, and because in this tiny Patrol of six girls, their leadership counted for so much. Only in a queer way we remained friends, and there is always hope in Prayer ...

[Sunday] evening Cecilia didn't get home for supper, but instead James O[gilvie][11] arrived with Ginger, bearing a note to say that she was staying with May and had Chicken Pox! Poor Cecilia, wasn't it maddening? Two weeks quarantine and such an ignominious complaint, evidently given her by her little lambs at Taylor. The angelic May kept her, to look after her and save us all from quarantine ...

About halfway up [the Pine on Monday] we came across a waggon, or rather a hay-rack, of which two wheels had slipped into a mud-hole and there it was stuck immovable. The man and woman, a young Norwegian couple,[12] were just coming in to their homestead. They had driven up from Alberta, bringing all their possessions in the hay-rack and driving their one cow. At the river they had first been daunted, and camped four days on the other side, hoping it would go down much lower. But instead of that, their food and their horse feed ran lower, and they couldn't afford to wait any more. So they had taken the hay-rack to pieces and crossed it and all their possessions piece-meal in the boat. Then they had driven the horses across and finally the cow, who is apparently the best swimmer of the lot. Then they had started up the hill – full of joy with only about 12 more miles to go, and then this frightful trap of a mud-hole held them fast.

The rack was all down on one side and the wheels completely buried. The thin and exhausted horses could do no more than just hold on; the woman was throwing out all she could to lighten the ship, while the man cut down a tree to make a lever. I offered to help and was most rapturously welcomed, as they were almost in despair, poor things. Then we had a high old time, of the sort that you all know well, though probably with cars and not waggons. We cut levers and blocks, and hauled and balanced, and tried to drive wedges under the wheels. Then we took *everything* out – bed, stove, trunks, sacks of flour and potatoes, tools, boxes of grub, oat-sheaves – and started again digging and levering, cutting brush and trying to make a new footing for the wheels. They were a sweet couple, so full of hope and good humour, especially the man. The poor little woman was brave too, but dog-tired, and she was really in no fit condition for that kind of work.

At last, after about two hours, we came to the conclusion that to pull out forwards was simply impossible, and had to make the rather reckless decision to hitch the horses behind the hay-rack and pull her out *backwards*, i.e., downhill. It was a bit reckless, because you see there was no pole behind, and no brake of any sort, so neither we nor the horses could prevent her from running right away if they pulled her one inch too far. However, we did what we could by building a solid bar across the road, and then Mrs B—d and I stood ready with blocks to shove under the wheels, while Mr B.

urged the tired horses. For a moment or two it looked as if the wheels wouldn't come out backwards any more than forwards; then they came out suddenly and it looked as if the whole rig must jump the bar, kill the horses and crash down the hill into the river. Then by a miracle, it was checked by a little rise in the ground; we thrust in the blocks and the game was won.

Even after that it was doubtful whether the horses could make the top of the hill. Mrs B. rode Puck and herded the cow (who would take no orders from me), while I followed the waggon with a good-sized block and thrust it under the back wheels every time the horses played out. And so at last, at mid-night, very exhausted and filthy but very happy and triumphant, we reached the top of the hill.

There I left them to sleep in their bed in the waggon, and would have camped there too, but had brought no bedroll, and they didn't seem to have anything extra, so I rode on to seek my fortune.

Just before one I reached the Solorenkos ... Later the [next] afternoon I ... rode off six miles South East to the Kemps[13] for supper. Mrs Kemp ... is one of the sweetest women in the whole country, entirely selfless and generous in all her thoughts, let alone her acts.

After supper I wanted to visit one or two needy families further North ... All recent settlers, two were desperately poor, in fact, pretty near starving. One couple had nothing to eat in their house but half a bag of flour (really a loan), and the other, with four little children and the woman soon expecting another, was nearly as low. I was able to give both of them emergency relief orders from the precious fund you send me from Home; to promise to see the Government Agent about help for one man, and to invite the expecting mother to our house as soon as possible, so that she may be near the hospital and not have to make that awful rough journey with the hills and the river to cross, too near her time. She is such a charming woman, I quite look forward to her coming ...

But one new problem had arisen which seemed to me very urgent indeed – the problem of *seed oats*. You understand that, owing to the dearth last year and the long hard winter, practically all the oats North of the Peace and entirely all North of the Pine had long been consumed for feed so that *there was nothing left to put into the ground.*

... Then a new fact emerged. The Government had been issuing seed-grain orders to applicants at Fort St John who would sign a promise to pay back for it in so many years. But this seed had to be hauled from *Dawson*, 55 miles from Fort St John, 75 from Northern Transpine, with a dangerous river and a broken-down bridge in between. All their horses were half-starved; they simply couldn't do it ...

No crop would mean NO FEED next winter. Last winter was bad enough, but NO CROP would mean straight famine – death to all the stock, and utter ruin to the country. What were we all thinking about ... I went to see George Teather and got from him a list of the men in need of seed oats with the quantities required. It totalled over 800 bushels.

'Could *any* of these men haul from Dawson?' 'No, not one. The horses are half-starved, and we are working them now on grass ...' 'Why didn't you let the Government know?' 'We were told [the seed] was being hauled to the Peace, and some of us could have made it there and hauled back for the rest.'

... I reached Fort St John at five, and went straight to Mr Pickell [the Sub-Government Agent][14] about the seed grain. I discovered a situation, which, if not tragic, would have been Gilbertian ... The Government seed was promised long ago, orders issued at the Post Office after the usual forms were filled up, and arrangements made for two railway trucks of oats reserved for the North Peace to be shipped to Dawson and then to be brought the 50 miles to the river itself by Government trucks (lorries).

Pickell told me that the oats had arrived at Dawson, and the trucks were ready to load – when a telegram arrived from Victoria cancelling the whole arrangement, removing all authority from Government Agents, and putting the POLICE in charge instead.

On the same day it was discovered that the whole of the grain earmarked for *this* side had been disposed of at Dawson, and to complete the confusion, I learned that our solitary Policeman, Constable Smith, was to go South next morning, and not come back for at least a fortnight. So just at the moment of sowing, all our promised seed vanished into space, and the only man authorized to do anything about it was about to vanish too! Poor Pickell was foaming at the mouth, and no wonder ...

So I started in on the Constable, who was almost as bewildered as Pickell, having had nothing to do with either Relief or grain before. The only help he could produce was a telegram just arrived, to say that there was grain to be had at the Gundy Ranch, a place 80 miles from Fort St John, *to be fetched by the applicants themselves*. We talked this over and he agreed to its complete impossibility, at any rate for the men across the Pine.

If *only* the Government hadn't countermanded the trucks (lorries)! We talked it round and round, and at last it seemed that nothing but Trust No. 2 (your gifts from Home) could save the situation. I did wonder whether you would approve or whether any would think it an unspiritual bit of work; but I couldn't think so after the Feeding of the Five Thousand.[15]

... Finally all the minor difficulties were cleared away and only one big one remained – how to induce the Gundy Ranch to release the grain to truck drivers and not to individual farmers as per instructions ...

At last we realized that the individual orders would have to be collected from the individual men and divided among the truck drivers; and Mr Smith promised on his journey South to see that orders so carried, were honoured at the Ranch. But there arose a difficulty about the signing of the promissory notes – but we fought that down, and I got home to supper at 9.30 ...

Next morning it poured and poured and my spirits began to sink. Everything in the little conspiracy depended on Mr Spence coming [from Transpine] ... and it began to look as if he wouldn't come. So Miss P. [our temporary housekeeper] and I did a tremendous lot of house-tidying, in the midst of which my conspirator arrived – soaked to the skin and rather exhausted. His horse had deserted him at the river and swum back again, so he had walked the last nine miles in a steady down-pour. We fed and dried him as much as possible, and then with admirable spirit, he started to walk home again, promising to get all the Transpine orders collected up somehow on Saturday, and to meet me with them on the South Bank of the river at noon on Sunday ...

Meanwhile Cecilia's quarantine was at last at an end, so I rode over to May's and took Ginger to bring her home. It *was* nice to get her back after a whole fortnight away – the longest time of separation since she joined me nearly two years ago ...

On Sunday morning, instead of going to Sunday School from which we were both debarred by medical authority, Tony and I rode off to fulfill our assignation on the banks of the Pine ... It was rather fun, as we felt more like characters in Sir Walter Scott or Stanley Weyman[16] on some desperately secret errand than banal Canadians going to talk about oats.

There on the top of the great hill 800 feet above the river, sat Mr Spence in his huge Western hat, hide coat and moose gauntlets, looking as perfect a Cavalier[17] as you could wish to meet in any historical novel – and what's more, perfectly unconscious of his own unreality.

We sat on a bluff together discussing the secret documents, and soon discovered a fresh crisis. There were only 13 *orders*; but at least another 20 more men desperately needed the oats and hadn't got orders ... So then we conspired again. Mr Spence drafted an impassioned telegram as from the Farmers' Institute,[18] and I drafted a letter, both demanding that someone be authorized to act in the Constable's absence. You might have thought that this would be a matter of course. But on the contrary – so beautifully law-abiding are we supposed to be up here that when the Policeman goes away for a fortnight he leaves 3000 square miles in sole charge of the Game Warden, who is at present completely incapacitated by a broken leg. And even *he* was not authorized to issue seed orders.

I planned with Mr Spence that three trucks should, weather permitting, take the grain right down to the river, and he for his part undertook to have the men there ready to measure it at once, *whenever* it should arrive, as there was no building of any kind that could be used for a granary.

Then he went back to collect the men, and I rode back to Fort St John to meet the truck men. Next crisis – two of the three failed to meet me at the hotel as agreed – no reason and no sign of them. So Mr Bowes had to take all the orders; and instead of an instantaneous fleet of three, I had to be content with one truck, making a succession of journeys. Drawbacks? Possible breakdown of the weather over the longer period, possible disputes at the bank among those waiting for the seed. Both these had to be risked (and both took place) ...

Meanwhile it began to rain, and soon continued all day. I trembled, thinking of the truck stuck tight on a hill and all the Transpine men waiting indefinitely at the river bank. Next morning I rode into town and learned that, owing to a trial at Rolla, *no Policeman* had been on duty at Dawson, so no permits for seed had yet been issued and nothing could be done.

However, that righted itself next day, and moreover, a telegram came at last – appointing, who do you think, to act for Constable Smith? – Mr Pickel!

It was too late to let the men know that night, so I arranged to do it next morning. Then, once more as we were going to bed Mr Bowes arrived with his brother-in-law who actually drives the truck, just back from Gundy with 200 bushels on board. He said the road was fearful and he couldn't possibly attempt the Pine Hill, so had taken the grain straight to his own garage in the town, where they proposed to make a bin and store it.

Meanwhile I thought of the men still waiting on the Pine bank; so first thing next morning rode there again, bearing both good and less-good news, i.e., 1) that fresh orders could be obtained if applied for at once; 2) that they would have to fetch the grain from Fort St John. The latter was hard on some of them of course, but after all it was only nine miles from the Pine instead of 90.

Finally, we had to get a trustworthy steward to distribute the grain according to the orders. Luckily Mr Bowes has a charming oldish father-in-law, Mr H[erron],[19] who lives next to the garage, and had no job at the time. Him I appointed to be Patriarch Joseph and minister true justice to the People. And really it was rather a patriarchal sight to see them lumbering up – not with asses it's true, but with shrunken horses hauling heavy waggons. And there was Benjamin and Manasseh, looking a little unusual in battered cow-boy hats, but busy cobbling up the same old torn sacks – flour sacks, sugar sacks, any kind of sacks, into which Joseph measured them so many bushels apiece[20] ...

N.B. The Government, stung by our action, have just hauled seed up for the rest of this country, but they would have been too late for across the Pine ...

Month of June

... At Hudson's Hope we found no small stir, and for the first time in history, the hotel was *too full to take us in*. True, it only has six bedrooms including the proprietors', but still it takes a mort of people to fill six bedrooms in this country. The cause of this great influx was what is known as the 'Indian Treaty Party.'[21]

You probably know that by solemn treaty the Canadian Government pays a small grant (about equal to £1. I think) to each Indian every year, that is, so much to each man and woman and something for each child. The Indian Agent travels all over the country to meet the Indians and pay it, and up here anyway, this takes place at the end of June. I believe it used to be a very big day, the Indians coming in to various centres from hundreds of miles round, and joining in games and feasting. And so it ought to be now, but owing partly to the general decline in numbers, prosperity and virility of the Indians, and partly I suppose, to the general retrenchment, the whole thing has shrunk down to a miserable little business affair, with no ceremonial or fun at all. The Indians just camp in the bush a mile or so away from, and all around, the pay centre, and come in throughout the day like ordinary employees to receive their money ...

But the actual Treaty Party remained, having come by aeroplane with the intention to fly South to Moverly Lake next day. The party consisted of the Dominion Agent, the Provincial Agent, our own local doctor, the pilot, a rather distinguished airman called *Wop* May (?)[22] and with them were two gold prospectors belonging to some Eastern Company ...

But it was the Indian Agent that I was especially glad to meet because of the Indian School question which had been on my mind ever since the winter. So we had supper there and then I had a long talk with Mr C., who was most friendly and expansive about it all: He said that the Roman Catholics had definitely offered to run a school up here some time before we did, and that, if the Government could afford the expense of construction at all, the care of it would almost certainly therefore be entrusted to them ...

It was all very interesting and I learned quite a lot – among other things that, contrary to everybody's idea, the actual number of Indians in Canada is not dwindling but *increasing*.[23] He also promised to let me know if there turned out to be any way in which we as a Church could help.

Then I suddenly had a completely different kind of interview with our neighbour and friend, the Doctor. He is a very spiritually minded man, afflicted with what I hope I'm not prejudiced in calling a bad kink against our Church. In Fort St John we see each other constantly, but only for fleeting moments, each going about our own business. But at Hudson's Hope, 65 miles from home, there seemed to be the time and the place and the Unloved one, all together. So while we were admiring the view from the hotel verandah, he told me very frankly what he felt about ourselves and our Church. It's puzzling because he believes so strongly in God, and our Lord, and yet he is so sure that we have no common ground greater and more vital even than our differences. It is also puzzling and sad because his wife and children are among my best friends here, and yet he won't let them join the Church or even come to a real Service. We talked for about an hour and covered a colossal amount of country swiftly and incoherently, as you can imagine. We had three or four very narrow passages round a stand-up quarrel, especially when he spoke slightingly of Brother Wolf, and my temper began to break. It might have thrown me too, if I hadn't remembered what Brother Wolf himself would have thought of *that*.

Eventually we steered into calm waters, and made good friends, I hope, or at least convinced of one another's sincerity and even tentatively agreeing that the Eternal and Infinite might be great enough to include both our views of Him ...

I left off on the evening of the 21st, when we reached Hudson's Hope ... The trails everywhere had turned into canals or swamps, so that our summer shoes very quickly became entirely water-logged, and we abandoned both them and stockings and went barefoot. I'm afraid this may seem to you a little irregular in a District Visitor, but compared with sodden footwear, it is warm and comfortable, and everyone here regards it as only common sense in wet weather. Cecilia had her fine Tyrolese cloak and hood to keep her dry, but I only had my cold corduroy land-coat, until the airman 'Wop' May lent me his slicker and air-helmet, in which I felt rather like Nebuchadnezzar's image[24] ...

We met at the school for Service and each slipped on a pair of borrowed shoes, in exact reversal of Moslem custom. Unluckily, as we had expected, the rain washed out the congregation, and only about ten people were there, including, however, Wop May, the airman ...

... [The next day, in streaming rain, we arrived at the Tompkins].[25] Mrs Tompkins was as welcoming as ever, made us take off all our clothes and endowed us with dry shirts and overall trousers belonging to her innumerable sons. They had finished their dinner, but of course she produced more for us ... The rain stopped during the afternoon, so after supper we went down to see how far the river had fallen, but were soon undeceived about that. The old Halfway, which at our crossing last Tuesday had been about 300 yards wide at most, now measured a third of a mile at least, and its boiling muddy waters were tearing past at sickening speed, carrying huge logs and piles of driftwood like corks into the Peace.

... Another long afternoon, raining all the time ... Mrs Tompkins was as sweet as ever and perfectly marvellous in coping with her immense party – husband and eight children, three hired men, an elderly lawyer from Pouce Coupé on a visit with his tiny son, a grown-up son by a former wife, and the two of us. For this party (apart from washing and mending and patching for all her actual children), she kept the house clean, made all the bread and the butter and produced three immense meals a day. She confessed to having baked during the last ten days *sixty-two loaves*, and this with an absence of fuss or effort that was quite uncanny ... But I think she rather enjoyed our being there, simply as *females*, as she only has one daughter of companionable age (13) and is otherwise completely submerged by men and boys. Think of this, you over-worked English mothers! ...

[The flooding river] was so strange and impressive that I had to try and preach that afternoon on the tragedy of driftwood souls – souls without God, being swept helplessly down the stream of time, dying or dead, and bringing destruction to any living thing in their path. And with them I tried to contrast a boat, made of the same raw material, also subject to the current, but embued with a new life, with control and purpose and power to save, if only the Pilot is in full command ...

Next morning we got up at five, breakfast for 17 at six, and then, accompanied by our saddles and bridles and bedrolls, Cecilia and I embarked with Mr C—e,[26] who had got down from the Hope at midnight ...

... Cecilia and I arranged that I should land at the Old Post and walk home up the coulee (only about two and a half miles), while she went on to the Taylor landing ...

I hadn't visited the McLeod's[27] [at the Old Fort] for ages, and felt rather guilty about it, so was touched by the welcome of old Mrs Mac. She made me warm up by the kitchen fire while she produced tea and toast, and then brought water to wash my rather cold and muddy feet. Finally the daughter said, 'You sure can't climb that stony hill with them feet. You must take my shoes. I'm only staying about the place and don't need them.' In spite of all protests she made me take them, and certainly I was thankful for them later, although not happy till I got them back to her two or three days afterwards. You see, spare or extra shoes are pretty well unknown now. It's like lending anyone your spectacles or your false teeth to lend your shoes ...

Then I was reminded of old Mrs Beaton,[28] wife of the original Hudson's Bay Factor, who now lives on their homestead about two miles West of the old Post ... Mrs Beaton was sitting huddled by a lighted heater (although the day was now hot), looking smaller and older and more Indian than anyone I have ever seen up here. She smiled at me wanly and told me through her half-breed daughter-in-law that she was very sick – yes, had seen the doctor – no good. Yes, had been to hospital – no good. Nothing any good – always sick now ...

Finally, in despair of keeping me quiet any other way, she [the daughter-in-law] said, 'Have you eaten?' and then succeeded in muzzling me for a little while with bread and butter and saskatoons (a black fruit, a sort of *extremely* poor relation to the black currant family). After that I began to feel in despair about Mrs Beaton and to wonder what I had come for – when she suddenly said something quite definite in Cree.

'What does she say?' 'She wants you to sing.' 'Me to sing?' 'Yes; she says Mr Beaton heard you sing in Church.'

Mr Beaton! When on earth? Then I remembered; 18 months ago in February I took Mrs B's funeral. She was a half-breed. Mr Beaton was there. As is usual here, no one took any part in the Service, so I had to sing three hymns all by myself. I suppose Mr Beaton thought they were intentional solos.

'What shall I sing to her?' 'She says, anything – hymns.' So I did, about five running, and then a pause for breath, while her eye gradually brightened and she spoke again.

'She says no one has sung to her *since Mrs Birley* was a little girl.' (Mrs Birley is about 36 or 37.) 'She says Bishop Hines[29] sang to her then ... – just those hymns you are singing and she had never heard them since. Go on singing.'

So I went on – and ON. But soon it appeared that Bishop Hines was a dangerous rival. Mrs Beaton began to expand and sway with the music, using her hands like a concertina. 'She says Bishop Hines played the accordion while he was singing. Don't you?' 'No, I haven't got one. Besides (hastily) I can't play it anyway.'

Mrs Beaton looked at me pityingly, but told me to go on. So I went on, and sang all the good hymns and all the bad hymns – in fact *all* the hymns I could possibly remember.

It was rather heavenly to see the little old lady growing vital again, her body straightening, her face lighting up. Gradually she began to whistle softly through her teeth, to smile in recognition, and finally to sing with me in a tiny crooning voice. When at last I ran dry, she spoke again. 'She says Bishop Hines read the Bible to her in Cree.' (I began to hate Bishop Hines.)

'Alas! I can read it only in English.' 'Read it in English. She can understand enough.' So I read to her St John XIV out of Father's little Testament, very slowly and clearly, trying to make it as much like Cree as possible. And then we ended with Prayer. I don't know how much she understood; but she knew it was Prayer anyway, and knelt with me; so that I guess our souls met at a Place beyond language barriers ...

On Sunday ... I collected Brother Wolf's little Starlight and Cecilia went to the Red Cross for Miss Claxton's 'Major' whom she said we might borrow for any emergency. That gave us two [horses for the long trail] but we required a pack-horse too this time, to carry tent, bedrolls and food; so set off to catch Robin, my intention being to ride him and pack the far more amenable Starlight. But Robin's intentions were quite different ...

At last, rather than wear out poor Starlight and Major for nothing, we gave up [attempting to catch Robin] and were both as near to losing our tempers as any Church Worker can be on a Sunday evening. Cecilia said for the hundreth time, 'Why on *earth* don't you get rid of Robin?' and I said, 'It's all very well, but he's a jolly good horse when – ' Whereupon Cecilia snorted, and went off to try and hire a pack-pony of some sort from Mr Mowick ...

After a little delay, Cecilia came back with a most amazing creature in tow – an immense gaunt brown nag called Bird. She looked about 100 years old, with huge haunches, head and feet, and a great bony Roman Nose. We stabled her with Major, who was very much offended at having to take under his wing that most unattractive old thing with a caricature of a face.

Next morning (Monday 24th) we got up at six, and mobilized bedrolls, tent, pack-sacks and food, hobbles, hatchet and tethering ropes. Our grubstake consisted of two tin cups and little plates, a Scout billy-can and little cook pot, some smoked bacon, some beans, flour and baking-powder mixed, and some cookies, i.e., home-made biscuits. The latter alas, got shaken out of the cook pot on the first day and nearly all lost.

The real excitement was packing the Hag, i.e., poor hideous old Bird. You see, it sounds like nothing to pack a pack-horse, but really it's quite an art, and neither of us had ever done it ... I needn't say the first experiments ... were not very lustrous, but really Cecilia was marvellously clever at it ...

We stayed with the Joneses for nearly three days – our one really English Country House Visit of the year. Of course, as English Country Houses go, it is a small house ... [but] the walls inside are papered and lined with books, so the whole appearance is wonderfully like Home. But more so still is the garden, a real little English flower garden with roses, mignonette, sweet Williams, pansies, and a whole border of tall delphiniums ... It is almost incredibly remote and peaceful, and so extraordinary to find in these surroundings, hidden completely from the river behind a grove of immense timber, this perfectly English home and garden – and Mrs Jones, who, with her perfectly English voice and clothes, welcome and culture, might be living in Rochester or even in Kew Gardens ...

We left on Sunday morning with great reluctance, already looking forward and planning a much longer visit next year ...

First Part of August, 1933 (July 30th to August 8th)

... We had dinner [at the Beatties] ... and had a good deal of fun with Mr Beattie over the packing of Puck ... [He also] gave us a rough map for our next trail.

This was to be quite new and much more exciting than any previous trip, being about 60 miles of pack trail with, at the most, two inhabited houses, and nearly 50 miles before the first one. Our aim was a Mrs Simpson,[30] the new Furthest North White Woman in the parish. She lives 70 miles up the Halfway River and has been in about six months, and none of us has got to her yet ...

The problem was to find the trail ... The sun was going down and we were beginning to get rather rattled; so finally decided to stop and camp for the night and start again with fresh eyes tomorrow. We found a good camping ground about 50 yards from the river, where Cecilia lighted a fire and cooked our bacon and dampers while I tethered the horses and put up the tent. After supper we looked to the horses again before going to bed ...

The night was warm and still, but very dark. Just at its darkest, we were awakened by some animal walking round. Suddenly there was a heavy plunging and we heard Ginger tear up the tree stump to which he was tied and bolt past the tent. Cecilia rushed after him, but could see nothing in the darkness, so we decided to wait till daybreak and then round him up. The sun rose and out we went to start the search, when to my dismay I discovered both Puck and Starlight had disappeared as well. There had clearly been either a moose or bear round the camp and all three horses had stampeded, Puck having pulled in half the stout leather of his hobble. While I was looking for him, Cecilia ran up the hill behind, and suddenly I heard a clatter on the stones of the river fore-shore. I ran down through the bush, and was just in time to see our three runaways stand for one moment at the water's edge, and *then plunge in and swim like seals to the further bank.* The current carried them down-stream, but they all landed safely and in another moment had disappeared in the deep forest beyond.

It was impossible to follow or to find them if we had. I turned back and saw Cecilia coming down the hill. 'They've crossed the river.' 'I know, I saw them.' 'We can't follow.' 'No. We'd better have breakfast.' So we did.

It was a funny position. The river was too deep and swift to cross ... and we had no axe to cut logs for a raft. So we were just marooned ... Then we remembered that Fred Cassy[31] was expected back before the end of the week, and the only thing to do seemed to be to wait for him.

Wasn't that ridiculous? So baffling as to be really rather fun. You know, I always like a hitch that jerks you out of all your preconceived arrangements. And as Cecilia rather bitterly remarked, I'd got my hitch now all right! We had plenty of food. The beans had gone mouldy but there was lots of bacon left and flour and one rapturous tin of sausages. We also had a good tent and blankets, Bible and Prayer Book, a book of Meditations by Father Lutyens, Wells' 'History of the World' (small)[32] and a silk veil that Cecilia was working for St Martin's. So there was no need to be either starved or bored for quite a long time.

We had our daily Mattins, complete with Mirfield Hymnbook, bathed blissfully in an ice-cold backwater, and then set out to look for the trail – just by way of something to do to keep up the Morale of the Troops ... In the course of [the search] we hit upon a very faint track of pressure in the grass and followed it with difficulty and many doubts as it disappeared across rocks and faded out among deadfall and deep bush. Finally, just when it seemed to forsake us altogether, lo! There was THE TRAIL – small and very modest but clear enough as it crept away under the trees and started to climb the steep hill-side.

Oh, then I longed to go – you can't think how much. But after a short sharp struggle I bowed down as usual to the false god, Common Sense. We simply had to wait and recover the horses somehow ... So we said Goodbye to that tantalizing trail – the symbol of everything found too late to be followed – and went back to our little waiting game by the river ...

We finished the sausages and worked and read again and then went to sleep. When we awoke, the sun was beginning to drop. I went down to the river for a bathe and was just going in when I heard a strange sound – a SHOUT! I jumped back into clothes and ran up the bank and there stood a young man – John Cramer[33] from Beatties – with Puck and Starlight, looking rather sheepish, in his train.

Apparently the three deserters had bolted through the whole 20 miles of forest and back to Beatties' pasture yesterday. They had been caught with great difficulty, and then John Cramer, who works for Beattie, had volunteered to bring them back and find us. It had taken him nearly all today to come, *and on the way he lost Ginger.*

This last was a sad blow. If he had brought Ginger we could have gone straight ahead with our journey ... There was nothing for it but to abandon all that little plan, and all our camp stuff as well, and to ride back to the Peace, hoping to find Ginger at Beatties once more ... I was sorry. It seemed a sort of enchanted place and I would gladly have been marooned a few days longer. But Cecilia was not sorry; she didn't like it much ...

Next morning we were up at dawn ... In less than four hours, i.e., before ten o'clock, we reached the Beatties, and got a good roasting from Mr B. for all our stupidity... However, they had caught Ginger for the second time. So after apologizing and thanking them for all the trouble we had given and they had taken, we took our leave, resolved to make Hudson's Hope that night ...

We got home to Fort St John at three o'clock on Tuesday the 8th, after 15 of the most interesting days I have ever spent in this country – not quite successful of course; but not quite a failure either ...

[Wednesday I] got home in the dark, so that I didn't notice that Eliza (my car) was not standing patiently a few yards from the gate as usual. But in the morning, it was only too clear that she was missing. 'Why ever didn't you lock her and take out the keys?' 'Because I was so much more likely to lose the key than to lose Eliza.' All the same, I did feel a fool, and couldn't think what could have happened to her, when, in sweeping the floor of the house, I found a scribbled note from Brother Wolf. 'Car broke down between Cache Creek and Halfway. Ventured to borrow Eliza' ...

Eliza has no side curtains left, and her back curtain has long torn adrift from all its moorings, and just flies out behind like the pennon of a ship. She has no wind-screen, because that was so splintered by sun and frost as

to be opaque glass so I had to take it out altogether. She has no radiator
cap, because that got lost somehow and I couldn't get another. But it's
wonderful what you can do with a green cotton comb-bag. Her battery is
nearly worn out, and her water-pump leaks. One of her doors won't open,
and another won't stay shut. Her hand-brake is too stiff to move and her
foot-brake is nearly worn out. She has a knock in her engine and a groan
in her steering gear (which is very loose) and her driving gear slips out on
hills – BUT Brother Wolf says she has a heart of gold and is ready for
anything. In fact, she's rather a typical Church Worker.

After all my old-maidish fears [the Wolves got to Hudson's Hope] and
back all right and in record time ... The Halfway itself was too deep to ford,
so they left her there, crossed in the boat and walked the remaining 30
miles to the Hope. There he held the Service, and then collecting some
drift logs in the river, made a raft on which they floated back to the Halfway, accompanied by Bay, their big police dog ... I was fearfully jealous of
Sister Wolf for rafting down the Peace before me ...

On Saturday morning Brother Wolf drove down to Dawson Creek to
bring the Bishop in, and that evening Mrs Williamson and I went to a
congregational reception arranged to welcome him ... In the middle
Brother Wolf broke the fairy ring to come across and tell me that he had
forgotten, while at Dawson, to get the Confirmation veils for tomorrow.
This was rather a shock, but luckily there was time to do something and he
was more needed to keep the party alive than I was. So I slipped out and
went to the Roman Catholic Hospital to ask the Sisters' help. They are
always wonderfully kind to us and ready for any emergency, even to lending us wine for our Altar. But they had no Confirmation veils, because
their children take them home and treasure them in their families ... I
knew that none of the stores had any white material, so we were a little
stumped until Sister Catherine with a sudden inspiration, suggested STERI-
LIZED GAUZE! Off we went to the little operating theatre and then the
kind Sister produced a whole bolt of soft white stuff, and cut off for me
four large squares ... [Next morning] the Confirmation was quite wonderful, the most moving that I have ever seen ...

After breakfast the Wolves were to take the Bishop back to Dawson Creek,
and then drive through to Ontario for their holiday at her home ... I had a
few odd jobs to do in town ... when Brother Wolf drove up alone in his car,
looking for him unusually harassed.

'What's happened? Where's the Bishop? Why haven't you gone?' 'I've
taken on too many passengers and they've brought piles of luggage and I
just *can't* squeeze them in.'

It was as we had feared. In this country whenever anybody is known to be going out (i.e., right out of the Block) by car, all the would-be travellers for miles round settle upon them like bees, asking for lifts to Dawson, Edmonton, Saskatchewan, or even right back East. Especially have they taken advantage of Brother Wolf ... They know he'll never refuse so long as there's a square inch left in the car, however inconvenient or expensive it may be to take them. So this time, besides Sister Wolf and the Bishop (a big man), all their luggage ... he had promised to take three women and a baby as far as the middle of Saskatchewan! You can imagine all the junk they brought. Well, no, you hardly can; because besides the suit-cases and babies' bottles that you know about, they also brought huge boxes of food, *eggs* and sacks of vegetables to eat on the way. He said he had tried for over an hour to pack them all in And It Couldn't Be Done. It would be all right after Dawson, because the Bishop and all his little Episcopal bags would disembark there ...

Well, wasn't it lucky that I had Eliza and a free day? It was as easy as anything. He made me drive the Bishop, the mother and baby in his car (which is closed) and he drove the other passengers and all the junk in Eliza and off we went ...

We got there a long way ahead because Eliza is so naked that you can't drive her much above 25 miles per hour for fear of her occupants being blown overboard. But they joined us at four o'clock ... Still as it was, both the running boards and all four wings and the fenders fore and aft were smothered with parcels, sacks and bags, and how the radiator was going to breathe I secretly couldn't imagine.

Finally Brother Wolf squeezed in under the wheel, grinned at us, and drove off with his harem. Not exactly ideal conditions for a first holiday trip with your wife – But neither of them would give a thought to that ...

Diary to the End of October, 1933
... At intervals during the holidays we had tried to find out [if Fred was coming back to school] because of other possible boys, but Mr Neilson couldn't make up his mind. Meanwhile Mrs Spence from across the Pine wrote and implored me to take her eldest girl, Jean (14) who had passed into High School. We can't very well combine big boys and girls, so I had to say, 'No – unless –'

On Sunday night before term, Mr Neilson told Cecilia that Fred *was* coming next day. But next day brought a note instead to say that he was not coming at all! Rather baffling, but no good to be angry. So I wrote at once to Mrs Spence for Jean – and then thought of Joyce Neilson, Fred's youngest sister, who had also just passed Entrance, and wanted somewhere to board. So after a few more messages and delays, Jean and Joyce both arrived, and were delighted to meet, because they had been patrol-mates and friends in [Guide] camp ... Jean is short and dark, eleven and vivacious ... Joyce is tall, fair and delicate ... very bright and sociable, and like old Fred, remarkably gentle and obedient.

We shall miss Fred very much ... I do so wonder whether we have been able to help him at all in any way that matters ...

Next morning, September 13th ... there was little Roger Hadland[34] to visit. He is seriously ill with some kidney trouble, poor child, and has been in bed a long time. After sitting with him and reading him a little story, I gradually became aware of a stupid headache. Mrs Hadland gave me some tea and cold bacon to take it away and we talked very pleasantly, but it didn't take it away. I thought it was caused by a kick on the head from Eliza's roof, this being a habit she has developed lately on revenge for loss of windshield, radiator cap and side-screens. Anyway, it wasn't really bad; so I went on to Mrs Ohland ... Finally, realizing that the plot was thickening rather fast, I drove rapidly to town ... interviewed a supplicant for clothing, collected the Mail, drove home, put the horses to bed, warmed up the Shepherd's pie, started the three children on it – and retired gracefully to bed – *for SIX WEEKS.*

... But by a wonderful providence, the Mrs Brisbin[35] whom I had engaged to come as housekeeper during our [projected] absence, arrived on Saturday night – and turned out to be an excellent nurse. She took charge of me and the house, leaving Cecilia free to carry on all our joint undertakings ...

But on the 19th day Dr Brown suddenly grew dissatisfied – not with them but with me. So he whirled me off to the Providence Hospital where I was X-rayed and X-iled from all human intercourse except with Cecilia and May. The Nuns were charming, as they always have been to us ...

Meanwhile the Guardians of the Peace, i.e., our three holiday substitutes had arrived (to be exact, on October 17th) ... Their names are Isa McArthur (called Mac),[36] Kitty Arnold[37] and Katherine Webber.[38] Mac has previously had two winters in Saskatchewan, which is a great help, but Kitty and Katherine are quite new to everything. They are all three so nice and tremendously keen and gallant. We can't be thankful enough to the Maple Leaf[39] for sending them out, and giving us this wonderful chance of leave without hindrance to the work ... Of course we knew beforehand what a plunge it must be to all of them – not merely the hard winter and somewhat primitive conditions, but also the wide scattered parish, and all the

Monica Storrs. Portrait taken ca 1920 in Rochester

Adeline Harmer, Monica's close friend and first Companion

The Lusk and Babcock families arriving by wagon train from Saskatchewan, 1932: '1500 miles in 89 days'

The Abbey, 1934. Notice the wood pile in the background, used for all cooking, baking, and heating.

Above left: Cecilia Goodenough with Theodore, standing in the doorway of 'Bethlehem.' The little church house at Taylor was so named because it was 'so small and simple and chiefly meant for children.'

Above right: Nurse Muriel Claxton (left) with Mrs Emily Crawford, owner of the XY Ranch and enthusiastic champion of North Peace River settlement

Gough Memorial Hospital, Cecil Lake, built in 1934 by local settlers with funds supplied by the Fellowship of the Maple Leaf, in memory of Prebendary Gough, who 'cared so much for the Empire settlers and their needs'

Tommy Hargreaves, taxi driver, trucker, and rancher, with his 'snowmobile,' March 1934

Cecilia Goodenough (left) and Monica Storrs (back row, right) with children from St John's Church Sunday School, Baldonnel, 1935

Boarders at the Abbey, 1936: Eileen Brisbin, Micky Flatt, Phyllis Freer, Tony Flatt, Roy Cuthbert, Rosaline Beck, Percy Freer, Alf Cuthbert

Above left: Elinor Higgenbotham (left) and Rosemary Owen, Companions, at Taylor, 1936. Overalls, the usual household wear, were not to be worn away from the Abbey or 'Bethlehem.'

Above right: Priscilla Oldacres (left), who later married the Reverend Russell Brown, and Nurse Agnes Ayling, soon after the latter's arrival from England, 1936

Doris ? and Companions Hope Onslow, Monica Storrs, and Priscilla Oldacres, with Monica's dog, Kristin, in front of the Abbey. Hope is dressed for entertaining guests.

Hope Onslow, who married Bob Symons, local game warden, artist, and author, leaving their ranch for the forty-mile drive into Fort St John

Fort St John's Main Street in the late 1930s, showing C.M. Finch's store, Hunter's restaurant, a second-hand store, the bank, Titus's store, and Bowes and Herron's garage

Hugh (Horst) Schramm (left) and David (Arwed) Lewinski, Monica's two 'adopted' refugee boys, newly arrived in England from Germany, 1939

tiny units and individual problems to be followed up. That was why we had arranged that Cecilia should go Home first and come back first, so that by over-lapping we should be able to help through the early difficulties both of winter and of spring ...

But God's plan was quite different. Why I should get pneumonia is on the physical side a mystery. The weather was warm at the time and I was living an *exceptionally* innocent, sheltered, almost suburban life, just pottering round on odd jobs with Eliza ... Not only was I put out of action for all those weeks; but Dr Brown (with grim satisfaction!) insisted that I should be of no use for any more work in Canada this winter. And, alas, May and the Hospital Sisters said the same. So there was nothing for it but to cook up enough vigour for a journey Home with Cecilia at the beginning of November – and it's a poor heart that never rejoices – .

Meanwhile Cecilia trained the Guardians for one intense fortnight, and a pretty tough breaking in it was for them. For three days after their arrival winter arrived too, cold on their heels so to speak. It began with a sharp drop to zero, and went on with a week of almost continuous snowfall which came to stay ...

I was allowed to leave the Hospital after 19 days, but not to go home. So I spent the last ten days in a very blissful convalescence with May, under a regime of such angelic tyranny as was never known before ...

On Monday morning, October 30th, Cecilia called for me with a team and cutter. It was four days before the train. But the Peace was getting so full of ice that it seemed to be advisable to cross when we could, lest it should reach the impossible stage and we should lose the ship.

May and Nina saw us off at the gate; and I did hate to say Goodbye to them. Nothing can exceed the loving kindness they have shown us all this time ...

We reached the river at about two o'clock; and sure enough it was swollen, racing and chockfull of ice ... So we slept at McKnight's hoping for the best ... At 11 o'clock [next day] the little tug that usually pushes the ferry was obliged to make one journey ... so we made her take us back. And the snow-covered floes scraping past her sides gave us cold farewell kisses from the Peace[40] ...

On Friday the train came in as usual ... and out of it who should come but Brother Wolf. He had been 17 days on the road, sleeping in the car, which he was finally obliged to abandon in a drift 200 miles away and take the train. Luckily for her, Sister Wolf, being a little run down, is staying at home for another month, but will join him before Christmas.

He was in glowing spirits as usual, and stood quite serene, while we each poured out our respective reports, complaints and instructions about the parishes ... Then he stayed in the train much too long, conferring Farewell Blessings; and jumped out when she was going at a sickening speed – on to the icy platform.

Don't forget to pray for him sometimes – and for the three Guardians of the Peace. They have all got a pretty tough winter ahead ...

Goodbye for the present. With most grateful love to you all, from Monica

1934

Fortnight Ending July 16th, 1934

I have been back here exactly a fortnight, and already can hardly believe I ever went away ...

It was an odd feeling coming back. I had been away just too long for it to seem obvious and natural, and to tell the truth I dreaded it rather – all except Cecilia and Kristin!

But ... in the train coming on I found Mrs Johnny Brown of Fort St John returning from an operation in Edmonton Hospital.[1] All that was somehow encouraging. But when at 10 p.m. that night part of the train ran off the tracks and we settled down to a nine hours' pause until help should come, all strangeness departed and I felt *quite* at home once more.

Mrs Johnny Brown is quite a middle-aged woman ... and what *do* you think she did last year? She and her husband were employed by a trader to accompany a whole lot of livestock down the river to Fort Resolution about 600 miles away. They built a big scow (small barge) and loaded it up with six milch cows, a 'bunch of steers,' over 100 hens and 53 pigs, including of course all the feed as well as all their own food; and off they went for months and months like a very protracted Noah's Ark – in fact Mrs Brown didn't get home again for a year. She said it was a bit monotonous, but quite comfortable; they kept the Ark *scrupulously* clean and reached the Fort with everything alive ...

Oh, I haven't even mentioned Gwen Hampshire.[2] How dreadfully self-absorbed! Well, here she was with Cecilia, looking as if she had never worn anything but smock and breeches and already three parts Canadian. She has settled down most wonderfully and I do think is really happy ... She is a charming, serene Companion, immensely interested in the country and people, and has already taken to riding Puck on errands to the City – this after telling me she never had ridden and didn't intend to begin! ...

Meanwhile, Cecilia is doing a bit of building. She is having a little shack put up alongside of the Good Shepherd. It is to be 14 by 16 feet, and will be a one-room 'manse' where she can hold small meetings, Guides, etc., keep things, and sleep pretty often in the winter ...

And now I must tell you our sad news. Brother Wolf is leaving in September. It's not sudden, because he wrote to me about it during Lent, and even hinted at it before I left last October. I think his three years here have exhausted him quite a lot and both he and she certainly need a good holiday ...

I needn't say how much we shall miss him; in fact I can hardly *think* of the parish without him yet. But the new man is appointed, a Mr Nose-worthy (!)[3] and of course we must welcome and back him to the utmost of our power, all the more because it won't be easy for him to follow Brother Wolf ...

Diary Beginning July 15th, 1934

... [On Sunday] among others I visited Mrs Middleton ... Unluckily she was out, but I found all the children and had a delightful hour playing with them. They consist of five boys ranging from four to 14, and two girls – Margaret, confirmed with her mother last year, and Lucy aged seven, who is about the sweetest little girl in the country. She is amazingly loving and welcoming, and full of daring and fun and comradeship. They are all curiously friendly – more like East Londoners than the reserved independent children up here; so ... they all gathered round and we sat in a ring among the wild flowers outside the house and played games ...

Tuesday was the day before the W.A. Stampede at Sunset Prairie, South of the river and about 80 miles away. And as it was to begin with a Eucharist at noon, our little contingent had decided to start the day before and get to Dawson Creek first ...

Mrs Middleton came in a state of great flutter, part genuine spiritual zeal, because Religion really is her life, and part frank excitement at the trip, because she hasn't crossed the river for years and years. Unluckily, it was all rather too much for her, and she felt dreadfully car-sick all the way and was only happy each time we stuck in a mud-hole and she had to get out and walk. This happened about six times; but even that didn't prevent her from reaching Dawson in a state of collapse. She was put straight to bed at the Proctors, where it was agreed that I should stay too, while the other ladies went to the local hotel for a spree and had a blissful evening at the Talkies ...

I joined Mrs Middleton about mid-night and found her wide awake and quite recovered. She said that no amount of car-sickness could make any difference to her joy in coming; and her only prayer was that she might not be too ill again, after the extra 30 miles tomorrow, to be present at the Eucharist. And then for about half an hour she talked to me with her broad Sheffield accent ... I was amazed at her understanding; for she is not at all an educated woman; but I have never been so deeply impressed as by her simple and utterly sincere expressions of faith and love and thankfulness.

Next morning at about ten we all set out for Sunset Prairie[4] ... About 60 women rolled up, which is quite good considering the distance and general poverty of everyone, and the Church was quite full. Mrs Middleton arrived in a state of complete collapse; but before the bell stopped she had recovered enough to achieve her heart's desire. It was a Sung Eucharist, *not* good music or well sung; but it was all right for all of us, and for her it was the Gate of Heaven ...

Our next great event was the *Bedeaux Expedition.*[5] Mr Bedeaux is a Franco-American millionaire almost or quite identical with Citroën Motors, which he advertizes by tremendous stunt journies ... but now his plan is to blaze a brand-new route across the Rocky Mountains with five Citroën caterpillar tractors. The whole thing has been planned for months and on an enormous scale. The actual party was to consist of Mr Bedeaux, his wife and a friend and a Spanish maid. But their train included a geographer, a radio expert, a cameraman, an airman, a minerologist, botanist, etc., besides innumerable aides and mechanics and cooks, and TWO Pack-trains of over *60* horses each, laden with supplies and controlled by at least 20 'Wranglers' as they are called.

Well, the blissful part for us was that all these forces were to mobilize at Fort St John and really start from there, giving a lot of employment in repairs, feeding, etc., buying a lot of horses and engaging about a score of our young men to take charge of them at the princely salary of four dollars a day.

You can think what a stir all that made, and how glad Fort St John was to welcome them. So much so that the Board of Trade decided to give a banquet in their honour directly they arrived. So when I got home on Thursday, I heard that this banquet was fixed for next day and honour demanded that we should go ...

Even getting [to the Fort St John Hotel] was quite a chore as the deluge was still on, the trail was a canal and the road a quagmire. So for the first time we broke our Rule and rode to town in overalls (Gwen looking enchanting in Cecilia's enormous pair!) and bare legs, taking stockings, shoes and party smocks rolled up in a haversack; and found a corner in the hotel to change. I wish the weather had permitted me to photograph Gwen as a Church Worker starting for a Civic Banquet. There would have been a new relic for St Christopher's[6] ...

On Saturday evening, the 29th, just as I was crossing Holland's coulee about six miles from town, I met a stranger, who, after the usual greeting added, 'Have you heard about the two kids drowned yesterday?' 'No, what kids?' 'Lucy Middleton, I guess, and Tommy Kingsley.'[7]

Lucy Middleton – !

I came back as hard as possible to the Middletons' home and found one small boy, Walter, minding another. They were quite placid and evidently hadn't realized a bit. Their mother was not there, so I went to the Church House and saw Brother Wolf, who said it was all too true, that the funeral was to be next morning at ten and that the bodies were at the Kingsleys and Mrs Middleton was probably there too ...

Before I got there I met Miss Claxton bringing Mrs Middleton home in Eliza. I jumped off and ran and kissed her, and all she said was, 'She's safe with Jesus. I'm just holding on to that.' Miss Claxton said, 'I'll take care of her. You go on to Mrs Kingsley – she isn't bearing it so well.'

Mrs Kingsley is a refined delicate woman and Tommy was her only child. All this time I knew nothing of how it had happened. That didn't seem to matter yet. Outside the house, under the trees, I found a neighbour making two small coffins of rough lumber, and two or three women sewing white stuff together to cover them. Inside were three rooms – the living room with a group of people having supper, and two little bedrooms – Mrs Kingsley prostrate in one, and the two children in the other. Two neighbours were sitting with her crying. They kindly made way for me and I sat with her for some time and learned her pitiful story.

These two mothers are very great friends, and Tommy and Lucy were great friends too, though he was eleven and she only seven years old. It seems that Lucy was on a visit to the Kingsleys and the two children were doing what all children do here in the summer – playing in the dam. Lucy was a first-rate swimmer but Tommy had never swum yet. So Mrs K. had strictly charged them to keep to the shallow end, which shelves gradually from a few inches to 12 feet.

She watched them from the house close by and saw that they were really paddling about to Tommy's knees. Then suddenly, taking her eyes off them for a moment, she heard a little cry, ran out and saw *both* children struggling in the middle of the deep part. She herself was unable to swim, but jumped in at once fully clothed, grabbed at the children and tried to drag them out. But their struggles were too much for her. They dragged her under, and when at last, nearly drowned herself, she reached the bank, there was nothing to be seen of them.

Mr Kingsley was out and she was alone. She rushed half a mile to the nearest neighbour and *she* rushed on another two miles to Miss Claxton, who happened to be at home. Miss Claxton collected a man or two with ropes and they all flew back to drag the dam. All this time poor Mrs Kingsley had been desperately trying to find the children herself; but it was a full two hours more before the little bodies were discovered and brought to land. Meanwhile someone had gone to fetch Mrs Middleton and she arrived just as all attempts at artificial respiration had been given up.

Mrs Kingsley said she dreaded to meet her friend, fearing that reproach and bitterness might be added to her own despair. She didn't look up at her but just stayed bowed down with grief. Then Mrs Middleton ran to her, put her arms round her and lifted her up, and they mingled their tears together ...

The funeral on Sunday was wonderful. Dear May brought masses of flowers and we made the Church like a garden. It was packed with people of course, and there was only just room for the little coffins to be carried in and out by four boys and four girls chosen to do it. Brother Wolf spoke of Christ's love for the children and their happiness with Him, and of all that sorrow calls forth of courage and faith ...

Then we carried them out to their single grave; and the boys and girls led the way after Brother Wolf, carrying all the flowers ...

Mrs Middleton was marvellous [when I visited her next day] – so welcoming, so worried about me being wet, so natural in both her grief and her beautiful faith. The other children had gone out before the rain to get berries so before they got back we could talk quite peacefully, and she said two wonderful things: 'You know she was just everything to me, my sunshine that never failed. But I do feel that I mustn't grudge her this happiness, just the same as when Mrs Kingsley asked her to stay, I wanted her at home badly just then for company, and then I saw her little face so eager, and I thought I mustn't grudge her such a fine treat. Well, it's like that now; I couldn't be so selfish as to grudge her *this*' ...

Soon after that the other six came home soaked to the skin. So we dried them and changed them and had supper all playing quite naturally with Lucy's little kitten 'Caruso' – so named because she had said he sang so beautifully ...

August, 1934

... On Monday 6th, I had a night with May, such a treat. We each went in turn that week; stayed in bed late and behaved for a few precious hours

like the Decline and Fall of the Roman Empire; that is, Cecilia read dozens
of novels, I played tennis with Douglas,[8] and I don't know exactly what
form of debauchery was enjoyed by Gwen ...

Another outing was to Edith Stewart's[9] 'Can Shower.' Perhaps you don't
know what that is. Well, when anyone is married here, you don't see rows
and rows of presents in the bride's house, sent beforehand by those who
were invited to the wedding. But *after* the marriage is safely accomplished,
some friend 'puts on a can shower' in her house, that is, a party to which
all the other friends of the bride and groom come and bring their gifts.
This was the first I had ever been to and was awfully nice. All the Baldonnel
and Taylor ladies were there and a handful of men ... Cecilia and I took
kitchen pots and a garment or two for Edith, who wore her blue wedding
dress and looked very sweet and happy ...

The next important event was a Farewell Social given at Baldonnel for
Brother Wolf on Tuesday the 14th ... We found an immense crowd there,
all waiting for Brother Wolf who was badly overdue. Cecilia thought he
had forgotten, but having just come over the road, I feared he must be
stuck too. Anyway, he didn't come, and the Hall got fuller and fuller, and
being almost dark (only one gas lantern), became rather bewildering. At
last we found two men with accordions and persuaded them to play familiar songs which gradually led the people to join in some choruses ...

Just when these were running dry Brother Wolf arrived, his face and
hands and Farewell-Social-clean-clothes plastered with mud. He had stuck
in a far worse hole than ours ... and his battery had caught fire. Poor Tess
(as we now call Sister Wolf) looked frightened and tired out already. She is
expecting a child in November; and this kind of struggle has been going
on all summer, which I'm afraid, softens her regret at leaving the Peace
River.

However, there was no time to waste, so the poor Dears were hurried to
the platform for their presentation. Bert Hadland[10] read a very nice letter
of appreciation and regret which had a great number of signatures, and
handed them our offerings – a handbag for Tess and for Brother Wolf
a strong chromium wrist watch, said to be dust-proof, frost-proof, shock-
proof – in fact, all but Wolf-proof. Dear Brother Wolf was so pleased. Apparently he hadn't had a watch for over a year, which may partly account
for a certain optimistic vagueness about time.

[On Wednesday the building of] the new Chapel [was completed] – a
stately edifice of 18 by 10 by about 12 feet high. Outside you may not think
it's very exciting, but inside it's a dream ... We made an Altar step of three
spare logs and new benches of all the log-ends, six benches now as well as

new Altar rails. You can't imagine how I loved making those, and who do you think helped me? HARVEY.

He came home from the Industrial School just before I got back, and I had seen him once or twice, but not properly. So I sent word to ask him here for a week as soon as his father could spare him, and he turned up last Friday just in time to be with us for the climax of the year. He is now 15 and very tall and strong and nice-looking and I think glad to be here. He carpentered with me and weeded and worked at all the chores and came to Prayers and sang the hymns and seemed completely at home again ...

Diary from August 18th
On Saturday morning the 18th, Brother Wolf brought the Bishop straight to us from Dawson Creek ...

The Service [of Consecration] was wonderful; and to our great joy the Bishop consecrated our tiny Chapel as fully as any parish Church, for baptisms, for marriages, and for funerals, and any other sacred purpose; and dedicated it with the name of Holy Cross Chapel by the Peace River[11] ...

After that we had the Bishop with us for four Services ... But best of all was the Confirmation in the evening ... Three years ago, as you know, the Church of the Good Shepherd didn't exist, and the Bishop's visit to Taylor Flats could only draw seven people to Service in the school house, four of these being children. On this second birthday of the little Church, the porch was full of men standing, and the congregation was over 70. Mr and Mrs Hoffstrom were there, of course, and Mrs Middleton had got a lift all the way from Fish Creek ... Oh, and one other thing I nearly left out – the Blessing of Cecilia's little shack. I told you she was building one alongside of the church, to be her base at that end of the parish ... It is to be called Bethlehem because it is so small and simple, and chiefly meant for children ...

One of the delights of this whole Sunday was having Harvey with us again. He loves the new Chapel and ... had been present at its Consecration and the Eucharist. Well, after breakfast I told him he was quite free to visit friends or stay at home or come to another Service. He came with us to St Martin's and then said he'd like to ride on with me to St John's. After that Service I suggested he should visit in Baldonnel where he used to go to school, and then go home to supper. But later, when I got down to Taylor Flats, there was Harvey in the congregation. His voice has come on wonderfully, and he seems more alive and happy than I have known him before ...

For the next three days the Bishop and Brother Wolf were on the river visiting Hudson's Hope and the intermediate settlers. They were due back at Fort St John for a farewell banquet on Wednesday [for] Brother Wolf, to which Canon Proctor was also coming, and on Thursday morning, after the Eucharist, the Bishop was to take his departure with the Rural Dean.

The Wolfendales were also to leave that day, because Canon Proctor had, rather cruelly, arranged a farewell party for him at Dawson Creek. So poor Brother Wolf, after three years, had no time to pay his bills or pack up or do any private business until the actual day of his own final departure. Rather a stupid arrangement we all thought, but there's no controlling men ...

They were days full of sadness for me, but luckily not for Tess, who had not yet struck any deep roots here. But she came back and slept with me each night, so that I got to know her better than in all the two years before, and to love her gentleness and courage and complete unselfish trust in God and her husband. She's a capital companion too, when you are alone with her like that – full of shrewdness and humour which I had hardly suspected. I thought until then that I was only going to miss Brother Wolf, but now I know that I shall miss her badly too.

On Wednesday afternoon the Bishop and Brother Wolf got back from Hudson's Hope, and in the evening we all went to a 'Banquet' in honour of him and Brother Wolf ... One of the speakers was the Presbyterian Minister[12] ... He asked to speak, and then told us that when he first arrived, knowing nobody and quite bewildered, Brother Wolf had welcomed him to his house and spent two or three days driving him round to find all the Presbyterian families. Then a little later when he was out of funds and his salary had failed to come through, Brother Wolf had lent him enough to tide him over his troubles. All this was news to us of course; and poor Brother Wolf was getting dreadfully embarrassed, when the Bishop, to ease matters, said, 'It's the first time I've ever heard of an Anglican clergyman in Canada having money to lend.' Then Brother Wolf, in despair, jumped to his feet and replied, 'But I must confess, Sir, that money was borrowed.'!

Finally Bert Bowes, the garage man who is President of the Board of Trade, read a letter from the people of Fort St John and presented the astonished Brother Wolf with a purse of thirty dollars ...

Thursday the 23rd ... Cecilia and I walked with [the Wolves] to the gate where they both kissed us both, and drove off quickly ... He has a good deal still to learn about method and punctuality and the planning of work – but very little indeed about I Corinthians XIII,[13] and I can imagine no circumstances in which he would fail in generosity or courage. We may get a better priest; but I don't think there could be a finer Christian or truer comrade anywhere.

August 24th – September 6th

The afternoon following Brother Wolf's departure we set out on our annual trip up the Western trail to Carbon River ... [I visited] a woman who frankly acknowledges her husband to be alive in the States while she and her four small children live with another man here. These cases are so baffling. We have about four in the parish ... Cecilia and I find it awfully difficult to know how deadly a sin this is – I mean, compared with quarrelling and back-biting – and more difficult still to know what attitude to adopt towards these very irregular families ...

Next day we rode on over the portage, and the rest of the 35 miles to the Beatties ...

When we arrived, Mrs Beattie was on top of the stack working with the thrashers, and didn't come down till they all stopped for supper. She is a remarkable woman, a Russian with six children, the eldest married, the youngest six months old. She came into the house looking exactly like a short strong working-man, dressed in a man's shirt and overalls, and with a man's figure and walk, and her head tied up with a red handkerchief so you could see no hair. I was just thinking that it was hard to realize her as a Mother, when she stepped forward, picked the baby off her elder daughter's knee, opened her shirt, and gave it supper as beautifully and tenderly as any Madonna. In fact, for all her heavy work and uncouth clothing, she suddenly seemed to become the embodiment of Motherhood.

I said, 'Did you go into Fort St John for the baby's birth?' 'Why no. I never go anywhere. *Jim* has taken care of me for all my children.' 'How long do you manage to nurse them, with all your hard outside work?' 'Oh, maybe a year, perhaps eighteen months – sometimes two years.' (Two years!) 'And how often do you feed her?' 'When she's hungry, of course.' (Oh English mothers and nurses, what do you say to that?) ...

Thursday ... we only had about two more families to visit ... Mine was a Polish family called Polenenko[14] – *very* Polish indeed. I arrived about 11.[15] and intended to stay less than an hour; but Mr and Mrs Polenenko indicated quite firmly (though chiefly by gestures) that I was to stay for dinner ...

Her two little girls and a boy... knew a very little [English] and were most friendly; so I produced the simplest Bible stories with pictures which they enjoyed very much. When that was over and still no dinner, I had recourse to the shepherd's pipe,[15] and played various tunes including my two masterpieces, 'The Keeper' and 'Sellinger's Round.' The children adored that, and as it went faster and faster, looked as if they were going to dance – but didn't. I stopped and asked Mrs Polenenko, 'You like music?' 'No.'

Rather staggered, I asked why not. 'Jesus not like music.' 'Oh surely He does.' '*No. Jesus not like.*' 'But Jesus likes hymns.' 'What's that?' 'Jesus likes – Jesus-music' (illustrated by a slow chorale). 'Maybe; but Jesus *not* like –' (she waved her hands and moved her feet to indicate dancing).

We had no common tongue, so I couldn't argue the point, but 'Sellinger's Round' gave way to the most earnest hymn tunes I could think of until dinner was finally ready at *1.30*. It wasn't a lively meal, because Mrs Polenenko couldn't quite get over Sellinger; and continued looking at me with silent suspicion as if I might at any moment break into some new impiety. But Mr Polenenko, not having heard the Accursed Thing, was easier, and begged me to accept some tomatoes in exchange for children's clothing ...

The Rest of September
We came home to find a full house; for term had begun, and Joyce and Jean and Tony were already in residence, plus another girl, Peggy Cuthbert, aged 16, also from across the Pine. However, within a day or two there was great excitement – Joyce Neilson received an invitation from Isa McArthur *to go to England!*[16]

You should have heard how all the Welkin rang ... Everybody is glad for Joyce and most people envy her. For, rather sadly I think, England has come to be a sort of unattainable Paradise of Prosperity, much as the Golden West used to appear to some of us in the past ...

So Peggy slipped into her half of the bed, and within a week another third girl arrived, Rosaline Beck,[17] aged 13. At present I have no bed for her, but she sleeps very happily on the floor, and when I told her mother and asked whether she minded, she said, 'Well, she never sleeps on a bed at home. She hasn't got one, nor have I. You see, my husband's away washing for gold and I haven't got round to make such things as yet' ...

[Thursday] I visited out West in another neglected corner between Tea Creek and Deep Creek ... Three miles on and up a winding side trail I found the Claytons[18] in another one-room shack surrounded by bush. Mr Clayton is a University-educated Canadian, son of a lawyer, and himself, I think, trained as a surveyor. His wife is Scandinavian by blood, tall and fair and very plucky. A month ago she had a fearful accident which might easily have been fatal.

Mr Clayton had gone to the coast, taking their only child, a little girl, to stay with her Grandmother. Mrs Clayton was left alone, and went one day to haul a barrel of water from a spring a mile or so away. She did this in what is called a *stone-boat*, i.e., a heavy home-made platform on wooden runners, hauled by a team (pair) of horses. The team was borrowed, and she didn't realize that the horses were very unreliable until, while she was filling the barrel, they took fright and bolted into the bush. She followed and found them tangled up in willows and had to stand in front of them to disentangle their heads. Suddenly, while she was doing that, they bolted again and dragged her off her feet between them. For a hundred yards or so she hung on, hoping to check them, until realizing this to be hopeless, and fearing to be kicked to bits between them, she let go. But she forgot the stoneboat. The heavy stoneboat knocked her down and catching her under the jaw, dragged her along beneath it, over the stumps and stones and through the thick bush for nearly half a mile. Finally, by the mercy of Heaven, the horses swerved in their gallop, the stoneboat struck a tree and turned over, leaving Mrs Clayton alive. By another miracle in that lonely place, a man came along and found her, with every stitch of clothing torn from her body, plastered from head to foot in mud and blood, but still conscious.

I won't tell you all the stages by which they got her to the hospital; but you can imagine how long it took and how much she suffered. I found her there and we made friends and she asked me to go and see her when she got home again.

So this was the promised visit, and I took a bedroll to stay the night. I found her marvellously recovered, a little swollen and scarred still about the jaw, and a little stiff and sore in the back, but otherwise perfectly well and ready to make light of the whole event ...

Saturday was Michaelmas Day and FINE – such a joy, and everyone filled with new hope. The universal job was to dig potatoes; so Tony and Rosaline volunteered for ours and worked at it like Trojans all day without any goading or even supervision ...

Peggy and Jean are splendid too. I breathed something about the floors being dirty (like a ploughed field lately) and without more said they set to and scrubbed the whole house including the kitchen which was *filthy*. So after supper we taught them those two classic games, Up Jenkins and Dumb Crambo, and we had a very glorious evening ending with the gramophone. I am going to try and do this once every week – and who knows whether it may not humanize us all a bit?

I simply love the children and only wish we had room for more. Gwen likes them too, and gets on well with them all. Tony is more seraphic than ever – always happy, willing and courteous, equally ready to catch and ride a stray horse or to learn the Twenty-third Psalm ... Anyway, I wish I could buy him ...

Three Weeks or More Ending October 24th

... We knew the Noseworthys had left Montreal by car on September 12 and given good conditions might arrive in about a fortnight. But this summer has been so dreadfully wet that the 600 miles this side of Edmonton might take *any* length of time up to a month! So we made no urgent preparations beyond cleaning up the Church House ...

Next afternoon (Friday 5th) I was riding through Fort St John on my way to Fish Creek when Mr Pickell ran out with a telegram which actually announced the Noseworthys' arrival in a few hours – and to stay with us ...

We waited supper from six till about 8.30 and then I went out to light the Chapel for Prayers. Coming back I noticed that Mrs Crawford's familiar light half a mile off had suddenly produced *twins*. I ran in, collected Cecilia, Tony and a lantern and set off for the good old mud-hole. And there sure enough we found the car stuck tight in the classical manner; and by the light of their lamps and our lantern, discovered our new priest and his wife ... They were dreadfully tired, especially Mrs Noseworthy, after 2500 miles on the road, and the last few hundreds nearly all mud. So they were glad to have supper and go early to bed without very much talking. But we saw enough of them to like them at once, and now that the newness has worn off, we like them still more ...

After breakfast ... I took them to town to see their new home. They were awfully discreet and I don't know how the 'City' struck them, but he seemed agreeably surprized with St Martin's and the little Church House (parsonage) in spite of its being almost empty of furniture ...

His ministry so far has been four and a half years in a very well-run Montreal parish, with full crew of Churchwardens, Communicants, and every possible Church Organization – all going full steam ahead ... After his first Service at St Martin's, where we had the usual twenty or less worshippers, he observed mildly: 'You see, I do love crowds and *crowds*.' And then told me that his Sunday School in Montreal had 1100 children on the roll, and not more than 12 to a class – ! 'But I must say the average attendance is not above 850' – (Oh dear, how disappointing!) ...

For getting about he means to drive, if possible, and is looking for a buggy and a cutter ...

You will be sad to hear that *Eliza* has passed away, but not without making her will so to speak. You see, ever since I came back from England it was clear that her days were numbered ... Meanwhile I was negotiating with various seekers after her corpse which was in great demand for many purposes ... In the end, I drove a marvellous bargain with Mr Kisselbach,[19] our Church janitor. He is to have Eliza; and in return for her engine, he is to make me a Bennet buggy with her wheels, and a cutter for the winter, of lumber supplied by himself. So now you see what I mean by Eliza's Will. Instead of an aged but magnificent engine with practically no body, I shall have two smart new bodies with no engine ...

Tommy Hargreaves, the taxi man, says [the roads] are worse than they have been ever since they began to be made in 1927, and I can well believe it. Poor Mr Noseworthy, who hasn't ridden since his boyhood and is rather heavy, couldn't use his car for Sunday. So he had to start off by riding 26 miles in deep slippery mud, and got back to Evensong at St Martin's hardly able to stand upright. Nothing like beginning well, as we all told him sweetly, (including Mrs N.!) ...

[On Wednesday] I went on ... to Akisters. There I arrived (by intention) in the middle of the first birthday meeting of the Women's Institute branch, called 'Nor'pioneers'[20] ... Then Miss Claxton arrived and we told them the new plan about the tiny Red Cross Outpost which is now being built over there. The people have long been clamouring of it, and the men promised logs and labour, water, vegetables, horse-feed and other local produce. Then the Red Cross at Victoria authorized Miss Claxton to move across there as soon as the building should be ready, but there was no money anywhere for shingles, flooring, ceiling, windows, paper, nails, etc. – so everything was held up, while a correspondence went on via Claxton and me, between the Maple Leaf in London and the Red Cross at Victoria, B.C. We had just heard and were able to announce the happy result. Dr.Andrews[21] had written to announce the grant by his (Maple Leaf) Committee of £120 to finance the building in memory of Prebendary Gough[22] of Holy Trinity, Brompton Road, who had cared so much for the Empire Settlers and their needs. It is to be called the *Gough Memorial Outpost* and will actually be Church property, but of course will be run by the Red Cross so long as they need it, and of course, without any sort of Religious distinctions.

The Authorities at Victoria have accepted this; and it only remained for the people across the Pine to have it all explained. So we started with the Women's Institute, and the scheme had a most enthusiastic reception ...

One of Cecilia's *Brownies* received a *Certificate of Merit*. She is a dear little child of about nine, called Alma Alexander,[23] who had acted most courageously when the roof of her home caught fire and both her parents were out ... Hers is the *second* Certificate of Merit ever given to a Brownie in British Columbia, so we are all very proud of her ...

This is a stupid frivolous letter, all on the surface. But before it stops I do want to ask your prayers ... for Harvey Chiverton, who, alas, has run away from home and disappeared ...

November, 1934

... The wet Fall and the early snow destroyed all hopes of saleable crops, Government Relief is being much more stringently administered, and clothing is of course more worn out then ever [so] I hardly dare to go to town for the people meet me everywhere and ask if there is any hope of trading for underwear or overalls, footwear or warm stockings, and usually add, that without these they simply can't send their children to school. There are times when we are tempted to get impatient with these continual requests; but every long ride in a below-zero North wind helps to cure us of that, and the thing I'm most desperately ashamed of now is my own abundant warm coverings. Our Lord's Command about the two coats[24] suddenly takes on an urgent literal meaning, which makes you realize the number of things you have that you really don't need.

In passing I do want to thank you for the splendid parcels that have come already, especially those containing knitted sweaters and socks, heavy men's clothing, warm dresses, and even blankets.

Even the finery you send us is not wasted. I mean the occasional silk frocks and fine cloth suits. We had a little private Auction for them in this house a fortnight ago and invited the City ladies (storekeepers' wives and schoolteachers) to view the very latest European models. The excitement was intense, and I hope you would have loved to see the furious bidding that went on for that dress of yours. Anyway, it helped to raise 42 dollars which we are spending at once on mocassins and heavy men's socks, to meet the most urgent need of the moment.

Incidentally, one of the most successful 'lots' in the sale was my own old evening dress – that black lace affair which you and I bought together at Canterbury, Pet,[25] for the 49 shillings last Christmas. I threw it in anonymously as a make-weight, little dreaming what a furore it would cause. All the leaders of Fort St John fashion fought over it. Several tried it on and were heartbroken to find it too tight; and finally it was carried off in triumph by the Senior Schoolteacher, for whom it was also too tight, but nothing will make her believe it. She is so proud of it that I simply haven't had the heart to tell her that it was only mine, and not the gift of some distinguished Stranger. But I was rather stunned yesterday when the Postmaster's wife (a great friend of mine) said, 'If you should get anything more from that lady of the black lace dress, do let me have a chance to buy it – the fit is just right for me; and the style and materials are sure to be *swell*.'!

Wasn't that awkward! I replied lamely that we didn't expect any more from that quarter ... It would be such a hideous come-down for them all if they knew that the black lace lady was merely their own Church Worker in Moose-hide coat and breeches ...

In the very middle of the Auction party our new winter worker, Audrey Martley,[26] turned up ... She is a young thirty, was at St Christophers, and has been for the last two summers on Caravans[27] in Western B.C. We all like her immensely, and she will make all the difference in the world this winter ...

... December 20th and 21st are days usually sacred to the school concerts, and of course we have to attend as many as possible between us ... The concert [at Charlie Lake] was very nice and just like all the rest. But a great feature of the Christmas Tree was that every child had a toy made in the district by members of the Women's Institute – such good toys too – hobby horses and rag dolls and birch-bark canoes, immensely creditable to this absolutely penniless region.

Then followed the dance and I began to wonder about the chances of a bed; but alas, all the world was there and no one showed any sign of going home before morning. However, at two the nice Russian Mrs Solorenko intimated to me through her more English-speaking daughter that she was going home to bed and would I like to go too? Would I??

But when we arrived at her house *Mr* Solorenko (who despizes [*sic*] dances) looked very dubiously at Robin and my heart sank again. We went to his barn, and not only found the whole alley-way chocked up with visiting horses (no one asks leave on these nights). But Mr Solorenko's own best cow had been literally crowded out of her stall and had climbed into the manger, where we found her sitting and staring resentfully at the intruders. Mr S. was resentful too, and for once I was glad I didn't understand Russian.

... We led Robin away, and he passed what remained of the night in a very small shed full of pigs who seemed just as outraged as he was by the arrangement.

They are great fun [the S's], most friendly and he full of talk, but *so* Russian that it keeps you guessing to understand him ...

I reached the Kemp's gate about 8.30 [the next day] ... They got me supper and we had a lovely evening and for once the nice daughter Dorothy was at home.

Dorothy is a nice gentle girl of about 19, who has for sometime been 'going with' a young Scot called Pete Smith.[28] On Sunday morning, just as Stanley was saddling up for us three to ride up to the store [for] Service, Dorothy asked me casually, 'Shall you be in town tomorrow?' 'Only for an hour or so.' 'I wondered whether you would be Witness at my wedding.' 'I never knew you were going to be married tomorrow.' 'Well, no. We've only just thought of it – as a kind of surprise for the folks here.' 'But who's going to marry you?' 'Sure Mr Noseworthy I hope – if you'll ask him for us; if he can't, perhaps *you* could.'

I explained that that was quite impossible, and Mr Noseworthy most improbable on Christmas Eve ... Finally I agreed to ask Mr Noseworthy for Wednesday and to be present myself as Witness, and not to let out the secret to anyone across the Pine ...

Then Stanley and Dorothy joined me and we galloped the two and a half miles to the store; the cold, about 30 below, being just enough to excite the horses and to freeze one of my ears ...

The store is very tiny, but alas, big enough for the congregation which was only 13 ... I officiated from behind the counter with a large flat home-made cheese for lectern. For pews we had a few wooden boxes, and nail kegs, two or three flour sacks, an oil can or two (the least comfortable) and a saddle sitting on the ground ...

St Stephen [morning] it would have been quite nice to stay at home, but Dorothy Kemp's wedding prevented that; so I went to Town a little before noon, and found an interesting situation. The Young Couple had just arrived in their little home-made 'caboose' or enclosed cutter – the funniest little rig you ever saw, with a tiny stove and chimney. But Mr Noseworthy found he couldn't legally marry them because, although he had been just three months in B.C., he hadn't yet received his license to perform marriages in the province.

So with great resourcefulness he collected Mr Simpson,[29] the Presbyterian (who has been in longer and is licensed) and arranged a combined Service *but all Anglican.* So the two Ministers stood side by side in the Chancel and Mr Simpson performed the legal part of the ceremony using the strict Prayer Book form, and Mr Noseworthy completed it all with Prayers and Blessing ...

Dear Dorothy, I do hope she will be happy ...

My last event of the old year was the Carol and Tableaux Service in St Martin's on Sunday night ... The tableaux took place in the small Chancel just West of the Sanctuary step, and had of course no background or scenery of any kind, only the rough little Manger with a strong light in it to symbolize the Incarnate Light of the World. Aline Darnell[30] made a very sweet grave Madonna; and her sister Betty and another girl stood as Angels quite motionless on each side of the Sanctuary step throughout the Stable scenes.

Three little Wise Men came one by one up the Church from the West door, *not* a long distance, as you can imagine. But the Wise Men learned their lesson of slow movement so thoroughly that Mrs Kirkhoff had to play several supplementary verses to 'We Three Kings' twice over, before they all arrived at Bethlehem. While Mr Noseworthy's big bass voice was singing 'Gold I bring to crown Him again,' I could look through the curtain and watch Walter Middleton, aged 11, dressed in a long red robe and turban, carrying up his little golden crown (née jam-can) with infinite reverence and concentration. George Middleton looked much more ecclesiastical, wearing my Cyprus bed-spread as a kind of cope, and swinging a silver censer which had once been an Antiphlegistine tin. Harold, the Myrrh King, was entirely enveloped in a beautiful length of purple cloth which one of you had sent in a clothing parcel ...

It was all wonderfully reverent and unselfconscious, which mattered more than any technical perfection, and filled me with thankfulness.

And so ended 1934; but I must tell you one bit of news about Brother Wolf. We heard from him just before Christmas, that he has a little daughter. She is called Hope, but one of her other names is Monica.

And now this really must end at last ... From all the Companions by the Peace ...

1935

January 1935

This has been a scrappy sort of month as regards doings – at least for me; and chiefly dominated for all of us by the steady cold snap ... with not much fresh snow, but an average temperature of 20 to 30 below zero and dropping several times to 50 and 60. In one or two places it fell to 74 below, but I wasn't there, so I can't take any credit for these excesses ...

Of course we have no bedroom doors [in the house] but only curtains, and these are drawn back as much as possible to circulate the heat. Even so, the boys' and girls' rooms are perishing in the morning, and I have let them come and finish their dressing round the stove ...

At 6.30 I light the heater and then call the family, all very sleepy except Gwen who is apparently waiting to get up all night ... Gwen lights the kitchen stove simultaneously; and directly the children have any clothes on they come and cluster round the heater for the final struggle with socks and mocassins. All the downstairs dwellers take part in this preliminary act of stove-worship, i.e. besides the five children there are Audrey and me, Kristin and all the cats. It sounds very decadent, but if you were staying here, I bet there'd be one more.

At seven everyone is on duty, one girl cuts the school sandwiches, another tidies up their room, and the third is 'Queen of Spuds' and peels as many potatoes as she can in 20 minutes. Fred is Master of the Horse and takes out Demon to the stable. Tony is Vestal Virgin[1] and goes with Wolf to light the Chapel fire. Gwen heats the porridge, toast and coffee, Audrey lays the table; and I interfere generally and keep everybody up to time (much the hardest work!).

At 7.15 or so we three go over to Chapel, and the rest follow at 7.25 for private prayers ending with the Lord's Prayer, hymn and Gloria in Excelsis.

At 7.50 we come back to breakfast, at eight the girls wash up, and the boys get in wood and snow, and we do the housework. At 8.30 we go back to the Chapel for our hour, leaving the children to go to school when they are ready ...

At six everyone who is home has supper. After that, homework and games till Prayers at 8.30, and then at intervals after that, BED ...

It's odd how laborious and slow the cold makes every occupation ... Clothes are laborious also. Two pairs of stockings plus one pair of socks, plus moose-hide mocassins. On the hands one pair of woollen mitts and another of horse or moose or sheepskin on the top – *so* clumsy. Over our smocks a thick sweater (or two) ... and a moose-hide or sheepskin coat ... On to the coats we have stitched canvas hoods (like the Eskimo parka) which, when pulled up over the head, make a wonderful windbreak and save your face and ears from freezing more often than necessary ...

Diary for February, 1935

... [At the Outpost, Muriel] had already decided to take Mrs Thompson[2] into Fort St John that day for an X-ray examination. It was going to be a pretty hard trip for the old lady in her brittle condition, as the hill was still practically a glacier and none too safe for sleighs. However, she has three grown-up sons; and these with their friends got on the hill first thing in the morning, cutting groves in the worst places so as to prevent the sleigh from sliding over the edge. Then they got an extra horse and hitched him to the back of the sleigh to hold it back as much as possible. And so, after half a day of strenuous preparation and most careful driving, they got their mother safely to the bottom of the hill. The climb [up] the other side was heavy but not dangerous, and by evening they got her into hospital at Fort St John ...

Lastly, while I remember them, these rather nice childish remarks:

... Miss Claxton and Phillip Hadland,[3] a very delicate boy of eight, who stayed with her for some weeks before going out to the Solarium on Vancouver Island.

Phillip. 'When I come back you'll be 60. *Then* you can be an Old Maid and I will come and be your husband and do the chores.'

Caution. Muriel. 'Phillip, don't be surprised if you feel strange in the Solarium at first. You may not like it *at all* for the first two or three days, but don't be disappointed.'

Phillip (several hours later). 'I wonder why we always expect to like Heaven at once when we get there. I don't suppose we shall like it *at all* for the first two or three days.' (You'll be glad to hear he adores the Solarium now.) ...

Diary for March written April 29th (Rather an effort)

... It's lovely to get up by daylight, and yet the glory of the sunrise is one of the compensations of winter which I am sorry to lose. Another is the night sky, such an enormous and clear expanse up here, with Orion and his neighbours sparkling like diamonds in the intense frost. Then there are the Northern Lights, often stretching in a great arch from the Eastern to the Western horizon, and full of life and movement ...

And even the day sky often has its interest. There have been a lot of sundogs this winter, that is, twin reflections of the sun at a distance of perhaps 20 degrees from him on either side. Once or twice they have been so bright that it really did look as if there were three suns in the sky. And one morning they developed into a great halo or rainbow round him, from which grew another halo, curving the opposite way. I might have missed this altogether by over-devotion to housework. But looking through the window, I happened to see Fred in the act of bringing in snow, suddenly stand gaping at the sky, apparently in a trance. I hurried out with a few winged words on my tongue (for Fred is rather too easily entranced) but for once they were not spoken.

... The next day Audrey and I scrubbed and re-stained the Chapel floor ... I then issued old copies of Punch to be used as kneelers pro-tem. Just then Tony became *so* assiduous in his duties as Vestal Virgin that I couldn't help wondering a little. And sure enough, on the third morning when I went slightly early into Chapel, there was the little Levite[4] blissfully *reading the kneelers.*

Diary for April, 1935

... For the first three days of April I was across the Pine ... I called in on the Solorenkos who, alas, are leaving and intend to sell all their possessions next Saturday. It's a dreadful pity, as they have been in four years and proved up a good homestead, with a decent house and buildings, lots of stock, and everything well started. But Mr Solorenko is a restless, disinterested type of Russian, always wanting to move. He is now sick of real farming and wants to raise chickens near a city – just as if every Canadian city wasn't already ringed round with chickens and eggs. He [wanted] to sell me all kinds of things; but I only wanted to look at his kitchen stove – and something else – and to try and find out what was going to happen to the two girls. I had heard a rumour that Jenny aged 15 ... was going to get married at once, and wanted to know the truth ... As for Nellie, the elder one, she really didn't seem to have any plan. All she said was, 'We can't pull out anyway till the snow goes, and that won't be for another month, so I needn't think of anything yet.'

I said, 'How will you manage here after the sale before you go away?' They told me they were borrowing a little stove from an absent bachelor and keeping a couple of cooking pots and a few plates and cups, rather a wretched business, with no real plan ahead. I gathered also that Nick, the father, had an ungovernable temper, and no love for his children, so there seems to be a blank future for them any way.

The sale was on Saturday the 6th, and billed for ten a.m. sharp. Gwen and I had our reasons for attending it. We got there about one and expected to be late – but bless you, no – the *Auctioneer* hadn't arrived yet! ...

Luckily it was much warmer, only just freezing, so we could all sit round on the beds and tables and turn it into a sort of garden party, with Mrs Solorenko and the girls 'receiving.' It seemed a little sinister, though, to be talking brightly to them about their plans and prospects, while all the time you were trying to discover whether the stove was burnt out, and how many holes the kettle *really* had!

At the end, Gwen and I found ourselves the proud possessors of – A pail, A roaster, A scythe blade, Baking tins, A cooking stove, A well-wheel (you never know when you might not have a well), and a BAY MARE! Not a bad bag for one's first day out.

I had seen the mare before and tried her for a couple of days, which decided me that she would be a real improvement upon poor Robin ... She is a good deal bigger and heavier, with a long body and large feet – NOT, as you may gather, a Venus of Milo – but as she is to be a Church Worker, that's hardly necessary; while for combined strength and gentleness, she is a model Anglican ...

[Later]: Mrs Stokke,[5] one of our local ladies, went two years ago to Fort Nelson with her husband and two children. He is running a store for the Indians, and she is the only white woman there since the Policeman's wife went away. Last February she arrived in Fort St John again to see her mother, and leave her little girl to go to school. She had quite a jolly month seeing all her friends; and in March started back with her son aged 13. There's nothing between here and Fort Nelson but an old trapper's cabin and a few Indians. Three hundred miles straight North in the teeth of the wind, alone with six dogs and a boy, camping in the snow at night in order to live where there's no other white woman at all. She's a young, good-looking woman too, lively and rather delicate. All the food at Fort Nelson, except wild meat and fish, is canned. They can't grow vegetables or crops, so they can't keep cows or chickens, and flour is a colossal price ...

I asked Mrs Stokke whether she liked living there and she answered quite simply, 'Well you see, it IS our living.' Consider this, all ye who find life dull in an English village, or can't exist out of reach of the movies ...

Next morning ... poor Nellie came and wept to me about her home. It seems that since the Sale old Solorenko has got more morose than ever and a few days ago threatened his daughters *with an axe* unless they cleared out. He was bad enough to frighten them all out of the house for two days, during which Jenny actually sought safety and a new home in marriage,[6] and Nellie found a temporary job in a store. But she wants me to help her find permanent work and that I must try to do. Mrs Solorenko rather bravely went home. I visited her and found her unhappy and dreading the future, but in the fatalistic way of most Russians. He wasn't at home; so I could form no direct impression of his state of mind, but could only gather that he is sane and courteous to all outsiders, but impossible to his own family ...

On Saturday ... afternoon we heard of a terrible accident. Roy Taylor,[7] a farmer at Fish Creek and step-father to one of the Guides, was cutting logs near Charlie Lake when a big tree bounced somehow off another and fell upon him, smashing his hip-bone and pelvis to pulp. He was with two other men and about two miles from the nearest road. They had to make a stretcher and carry him to the road; and then convey him on the rough-log sleigh for several miles to the nearest house. Then get a better sleigh and take him the last eight miles to the hospital. The roads being at their very worst owing to the thaw, it took seven hours to get him the 12 or 13 miles in. Then Dr Brown found he could do nothing for him, and the only chance for his leg, perhaps for his life, was to be taken by aeroplane to Edmonton.

An aeroplane costs 300 dollars to start with, and Mrs Taylor has next to no money; well, I'm thankful to say everyone played up, that is, everyone who could – the storekeepers and a few others lent or gave all they could, and enough was collected to wire for an aeroplane. So all of Sunday between and even during Services we couldn't help cocking half an ear for the sound of its coming ...

We had a delightful Easter Evensong, quite full and very happy. Mrs Taylor was there, straight from her husband's bedside. The aeroplane had come, but couldn't rise until the early morning frost. She said her husband was suffering terribly and dreading the journey; but she and the little boy were going with him and hoping for the best ...

Easter Monday, the 22nd, was slightly wrecked for us by a grand Cabaret put on by the W.A. (if you please!) for Church funds. It sounds rather awful, but really was quite harmless, just a few rather pretty dances got up by Mrs Kerkhoff[8] and wedged into the usual general dance. The only fiendish part was that all the members of St Martin's had to go dressed as *gypsies*! So you might have laughed to see Audrey and me laying aside our chaste smocks and putting on all the loud-coloured petticoats and blouses and silk handkerchiefs we could rustle anywhere, and calling pitifully for Beads in a perfectly beadless house. But then, on the top of all this tawdry finery, we had to wear overalls and rubber boots in order to ride through deep mire to the show ...

Altogether it was a great success and a real help to funds as well – something like a garden Fete, only quite different! ...

Diary for May, 1935

I've never minded being out of England so much as I did last month. From 1897 onwards, thanks to Mother's[9] splendid determination, I had hardly missed a single great National procession, and it really seemed almost an outrage that the King could contemplate a Jubilee without me!

Still, we did our best in a tiny way to join in the fun ... for in the middle of my address [at Charlie Lake] about the virtues and example of the King and Queen,[10] [Mrs Soman] walked in with four friends, two immense iced cakes, a big bowl of cookies and a two gallon pail of milk. We finished Sunday School with due decorum and then had a most wonderful feast which I'm sure did more than any words of mine to strengthen their loyalty to the Throne. The dollar was absurd payment for so much, but Mrs Soman is like that, and it's all the more remarkable because she is a devout Roman Catholic herself.

After that we hurried back to St Martin's for Jubilee Evensong ... [We] were combining with the Presbyterians, so Mr Simpson, their Minister, preached. He did pretty well for an American-born Canadian; but we heard that the finest and most moving tributes paid to the King and Queen were by the new Roman Catholic Priest who is an Old Country *German*[11] ...

The next great event was *Priscilla's*[12] arrival ... On the 22nd I took [her] across the Pine ... The following morning we had intended to push on to Erinlea, but the torrents all night and still continuing convinced us that no children would get to school ... So we went only two and a half miles to the Kemps, and arrived soaked through our waterproofs. We found the poor Kemps very little drier, because this is the time of year when their roof leaks all over and they make their annual resolve to build another house.

They were moving the table disconsolately round and round the living room trying to find a reasonably dry corner for dinner; and were rather cheered when we came dripping in, to see that people could be found wetter than themselves. Of course they fell for Priscilla and we had a splendid time, culminating after dinner when we made Mr Kemp and Stanley play their fiddle and guitar and Priscilla danced the Irish Jig ...

Diary for June 1935
This has been a prosaic but pretty lively month with a lot of coming and going, and no danger of loneliness. In fact, it has once or twice made me long for the rustic seclusion of a London season ...

Monday the 3rd being the King's Birthday was a general holiday ... After supper Priscilla and I had to go back to town to the concert got up for the Hospital. We arrived late and stood outside the hall listening to the Fort St John ladies singing 'Sweet and Low.' Instantly Mr Watson,[13] a Sunday School father, joined us. He has come into some land near Edmonton and is also quitting at once with his family of seven in a covered waggon. I asked him how soon they were going:

'As soon as I can sell the cow.' 'What do you want for the cow?' 'A saddle horse for Donald to ride to Edmonton.' (Alas, poor Robin) ... At last we arranged that Priscilla should inspect Ruby [the cow] at Charlie Lake on Wednesday, ride back to town and telephone to the Gough Memorial (Rest Outpost) across the Pine, that I should pick up the report there, and if favourable, set out at once to recover Robin and bring him back next day.

Priscilla was awfully thrilled at the extraordinary powers conferred upon her; especially as she was also to take Service at Peace View next Sunday. She said, 'To think that before I've been here a month, I should take a Whitsunday Service AND trade a horse for a cow!!! Could any Church Worker's ambition go further?' ...

Her report was first-rate. She said that Ruby was a RED cow (surprising), plain-looking and lean, but obviously virtuous ... On Saturday, June 8th, the dreadful deed took place and Robin turned into Ruby.

I had Robin carefully shod for the long journey; then groomed him very thoroughly for the last time, and feeling rather sick and miserable, sent him off ridden by Fred, to meet Mr Watson who had promised to set out at the same time with Ruby.

Darling old Robin has served me for four years with splendid vigour and endurance. But I don't think his heart was ever really in Church work and from the cynical way in which he received my last embraces, I really think he was looking forward to retirement, and a secular life for his declining years ...

A few hours later Ruby arrived and was installed in the former garage, now cow barn ... and we soon found that all we had been told about Ruby's productiveness was under statement [sic]. The amount of milk she gives twice a day was at first almost terrifying; and I would come in to find poor Gwen hunting the house for extra bowls, pails and jugs, while at the same time imploring everyone she saw to have a drink. In fact we were driven to adopt that dreary old slogan DRINK MORE MILK and to make it almost a binding rule with the boarders to consume so much a day ...

Do get a cow whoever you are. Trade your old car for one. It's worth it every time, besides giving the finishing touch to any true home ...

Coming home that night I heard very sad news. Do you remember the Leas, who live across the Montney about ten miles North of Fort St John? Their little girl lost her eyesight completely five years ago, through an accident with scissors ... Well, on Sunday night I learned that [Mr Lea] had been brought by a neighbour into hospital and was found to have a tumour on the brain. The school teacher who told me (and who had once lived with them) said that Dr Brown THOUGHT it was inoperable but added a brain specialist MIGHT operate if he could be got to Edmonton, but he thought it improbable. Anyway, he believed that the journey to Edmonton by road and rail would kill him. Of course our thought flew to an aeroplane and in a few minutes Miss Rutherford and I agreed to make ourselves responsible for raising the money needed if there was the slightest hope of a cure at Edmonton. She promised to get this through to the doctor (VERY anonymously because he doesn't like me) and I arranged to ride out next day to visit and tell Mrs Lea, for what comfort it might bring her.

So on Monday morning directly after Prayers I set out, crossed the deep and beautiful Montney Valley and climbed up to their home which is high up with a splendid view.

I found Mrs Lea, not alone and repining, but hard at it feeding some neighbours who had come over to finish some new fencing just started by her husband. I joined them and we talked generalities till they had gone out again and we were washing dishes ... Muriel is at a blind school in Vancouver, but coming home in a fortnight for her annual holiday. Jimmy the only boy is eleven. He is home from school and working splendidly, but too young to carry on the farm, and she had at her breast the baby girl six weeks old. She was very quiet and controlled but looked terribly drawn and strained and broke down a very little before I left. I told her of our guarantee that if anything in the world could be done to save Mr Lea we would see it through. And she said she was glad, but a little bewildered, unable she said, to plan or settle anything till Mr Lea's brother 'Stan' should arrive, and he had wired that he was coming on the Tuesday train. Meanwhile one of the neighbours brought a waggon to take her into town for a few days, and little Jimmy was left alone at home to mind the stock of which they have a good deal – cows, horses, pigs and chickens.

So she promised to tell Stan of our offer and I was to see him after he had seen the doctor.

Well Stan did arrive on Tuesday evening. Mr Noseworthy drove out to Dawson and brought him in, and on Wednesday afternoon I went to see him as arranged, to hear the doctor's report and repeat our offer. But alas, one glance dashed all my hopes ... It was the helpless look on his face that baffled me. We talked for over an hour and I begged him for *her sake* to seize on any crumbs of hope. But he insisted that Dr Brown said there was *no* hope and nothing could be done. Bill was already a dying man, and if he were sent to Edmonton, could only die there.

I minded so much that I could hardly believe it. Still, it would be worse than useless for me to tackle the doctor. SO I could only implore Stan to stay as long as he could, and watch and pray. He stayed a week, and had to go back to his own work and family, Dr Brown having decided finally against any possibility of saving his brother's life. Mr Lea is still alive (July 6th) and in hospital, but unconscious. His wife is waiting for little blind Muriel's return, who doesn't yet know that she has gained a baby sister, and lost her Dad ...

Mr and Mrs Kisselbach had decided to leave the country and go back to the South. They are very nice Lutherans of German race who, with their four tiny daughters, lived next door to St Martin's Church. He is a pretty good carpenter and has for the past two years been janitor to the Church. The elder children came to Sunday School and the baby, 'Julia Monica,' was baptized there a month or so back. Well he got despairing of any future here, and like so many other people, thought there *must* be prosperity anywhere else. So they sold their house, as from last Saturday, and billed an auction for the same day of practically all their possessions, intending with part of the proceeds to buy an old car and leave immediately.

But you can't arrange things so easily as that either, for in the first place Mr Kisselbach found he had a good many debts still left to work off (chiefly with the doctor and hospital for Julia Monica's birth) and secondly the June rains arrived with such vengeance as utterly to destroy the roads once more. So last Friday I found Mrs Kisselbach faced with the prospect of turning out with her four little girls into empty space, and on the very next day.

I said, 'You're wonderfully peaceful about it; what are you going to do?'

'Hasn't Julius seen you?' 'Seen me – no – what for?' 'Oh well I guess he hasn't had time. The fact is we *figure on coming to your place*.'

So they did, the six of them, and it looks like a pretty long visit judging by the rain ...

The Kisselbach's are NOT good disciplinarians, and there seems to be always a yell on somewhere – generally two. But one gets used to it, and after all, it's what the homesteading tribes have to bear ALL the time with a fraction of our space and convenience. Priscilla and Gwen are marvellous about it, working in perfectly with Mrs Kisselbach and bearing the mud and turmoil and displacement of everything with unfailing good humour, especially as just now is meant to be their holiday ...

Diary for July, 1935

After all we were wrong about Mr Lea; at any rate it seems so. The doctor decided that there was no possible hope for him and said he was a dying man, which indeed he seemed to be at the end of June. But since the beginning of July he has mysteriously begun to recover. When I went to see him the other day he was quite conscious and cheerful and able to move a previously paralysed arm. Later I heard that he is actually walking about the hospital garden, not easily yet, but with increasing strength. Dr Brown is away on his annual tour among the Indians[14] and knows nothing about it yet. But everyone agrees that it is either a miracle or else there was no tumour at all. It might have been a stroke ... Anyway, no treatment of any kind was given, and it's very wonderful for Mrs Lea. Muriel got home and was allowed to see her father, and at his request to play to him on the hospital piano.

Roy Taylor is also recovering out at Edmonton (you remember it was he who had his hip and pelvis crushed by a falling tree on Good Friday). He is out of hospital and hopes to come home in two or three weeks. But of course he is still on crutches ...

We expected quite a good crop of [visitors] this year – not only Miss Newby[15] (who actually did come in August to our *immense* delight) but also three ladies called Brown, Moon, and Turner,[16] about whom Dr Andrews worked us up to quite a pitch of expectancy ... But alas! They never came; and we could hardly blame them. For the June rains submerged first the highway and later the railway at a point about 300 miles S.E. of here ... All through July and part of August we really were living on an island as far as communications went. The mail was brought by air to Grande Prairie about 100 miles from here; and then came on chiefly by waggon – a good mixture of Ancient and Modern! ...

However, we were not lonely because the same rains which kept Brown, Moon and Turner out, kept the whole Kisselbach family with us until near the end of July. Mr Kisselbach was away on carpentering jobs nearly all the time, but Mrs K. and the four little daughters occupied the girls' room and were very much in evidence ...

Diary for September, 1935

... This year we have had on the whole a really good harvest. Although a considerable quantity of crops haven't ripened enough to be thrashed yet there will be abundance of feed, and quite a good lot of wheat and oats did ripen and have been successfully thrashed ... But then there is a shortage of machinery – only one reaper (called here 'binder') to a dozen home-steads maybe, and only one thrashing machine to many more. So both machines and men travel round from farm to farm helping one another through the most critical days of the year ...

The only farms where so far a thrashing machine cannot get are beyond the Halfway River and across the Pine. So the people beyond the Halfway use the bulk of the sheaves as straight feed, and for seed and pigs, use the good old patriarchal hand flail. But across the Pine there were two *homemade* thrashing machines, of which one, the Cuthberts', was really rather won-derful. They made it entirely without cost from an old motor engine and other scrap iron; and for the driving belt, had collected about a dozen old car tyres, opened and flattened, and had sewn them together with wire. Just you see if you could do all that – and make it work! ...

We started term with four children only, i.e., Peggy, Jean, and Tony as usual, plus Peggy's brother Alfred who is 16. Fred was still harvesting for Mrs Crawford[17] and his future plans as usual wrapped in obscurity. Rosaline is still needed at home to help her mother, but may come back to us when the fall work is over and she can be spared ...

For the last week of the month Cecilia and I went up the pack trail to Hudson's Hope; and this time Gwen went too. I must explain to you that we were on the brink of losing Gwen. The truth is that over a month be-fore I had heard from another old St Christopher student called Sylvia Steward,[18] asking whether we could possibly spare Gwen as *she* was quite alone with no mate at all. She is working at a place called Ashmont, about 100 miles N.E. of Edmonton, where she has a disused Vicarage and little Church.

After some discussion and correspondence Gwen agreed to go about the middle of October, that is to say a week after the expected arrival of our new companion, Rosemary Owen.[19] It was a horrid decision to make all round, because we are all awfully fond of Gwen, and I think she has grown to love it here. But still the work is one, and as it happens Cecilia was at College with Miss Steward and liked her immensely. So we were pretty sure Gwen will be happy as soon as she gets used to the change.

So that is why she came with us to the Hope, because we couldn't let her leave without one visit to the loveliest part of the parish ... .

Diary for October, 1935

... The greatest event of October for us was Rosemary's arrival. She is Rosemary Owen you know, and I saw her once at St Christopher's when I was Home nearly two years ago ... Rosemary is 26 (I think). She is tall and fair, a *fraction* taller than Priscilla, who is herself a *fraction* taller than Cecilia. So they're rather a stately trio and look down a long way to see me.

The plan is for Rosemary to live and work mainly with Cecilia and for this purpose Miss Newby suggested that a bedroom should be built on to Cecilia's one-room shack, and herself most generously paid the cost of this addition. So when Rosemary arrived it was just finished. And there they live nine miles from us and close to the Church of the Good Shepherd ...

Monday 14th was Dominion polling day, not very exciting up here because Ottawa and all its ways are very remote and it's extraordinarily hard to find out truly what all the parties stand for anyway[20] ...

That evening Rosemary's luggage came and in it lots of treasures for the house ... But best of all, Audrey had sent me a glorious surprise present in the shape of a gramophone record of the Silver Jubilee procession and the King's Speech. We collected all the family for the first hearing of it, and it was perfectly wonderful. The bells and the bands and the King's voice would have been too much for some of us; but Tony saved us by his eyes and mouth opening *wider* and wider in astonishment at the cheering of the crowds.

... Priscilla is now housekeeper here, and a better one you cannot imagine. She is a born home-maker and never seems happier than when she is baking, churning, or washing the kitchen floor; her standard of cleanliness is rather terrifying, and so is her amazing methodicalness ... But she combines it with such light-heartedness and imperturbable good-humour that even such efficiency as might be unbearable in some people, becomes in her only a harmless foible to make fun of. As a sideline she is a real animal expert ... All the children of the house are devoted to her, and she to them ... Finally, though not good for shouting, she has a lovely singing voice, and a passion for really good hymns ... She sings alto except in the plainsong tunes. And when there is a descant, I try to sing that while Fred leads the boarders with the melody. Altogether we are getting quite choral, and when Cecilia and Rosemary are with us, we sing the evening Psalms antiphonally and feel just like a Cathedral Choir ...

[I must tell you about Robin Allen from near Hudson's Hope. He] is a ... devout Methodist, and I heard a fine thing about him the other day.

But first I must explain that when Gwen and I had ridden to the Hope the previous month we had passed a wretched little tumble-down shack with no door or window. And over the place where the door wasn't, some facetious resident had scrawled the name 'Seldom Inn.' I had often noticed it before as a completely deserted hovel. In fact, the name should have been 'Never Inn.' But this time we saw smoke coming from it, and as we rode by an almost terrifying figure ran out to greet us. At first it seemed hardly human – so ragged, hairy and utterly filthy. But it turned out to be a youngish man who tried to talk to us; but as he had a fearful stammer and seemed to be stone deaf too, that wasn't easy. He said he came from the East and was going to winter there, and his people were sending him money, but it hadn't come yet, and had we any tobacco. We hadn't of course, but decided to get some for him in Hudson's Hope. But there we found that everyone was frightened of him. They were sure no money was coming, and feared he was 'mental.' In fact they implored me to ask the Policeman at Fort St John to come and take him away.

On our way back two days later, we came to Seldom Inn again (Gwen bearing tobacco) but were surprised to find it deserted once more. The next family – four or five miles on – said, 'He's gone – good thing too.' And no one knew any more.

That was all in September; but in October what do you think we found? That Robin Allen had taken pity on the Stranger. He fetched him to his own little shack, burned his rags, scrubbed and sheared him, shared his own garments with him and kept him for a mate. It seems that the Good Samaritan sometimes takes people *from inns as well as to them*.[21]

Brother Wolf once told me another fine thing about Robin. A bachelor neighbour of his, called Charlie, had suddenly gone out of his mind and started off to drown himself in a big hole in the frozen Peace. Robin saw him go, and shouted to stop him; but he has a lame leg and knew he couldn't catch up in time. So at last he stood still and shouted with all his strength: 'In the Name of Jesus Christ come back.'

Charlie stopped; and he came back. He has since entirely recovered ...

Diary for December, 1935
... [I have actually] got my own cutter built. A cutter as you may know, in

this country is not a boat, but a small light sleigh on single runners, generally built to carry two ... Finally by grand inspiration I had it painted *scarlet* outside and black within. It really does look lovely and its name is *Rouge-dragon*. Barbary [my horse] as you know, has the body of a pincushion, legs of steel and the soul of a Nun, but she is rather nervous. I suppose Nuns are nervous sometimes though ordinary people never know it ...

Amongst other things Rouge-dragon contributed to a rather amusing business concerning Priscilla. Apparently her mother had conspired with some Montreal friends to send her an immense consignment of canned vegetables. The invoice arrived in October, but we couldn't trace the cans; Priscilla didn't mind a bit because she has a foolish hygienic prejudice against all canned stuff. However, the day Rouge-dragon made her maiden voyage, I found no fewer than *ten dozen* cans, all sitting outside the Mailman's house. They had all been there for six weeks through the sub-zero frosts and two big thaws. I brought them home in triumph, but when we unloaded them we found they were all frozen and *bulging* at one end. Mr Flatt who was staying that night, gave it as his opinion that any that plopped when you squeezed them were not safe and had better be dumped down the coulee. So we started a plopping test and to our horror, beans plopped, peas plopped, beets plopped, *grape-fruit*, asparagus tips, plop-plopped. By that test *everything was ruined. You should have heard the lamentations, the protests of the children*, to whom anything out of a can *is a rapturous mystery* and who had never seen – *far less tasted* – *asparagus or grapefruit*. But if Mr Flatt was right, we must take no risks. The ground was far too hard to dig a pit so I commanded the whole lot to be hauled away on the little toboggan and shot down a narrow ravine, 100 feet deep, out of the way of temptation. The family set to work on this at once in an atmosphere of funereal gloom, but gradually the fun of loading up the toboggan and rushing backwards and forwards to the coulee's edge was too much for them, and when it came to pitching those poor cans down that deep gully, the fun became so fast and furious that the hillside rang with shouts and laughter.

Next day I had dinner with Mr Birley and told him the sad story of the cans. He looked at me in amazement. 'Don't tell me they're thrown away! Why, if they're not *bust* freezing won't hurt *them. Flatt knows nothing about cans; but I worked in a store for years and* my canned stuff froze every year and was none the worse. You tell me where those cans are and I'll fetch 'em up and feed 'em my kids all the winter.'

I reported this to Priscilla that evening and we decided to consider a possible rescue party next day.

At breakfast I began to put the matter before the children, and questioned whether we should be able to get down the gully and fetch the cans up again. 'Oh we can get 'em all right,' said Tony.

'How do you know? Have you tried it?' Both boys were very pink. Tony: 'Well, yes – the fact is, we heard you tell Miss Oldacres last night about the cans being safe all right, so, later, after Chapel, us boys climbed down the gully and had a feast of tomatoes.'

M.S.: 'Oh you did – and what if they're not good after all?'

Alf (hastily): 'We should know by now, it only takes 12 hours doesn't it?'

M.S. (solemnly): 'About a week I believe.'

For a moment Alf's jaw dropped and I got my revenge! But that night we celebrated with asparagus tips and grape-fruit ...

Sunday the 22nd, was Brother Nose's Christmas across the Pine ... Consequently Cecilia and I were responsible for the Churches, and I took Evensong at St Martin's as a sort of preparation for Christmas. That evening I wore for the first time the black cap and gown which have been decided upon as being more suitable when we officiate in Church than the everyday breeches and smock[22] ... [At St Martin's also] I had to take the Carol Service in the absence of Brother Nose ... We had practiced quite a bit, so I hope they sounded better in Heaven than on earth. Fred was there and played his violin all through, and Priscilla got in from her milking just in time to sing a solo in the 'Holly and the Ivy' ... And then the 'Adeste Fideless' [sic] ended our Christmas Festival.

1936

Diary for January, 1936

This year began with a vile cold day, only about 25 below zero, but a stiff North wind and driving snow ... Then came a letter from Christopher[1] asking me to meet him at Victoria on his return journey from Western Australia at the beginning of February. So at the New Year's Dinner, to which I didn't go [because of illness] it seems that May and the others hatched a plot against me, that May should offer to go with me to Victoria if I would go at once and get treatment before his arrival. At first this seemed preposterous, ... [but] it seemed at last the most sensible thing to go. So it was decided that May and I should start together on Monday, January 6th, the Feast of Epiphany ...

But before I go on with that I must tell you about a typical thing that happened up here in the ordinary course of business.

You'll remember Mrs Bedier[2] whose baby was born in the Gough Memorial in December? She went home for Christmas; and on New Year's Day her husband Bill Bedier went out to haul a big load of firewood home. It was a beastly day as I have mentioned, about the worst this winter so far. But Bill got his load of big logs and was coming home when one of his horses (a green colt) took fright and they began to run away. It was so cold that he dropped one of the lines and as they were heading for the Pine hill, he at length decided to jump. But as he did so, the log he stepped on gave way under him; and the whole load rolled over upon his leg, pinning him down in the snow. His body was unhurt as long as the load didn't roll any further; so he held on to the remaining line to prevent the horses from pulling them over him. It was three in the afternoon when this happened and a young blizzard blowing. Bill shouted till his voice left him and struggled till he was quite exhausted, but there was no one on the trail that afternoon. I think he would have given up and let go the line but for two things – the thought of his wife and infant son, and the knowledge that the Mailman must go by next morning at about ten o'clock. So he kept conscious somehow all through the night, and held on *for 19 hours*, in the bitter cold.

Next day Tom Boychuk[3] came along with the Mail in his little caboose, as well as three children he was bringing back to Fort St John. The kids were looking out all round of course; and one of them noticed an overturned load of logs and horses standing by. Tom went over and found Bill, still alive and conscious. It was a terrible risk trying to extricate him from the logs without any help, and Bill knowing this, said, 'Don't spoil it now Tom.' Tom managed somehow without disaster, crammed his nearly frozen body into the tiny caboose with the children, and drove him the 12 miles to Fort St John. The miracle was that he was not dead, but it was feared at first that he would have to lose both his legs ... We were all dreadfully anxious about him, and Miss Claxton went at once to take care of the poor wife and child. But Bill must be amazingly strong; for when we left on the 6th, the last we heard was that he was doing well and might only have to lose a few of his toes ...

May and I left in the Mail-truck on Monday afternoon ... Of course we found a first rated doctor[in Victoria, and] ... after a week in hospital and three weeks of very mild drugs and a bit of X-Ray, I was as completely cured as Naaman[4] and I hope equally thankful.

Meanwhile May had to go back; and you can imagine how I hated parting with her, for there is no more wise, considerate, and delightful companion on this side of the Atlantic anyway ...

The only sadness in the month was the death of the beloved King. We heard of his illness through the radio on Friday afternoon; and somehow knew that it was the end. The actual news came at four o'clock on Monday, and seemed like a shadow over the whole earth ...

Diary for February, 1936

On the 8th of February I was still at Victoria waiting for Christopher, who had arrived that day from Australia via San Francisco and Los Angeles. It was rather exciting to see him after five and a half years; and he didn't seem at all changed. I wonder whether I did to him.

We spent the next few days at Victoria, went to the Cathedral on Sunday, paid various visits and went to several Talkies in the week. We dined with the Bishop Coadjutor (Sexton)[5] in the colossal Empire Hotel [*sic*], where we felt for the first time rather self-conscious about our clothes! We also dined with Sir Richard and Lady Lake,[6] who somehow found out that Wednesday was my birthday and surprised me with a delightful birthday cake covered with sugar primroses. But mercifully, they made no attempt at candles.

The most interesting thing we saw was the new Fairbridge Farm Colony[7] to which Deaconess Robinson[8] took us in her car ... We were very kindly received by Major and Mrs Trew and shown the school-rooms and the different cottages where the children live ... All the children came from the Old Country and their ages seemed to run between five and 14. We talked to several of them and loved to hear their North and West Country and Cockney accents. Of course they do all their house chores under the House Mother, and at about 14 or 15 the boys start on real farm work and the girls on full domestic training. They looked tremendously well and happy, and Major Trew said they were a splendid lot of children and no trouble at all ...

Christopher and I left Victoria on Thursday night and spent Friday in Vancouver ... We arrived [at Edmonton] on Saturday night and had the loveliest welcome from the Bishop[9] as usual ... Christopher also went to hear the Premier, Mr Aberhardt,[10] prophecy at one of his crowded Sunday evening meetings. The prophecies were lengthy and rather incoherent; but Christopher listened very patiently for more than an hour before he found out that it wasn't Aberhardt who was speaking, but only a Minor Prophet after all! ...

On Monday afternoon we got into the train once more and turned our noses to the North West at last ...

We started [from Dawson Creek] at 7.30 next morning, which was steely cold, but clear and windless too ... We got out at Taylor, and there was Cecilia with a glorious welcome and dinner for us at Bethlehem. Christopher was interested in the little two-room house full of books and pictures, and got on awfully well at once with Cecilia, who was alone, Rosemary being at the Abbey with Priscilla ...

[Saturday] afternoon he and I walked round the coulee to visit old John McLeod. Do you know John McLeod? Well, he's a new friend and a most interesting man who has come to spend the winter with his son Henry McLeod. Henry is our neighbour to the South-West, himself a most attractive half-breed, looking just like a Fennimore Cooper Indian. But John is far more beautiful than Henry. *His* father was a Highlander, whose kilt and a bit of Scotch turf were buried with him; and his mother was a Cree Indian. He himself is 75 now, about six feet tall and quite broad and upright still. His hair and eyes are black and his skin a clear olive colour. But his features are a fine blend of Highland and Indian; and his face has the beauty of holiness, for John is a devout and enthusiastic Christian ...

He loves talking about the Faith and about his own conversion which took place about 35 years ago. His knowledge of the Bible is wonderful; but although nominally an Anglican he received his spiritual inspiration from some Protestant sect, which has tinged his views with a rigidity quite alien to his most generous and tender heart. For instance, he cannot easily believe that a man can be a Christian who smokes – or that a woman who wears trousers can be saved. And yet this puts all his relations and friends of both sexes into such a precarious position that his heart continually contradicts his mind ...

Presently the grandchildren trickled in from school, delightful looking kids with coal-black hair and eyes and round red faces. We asked John if they could sing a hymn to us, and he and they responded with a will. They sang three or four *very* long ones from a super Moody and Sankey book;[11] setting the most sacred of words to little jiggly tunes that would make Walford Davies and Harvey Grace[12] pass out right on the spot. But the children sang with such a will, their bright eyes glued to their grandfather's face and catching some of the light of his enthusiasm, that, sitting in that tiny log shack and listening to their little voices and his fervent one, I began to feel it was some of the finest worship yet offered to God in this country.

... On Tuesday the 25th, which was a vile cold day with a fierce North wind, Christopher departed ... It was a dreadfully short visit – only six days – and there was so much I had meant to do with him, and places and people I had hoped to take him to see. Still, short as it was, nothing could have been happier or more refreshing, not only for me and the Companions, but for our children too, and all the others whom he met here ...

Diary for March, 1936

... Our next excitement was ... Agnes Ayling,[13] a fully trained nurse and St Brigid's College Missionary, coming out to join our Companionship, but to work for the time being anyway with Miss Claxton at the Gough Memorial Hospital across the Pine.

Well, on Saturday, March 7th, Agnes arrived with the Mail. I had no means of fetching her and her luggage from Fort St John; so Mr Noseworthy had kindly agreed to bring her down in his cutter. And so he did in the early afternoon, but in a most unexpected manner.

I happened to look out of the window just in time to see Brother Nose turn in at the gate *on foot* leading a single horse, while our new Companion sat alone in the cutter like a Royal Visitor – only the odd thing was that she was holding the shafts bolt upright in front of her like two tall symbols of office! ...

Afterwards, poor Brother Nose explained that they had stuck so badly in a snowdrift that the shafts had both snapped. So for the rest of the way Agnes had held them aloft, while he had led the horse with the cutter banging at intervals into her defenseless heels ...

[Agnes] is about 26, slight and dark, with a pleasant voice (both speaking and *singing*), is obviously capable, very quickly adaptable to any new conditions and a first-rate Companion. Within an hour of her arrival (after 6000 miles) she was in Canadian overalls helping me scrub the Chapel floor, and fully appreciated what a high and intimate privilege she was sharing with me ...

All was well [that week], except for anxious news about France and Germany. Everyone here thinks that Europe is crazy; and it certainly looks like it is. But nothing that can happen, it seems to me, can be worse than the universal shame and tragedy of Abyssinia[14] ...

Diary for April, 1936
... On Monday we all rode to town for a big chicken supper put on by the Roman Catholics, and went to see a delightfully ridiculous thriller play called 'The Scarecrow Creeps' acted by the Noseworthys, school-teachers and others.[15] It was very ludicrous and very hair-raising and received with rapturous applause ...

On Saturday Cecilia and Rosemary left us and Mr Sprinkling,[16] the High School Master, came to supper. In the middle of that who should arrive but our new boarder from Hudson's Hope – Donald Peck.[17] Donald is an immense boy of 15, very high spirited and jolly and completely at ease with us in no time. He always wears a bright red shirt and a huge hat and brought his own little black horse on which he looks very delightful riding off to school.

The morning after he came ... I received from the Gramophone Co. in England a most wonderful present of records – including the Silver Jubilee Procession, King George's last speech and King Edward's first, Mr Baldwin's and the Archbishop's tributes[18] to King George, the Trooping of the Colours,[19] and the Ceremony of the Keys at the Tower.[20] You can imagine what a delight these were to all of us. Rosemary and I started by taking some across the Pine and playing them on every available gramophone there ... Luckily we had found some pictures of the Tower in an old *Sphere*,[21] and better still a full page *coloured picture of some Irish Guards* from which

Rosemary had skilfully cut away a huge bottle and other allusions to Black and White Whiskey. So in the stillness of our Northern bush, the children sat round the gramophone and with these two aids to imagination in their hands, listened to the voices of two Kings, the tramp of feet in old stone courts, and the strange sorrowful echoes of the Last Post – to them so meaningless – to us almost too full of meaning ...

Diary for May, 1936

... Next morning, May 11th, Cecila and I started for the Hope ... In the course of visits I saw two nice glimpses of rather primitive life, one typical of the new world, the other of the old. The first was a man scraping an immense bear hide which was stretched flat and nailed to the wall of his shack. He was scraping it quite clean with a blunt knife, the first stage in home tanning.

The other was a woman thrashing with a hand-flail which might have come out of any Egyptian tomb. She was Mrs Joe Selinka,[22] a Bohemian with very little English but lovely manners and welcome. They can't get a thrashing machine across the Halfway River, so Mrs Selinka thrashes for most of her neighbours in the true Biblical way ...

I joined Cecilia at the Ardills where she held as usual a little Bible class for the four charming children. Johnny, the eldest boy, had a wonderful wolf hide to show us – seven feet from nose to tip of tail. Johnny, aged 14, had gone out alone and shot it himself.

These boys are extraordinary. Vernon Peck, Donald's elder brother aged barely 16, shot a grizzly last year. He was in one of his father's trapper's cabins when an immense grizzly broke the little window, got his foreleg in and stole all the food cans off the table. Vernon, very indignant, went out and tracked him into the bush, found *two* of them, lost one and killed the other. Grizzlies are awfully dangerous bears and can easily kill a man if they get to close quarters. This was a record big one, so Vernon sold its hide to an American 'dood' (tourist) ...

Besides a good deal of sowing both spiritual and temporal, we had to rehearse a play for the Empire Day Hospital Entertainment. Mrs Pickell had asked us to do something, so under the name of 'The Abbey Players' our six rather hastily prepared, and performed a very silly piece called 'Iron Anne.'[23] ... It was our children's first attempt together, and what with lessons and chores we had simply no time to attempt anything better ... We made Donald the Iron Anne and he really was delightful. He wore a house-overall of Priscilla's and had tousled yellow hair made of unravelled binder twine coming down under a mob cap. His immense size and clumsiness were a great asset, and his impassive mask-like face and jerky movements really were better than anything we could have hoped for ... I think the audience enjoyed it, and I know the Abbey Players did ...

Diary for June, 1936

... The days that followed were saddened by the sudden serious illness of our dear Mrs Middleton. She didn't turn up as usual to the W.A. meeting on the 4th, and next morning we heard she was at the Hospital with a nervous break-down. It was so sudden that I, who had seen her nearly every week for months past, could scarcely believe it. But it was true enough. And as the Hospital was full, having 18 patients and two new-born babies, and the staff only allows of one night nurse, the doctor asked some of us to take turns there at night to help her should need arise. I began and Priscilla followed and then Mrs Noseworthy; and so we continued until it was decided to send her right away for more specialized treatment. She went off quite cheerfully, with her usual marvellous trust in God; knew us all to say Goodbye and asked me to look after the children and to write to her.

... And that was practically the end of June.

Diary for July, 1936

... The rain stopped on the afternoon of the first, and Priscilla and I rode to town to join in what survived of the [Dominion Day] festivities. The only amusing part was the bucking ...

The horses are all rounded up in one big corral and are *supposed* to be very wild and terrific. The riders are of course the local young bloods who turn up in the reddest shirts, the biggest hats and the grandest leather shaps [sic] and gauntlets and beaded moose-hide waistcoats they can posses or borrow. They really do look delightfully dashing and picturesque, like short-haired cavaliers or *very unpuritan* Roundheads.

These gentlemen draw lots for the horses they are to ride and gather near the corral, squatting on their heels awaiting their turn.

Then another set of men almost as flashy ride out and scatter round like the fielders in a cricket match. They are the 'Pick-up Men' whose job is to keep near the rider and *pick him off* his horse after he has stuck on for the required three or four minutes. That doesn't sound long, but if you *do* stay on (which of course I shouldn't for 10 seconds) you can be almost broken to bits by a true bucking bronco. However, our Fort St John horses are not really like that, being merely unbroken or rather lawless colts rented for the occasion, and I'm afraid, artificially irritated by the flank-ropes and other devices to make them do their worst. So the Pick-up Men are more or less ceremonial with us; but they certainly do add to the fun and excitement and no Stampede would be complete without them.

While all is getting ready a Master of Ceremonies rides round the ring with a megaphone and does a lot of talking. This is usually a very attractive Welshman called Ed. Thomas, who at other times is an excellent auctioneer. His appearance this time was enlivened by a bunch of balloons tied to his horse's tail (do try this next time you ride in the Row), and his auctioneering talent was admirably employed in working up the excitement before each successive horse, and giving them suitable *noms de plume* for the afternoon: 'Ladies and Genlemen,you are now goin' to see Poison Dog,' (or Blue Devil, or Grave-digger), 'the greatest man-slayer of the North. Believe me, Ladies and Genlemen, this horrse [*sic*] has already killed five men an' is waitin' for the sixth.'

Meanwhile, Poison Dog, or Grave-digger, is being driven into a close-fitting bottle-neck exit from the corral, called the chute, and is there saddled and bridled through the bars, while Ed. Thomas goes on : 'The fella who's tacklin' this horrse, Ladies and Genlemen, is Slim (or Shorty or Art or Pete). You can wish him luck now, for his bronk has never been ridden by any man before – an' it's no use feedn' him tame hay, for he will *not* eat it.'

Now, Slim (or Pete) glorious in his huge hat and flapping shaps and long spurs climbs over the bars and drops on to Grave-digger's back.

'Found the stirrups?' 'All set.' 'Let her go.'

The chute flies open, Grave-digger dashes out, and we hold our breath while he plunges and rears and kicks and sometimes roars. I am always terrified, even when the bystanders assure me afterwards that he didn't buck at all! When he can't kick any more he generally bolts off across country with Slim still on board, and the Pick-up Men flying after him like hounds after a hare ...

The next and very tremendous event was to be the arrival of our three *Visitors from England.* Mabel Causton[24] and her cousin Violet, and Christina Stubbington, whom I knew at Woolwich during the war, were all due to arrive at Edmonton on the 26th; and by their wish Rosemary (who is Violet's friend) and I were to meet them all there and go for a week to the ROCKIES. I was at first quite indignant at this suggestion, feeling that our old Peace ought to be good enough for anyone without starting aside to expensive Beauty Spots. It was all very parochial and stupid of me, and you'll be glad to hear that I have quite recanted since then ...

Really Jasper Park is (except for cars) a little like the Garden of Eden. There is perfect freedom, except to kill. So the lakes are full of beavers building away at their dams; and you meet deer and stags and black and brown bears at every turn, not only in the bush but right in the little town. The second evening, on returning to Camp from a walk, I came straight round a corner on to three immense black bears. They paused courte- ously in a graceful group, and then, seeing I had no camera, went on their way ...

During the Holy Communion on our second Sunday (August 2nd) it suddenly came to me that I must go and see Mrs Middleton, who is in a hospital near Vancouver. I had thought of it before, but it is a long way, of course, and I'm afraid I grudged the expense and the time away from the joys of Jasper. But that Service showed me the abominable selfishness of enjoying such a holiday and not giving what pleasure I could to such a friend.

So after Church I broke it to Mabel that I was going by the 2 o'clock train to Vancouver for one day, and would be back on Tuesday afternoon. She was not very enthusiastic at first, as we were starting for home on Wednesday. But after a bit, to my astonishment and delight, she suddenly offered to come with me 'to see the Pacific.'

There was just time to snatch up my things and a meal and off we started in a packed excursion train for the 19 hour journey to Vancouver. We ar- rived there at nine next morning and were met by a large brass band and a lady who bore upon her bosom an ornamental breast-plate inscribed: 'Official Greeter.'

Her greetings were, unfortunately, quite drowned out by the band; but [it] was very jolly to have at least a few hours' share in Vancouver's Golden Jubilee.[25] All the streets were hung with streamers and flags; and every- where in every sort of colour we were made 'Welcome to Vancouver' and reminded that it had been 'Fifty Years a City.' And truly it is a remarkable achievement to have become so great a city in so short a time.

We drove round Stanley Park in the morning, and Mabel had her (rather distant and sideways) view of the Pacific. And then we spent all the possi- ble time with Mrs Middleton. It was a delightful visit. She seemed so much better and there is apparently every hope of her return home before too many weeks. And I can't be too thankful that we went, for do you know she had been praying for three weeks that someone should visit her ...

Diary for August, 1936

... [Rosaline's] home life is in a state of upheaval ... The trouble is that her step-father, who is working at some oil wells right out beyond Calgary, has sent practically no support for the family during the past year; and Rosaline's

mother has been left with herself and three younger children and a homestead which she can't possibly work alone. She has written, of course, but
had no reply. So now in desperation she has started off to look for him. I
asked her how she proposed to travel the 800 miles or so each way. And
she said, 'Oh, I shall bum a lift when I can and walk when I can't.' I tried to
dissuade her from such a journey, but couldn't make the least impression,
and in the end all she would accept from me was a pair of old walking
shoes in the place of her own thin ones.

So Rosaline was left in charge of the little ones for an indefinite time,
and so far, poor child, has had no news of her mother.

The two Caustons and Stubbie ... fitted into the Abbey life most perfectly and were the greatest fun ... Mabel gradually ceased to look for a
bath-room and helped to hang new cleaned curtains instead. Also she took
the thick end of decorating our Chapel and two Churches for their Dedication Festival.

This was held at all three Churches on Sunday, 16th, being the Bishop's
one Sunday with us ...

Meanwhile, another small entertainment we were able to offer our friends
was the moving of Mr Donis' large house and store from half a mile out to
a site in the very heart of Fort St John.[26] It is a very big building, the biggest
in the town, I think, two stories high and very heavy, and it was hauled all
the way by two horses! Of course it was all done with the aid of blocks and
tackle and pulleys ...

It took about three days to move her the half mile into town, and another two to carry out the more complicated manoeuvre of turning her
right round amongst the houses, hauling her exactly over her big new
cellar, and finally jacking her up high again, taking out the huge skids and
setting her straight upon her new foundations. All this time the plants still
stood in the windows, and the family continued to live and cook and eat
their meals in their moving house ...

[Thursday] After dinner I set off on Starlight and rode across the Pine
for the Confirmation that night ... ..

Just before I reached the Outpost a big cloud burst and I was drenched
to the skin. Dear Agnes, having nothing else at the moment to replace my
soaking smock, lent me a bright pink pyjama jacket, in which I had supper
in company with the Bishop, Noseworthys, Mr Brown (the new priest)[27]
and a few leading members of the congregation ...

Sunday the 23rd was the Noseworthys' last Sunday, and the next evening
the final farewell party was held for him in Fort St John ... Two days later
they left by car for Montreal, to the general regret. We shall all miss his

kindness and humour and organizing ability; and perhaps even more her shrewd and dry wit which part conceal and part reveal a most generous and understanding heart ...

Diary for September, 1936

... Our school family rolled up once more, mostly on horseback as usual, with brothers or sisters to take the horses home. We have eight boarders this year, the largest number so far, and I think the biggest we can accommodate without changing from a family to an institution. This time we have five boys and three girls as follows: Alfred Cuthbert from across the Pine, 21 miles, aged 17; Percy Freer,[28] from Bear Flat, 25 miles up the Peace, aged 17; Rosaline Beck, from Tea Creek, 9 miles up the Peace, aged 15; Phyllis Freer (Percy's sister), aged 15; Roy Cuthbert (Alf's brother), aged 14; Tony Flatt, as usual, aged 14; Eileen Brisbin,[29] aged 11; Michael Flatt, aged 11.

There are two of each age as you can see. We were rather dubious about taking the two youngsters because they are naturally more responsibility, and can do much less in the way of pulling their own weight in the boat ... [But] I think the excellent tone of the elder boys and girls, not to speak of Priscilla's amazing blend of Ministering Angel-cum-Hitler would produce order and harmony even in Spain[30] ...

The regular duties are as follows:

Alf. Watering and feeding the horses morning and night, cleaning out the barn.

Percy (Caedmon).[31] Milking and general care of the cow.

Tony and Roy. Wood and water.

Michael (Vestal Virgin). Chapel sweeping, Chapel fire and bunk house ditto.

Elder girls. Wash dishes, prepare school lunches.

Eileen. Lay meals, put away dishes, tidy their bedrooms.

It all runs pretty smoothly, and when they go at their jobs with a snap, leaves plenty of time for homework and a little recreation as well.

Our time table is as follows:

6.30 Up and chores
7.25 Prime (so-called, i.e., Children's Prayers)
7.35 Breakfast
8.30 – 9.30 Matins (so-called, i.e., our Prayers)
6.00 Supper
8.30 Evening Chapel
9.00 Juniors to bed

9.30 Seniors to bed

11.0 Silence

... On Saturday mornings the girls wash all their clothes (boys too) and the boys do various public works like carpentering, general repairs, and finally tidy their own house and wash the floor with the girls' rinsing water.

On Saturday after supper we have an hour for foolish games – cards or Up Jenkins, or the gramophone or anything else they like ...

Forgive this rigmarole about routine. I have given it once more complete as far as possible, because you see it is the backbone of our life in this house, but I promise you shall not have it again for a long long time.

On September 1st, I was summoned to an almost all-day interview with our new priest – the Rev. Russell Brown ...

He is an Englishman by birth (Newcastle), but has lived in Canada from the age of nine, a very good mixture. He was in the Royal Flying Corps during the last year of the war, and after that in a Montreal Insurance Office for 15 years, and has only been ordained for three. When not in his cassock he wears an old R.F.C. uniform and looks just like an Army Chaplain ... He is tall and broad and very erect, with an entirely English voice and face and wonderfully serene and gentle manners ...

He is a strong educated Churchman, but so sympathetic and tolerant that the most un-Churchy men seem to be attracted to him and our rigorously Calvinistic Presbyterian Minister already feeds out of his hand.

He is an unexpectedly good preacher and, what matters more, takes every Service with reverent devotion better than any sermon ... His factotum is a nice lad of 22, called Jack Bennett;[32] ... he adores Mr B. (whom he calls 'My big brother') and though he can't cook any better than I can, he is excellent with horses and rough carpentry, and they seem to live most happily on that ...

Sunday was a real blizzard ... Of course all our transport was held up, and the Mail which had been going out by truck in three or four hours, got pitifully stuck in the drifts South of the river and was finally rescued by a Government caterpillar and hauled out to Dawson Creek, more than a day late for the train. Only one passenger from that train got through here, the indomitable Mrs Chancellor, our Rosaline's mother. She had started hidden in a truck which had refused to take her. After ten miles the truck got stuck, but she got on another ten miles in a buggy hauled by the caterpillar (coming to rescue the Mail). Then the buggy stuck and she came in on a small sleigh hauled by the caterpillar, later that deserted her and she had to walk. After that I don't know what happened, but I saw her triumphant in Fort St John after three or four days pretty hard going ...

Our next great event was the long expected visit of Dr and Mrs Andrews, and the arrival of our new Companion, Elinor Higginbotham[33] ...

Dr Andrews gave us a list map of all the other groups of workers connected with the Maple Leaf, so that through his visit we really can feel more closely linked with them in fellowship and prayer than we ever have before.

As Mabel and I left the river [some days later] we noticed a small open kicker boat moored to a rock, and a group of people scrambling over the rough stones up the river bank, carrying some one in a stretcher. I recognized some of the Tompkins family, and hastening to inquire, found that they were bringing their eldest son Eric to the hospital at Fort St John. He had been for five days desperately ill with pneumonia in their home 30 miles up stream. Of course they could get no nurse there; by a sad coincidence his mother had been just sent away for a much needed holiday at the Coast. That left only his younger sister Alice and a perfectly ignorant new hired girl to nurse him; neither of them had the least experience of illness. So in desperation they had brought him down in this little boat and were now going to take him up through 14 miles of mud to the hospital. They had wired to Mrs Tompkins and caught her at Dawson Creek just before the train started, so she had come right back again, and reached the river just in time to join them ...

That was Thursday the 24th, bright and sunny and the mud beginning to dry up at last. Directly after Chapel I left Mabel to finish packing [since, alas, the time had come when our visitors must leave] and drove to town to inquire about Eric; I found the two doctors had just seen him and said he was holding his own, that the journey hadn't hurt him and the good nursing might save his life. Then I drove out to May's and collected Violet Causton and her luggage, then back to the Abbey for Mabel and hers. When we were all loaded up, we suddenly discovered that we had to lead Mr Brown's black mare, Dot, to town as well; I am sure I cannot remember why, but it was so. Violet kindly volunteered to sit behind and hold the halter shank, and so we started at last with about an hour on hand for a quick lunch somewhere before catching the Mail. But on the way we had a slight misfortune, for which I felt very responsible and sorry. The horses were slack, so I gave them the usual tickle up with the end of the reins. They sprang forward suddenly and wrenched poor Violet's hand, the one that was leading Dot, hard back against the boards of the buggy and all but broke her wrist. She was most plucky and made no complaint at all; but the pain must have been extremely severe for before we reached the town she had fainted and collapsed into the floor of the rig. Mabel and I were naturally worried, not knowing whether she would be fit for the rough journey by Mail-truck in less than half an hour's time. So we drove her straight to the hospital for advice and first aid. But as we got to the door it opened and most of the Tompkins family streamed out with a look upon their faces that left no doubt. I sprang off the buggy and ran to the little school-teacher. Yes, it was true; Eric had died a few moments before, quite suddenly and in defiance of the doctors' hopes. Mrs Tompkins and Alice were still upstairs. Dr Brown had gone. Dr Kearney[34] was signing the certificate, and Mr Tompkins was with him. Poor little Miss Holt,[35] she was quite crushed by sympathy and sorrow for the family with which she lived on such close terms of intimacy.

... I said something very blundering I'm afraid, and was then obliged to concentrate on Violet who was still lying in the buggy.

Somebody helped us to get her to the hospital and at last I found a Sister not too preoccupied to understand (a) the accident, (b) The Mail, and therefore (c) the question. But of course she could say nothing without the doctor and he had vanished with Mr Tompkins. During these negotiations the horses got bored and walked off home with the buggy and all the luggage ...

It was all rather like a bad dream; I threw Mabel into a restaurant for anything she had time to eat before the hypothetical journey and continued looking for the doctor but found instead, first Agnes Ayling, who had just come into town and had a tooth out, then the bereaved Mr Tompkins ... Finally I ran Dr Kearney to earth and he promised to go see Violet and report in fifteen minutes.

A few minutes before the Mail was due to start he did sure enough, report that she was fit to travel, and indeed she said so too, though still looking quite white and shaken. So we tracked down the horses and transferred the luggage ... Five minutes later Mabel and Violet climbed into the small seat by the Mail driver and rattled off down the road, leaving me rather dazed. Then a voice said, 'Will you come and see Mrs Tompkins please' and I went back into the hospital again.

Half an hour later I went to the restaurant again for a bite, and the first thing I saw was Violet's small blue handbag. Something told me it held all their tickets and money. I looked in and there they were. In desperation I shouted at Mr Hunter, 'Who's got a car handy?' He answered at once, 'Why, old Parsons[36] across the road.' 'Mr Parsons, do you wish to earn undying renown?' 'I'd rather earn a dollar, but what do you want?' 'I want to catch the Mail-truck before it reaches the river.' 'Can't be done but jump in and we'll have a stab at it.' We sure did have a stab at it; it was the most breathless drive I've ever enjoyed. It had been raining again and the mud was as slippery as melted lard ...

At Baldonnel there was no sign of the Mail. It had left about 15 minutes before and having chains and big double wheels could make good speed. However, Mr Parsons' blood was up by now. The next four miles were alarming, and the hill almost terrifying, but as we flew round the corner at the bottom we almost bumped into the Mail, pulling out from the Taylor Post Office. I jumped out, ran across, and hopped on to the running board, and poked the blue bag through the window, much to the astonishment of both Violet and Mabel, who had not yet discovered their loss, and before they had time to take in what had happened, I had a fleeting glimpse of them both, and they were gone. This time for good.

... The next two days were mainly devoted to Eric's funeral and the preparations for it ... Everybody came to the funeral ... [I] was amazed at Mrs Tompkins. She is a Bristol woman, small and frail looking, with a very sweet face; she has been quite tearless throughout her trouble, but her gentle dignity and self-control showed most wonderfully at the Service (where it is rather the fashion here for mourners to let themselves go) and she sang all the hymns with an unfaltering voice.

Diary for October [and November], 1936

... The main event for us of that month, and tremendous loss to the Mission, was Cecilia's departure.[37] This didn't actually happen till the very end; but the anticipation of it certainly dominated the month for all of us, and made me at least feel that everything else was trivial ...

Meanwhile we had to acquire somewhere *two* new horses ... The first reason for this was that poor little Puck who with Robin had been one of the very foundations of the Mission, about August suddenly began to go down in health, becoming dreadfully thin and covered with sores ... So at the end of the year, after four months during which he seemed to be getting steadily feebler and more miserable, rather than expose him to the real cold weather, I agreed very sadly to let Mr Birley shoot him. One of the boys led him over there one day – and I never saw him again ...

Meanwhile Rosemary managed to secure a nice big four year old (whom she calls Tigger because his appearance is so nondescript) and Elinor was getting on very well with Starlight; but Priscilla and I were reduced to Barbary *between* us, which was at all times difficult and on Sundays impossible ... So I was rather at my wits end on October 4th when somebody casually remarked that the Hudson's Bay Factor had a 'single driver' to sell ... We went to look at him, and he immediately walked out of the barn to meet us – an enormous nearly black caricature of a horse, in height like a camel, with a head like a mule, a vast white blaze down his face, and rolling eyes with so much white as to be nearly human. He was so funny and so friendly that I took him at once *on a week's approval*, and led him home in triumph behind Barbary ...

He's not a saddle horse, but they said he could be ridden 'if a person didn't mind him being rather *rough!*'

So that evening I christened him ROFFEN ... I soon got hardened to his paces (although my breeches didn't) and the week after the Pine, rode him to Hudson's Hope ...

[We also have a new cow whose] name is Daisy. I had to get her to supplement and eventually rest up Ruby, who, after supplying us all with milk and butter for nearly two years, showed need of a vacation ... But [Daisy] is not nearly so tough; and in cold weather has to stay in the barn ALL the time and even be watered as it were in bed ...

The next day I took Audrey to town for ... Mrs Sowden's[38] shower ... [It] was a typical social event up here, though usually connected with a wedding. Mrs Sowden is a widow with five children who keeps herself and them off Relief by quite continuous labour as washer-woman and general cleaner-up of everyone in our city ...

Well, Mrs S. had at last saved enough money to have a little house built for herself and family, and no longer to be what everyone despises here, a *tenant.* She had just moved into it; and the other city ladies had secretly planned a SHOWER, i.e. a surprise visit from all of us together, bringing gifts for the new house, as well as cakes and sandwiches for an impromptu tea party. All Mrs Sowden knew in advance was that she had Better Be At Home that afternoon. It fell out very well. We all arrived about three leaving our parcels hidden outside until the Moment. Mrs S. showed a mild and pleasant surprise but no curiosity of course. We were then taken all over the house, a process which, with skill and tact, could be spun out to seven or eight minutes, and then sat round while Mrs Sowden brewed the actual tea. Then our sandwiches and cakes appeared (another surprise?) and we were all convivial. Finally (greatest surprise of all?) two chosen messengers slipped out and ran in again with a large wash-tub loaded with gifts and set it down before Mrs S. This is rather a fearful ordeal for a Showeree, for the donors all sit round and watch breathlessly while you open each parcel. However, the formula is really simple. You just say, 'A *tea-kettle!* Mine has a big hole in it.' '*Dish* towels! I've got none left.' '*Salt* shakers! How *did* you know, Mrs Bowes?'

This last is such a wonderful question. It means nothing at all; but conveys so much.

Then you pass the presents one by one round the room, and the donors have a wonderful half-hour handling, commenting, overhearing, and making secret comparisons. We gave from the Abbey coloured oilcloth for tables and a framed portrait of the King. It was funny watching them go round!

Afterwards we heard that Mrs Sowden had said it was the happiest day of her life ...

On Wednesday the 28th, being S.S. Simon and Jude, I rode down to Bethlehem for two last days alone with Cecilia ... It's impossible to measure what we owe to [her] or how we shall miss her everywhere. Only I think we all resolved not to dwell upon the loss to the Mission or ourselves, but rather on the gain that has come through her; and to try and go on building something worthy of the foundations laid. It's kind of enlarging too to our spiritual imagination (which gets pretty narrow here) that whatever greater work she is called to presently, will be in a sense our work too; for she will still be a Companion of the Peace ...

May and I said goodbye to Cecilia at Dawson Creek on October 30th ...

I stayed [across the Pine] for two days to visit, and then to take part in a mysterious event on Friday called a 'Box Social' ... The programme of a Box Social is first an entertainment (called a 'Programme'), then an auction of fancy boxes containing supper for two. Each woman or girl makes and brings a box; they are sold anonymously (in theory anyway) and the buyer has the owner for his supper partner. And after that they dance till morning. The purpose of the whole effort was to raise funds for the children's Christmas Trees in all three schools.

Diary for December, 1936

... On Saturday the 5th began the week of miserable anxiety about the King[39] ... Our only public source of news is the telegrams stuck up in the Post Office; and on the 5th for the first time the King's proposed marriage appeared in these. Of course we knew at once that this meant a crisis ... We could get no reliable details, as American radio stations were still dominating the air. The general opinion around us was intensely loyal to the King; and the people with least British background[40] were inclined to think it didn't matter whom he married, provided she made him happy...

You'll hardly believe it, but from first to last none of us knew that the King's proposal was a morganatic marriage. Even the telegrams stated that he meant to marry Mrs Simpson and make her Queen![41] But I'm sure if we had known it would have made no sort of difference ...

When at last the night of the 10th Tony brought back news from the Post Office that the King had abdicated, our relief was so *tremendous* that at first there was no room for any other feeling. Without understanding or knowing any details, we just felt that some tremendous victory had saved the Empire.

The next ... afternoon at three o'clock we went to the Pickell's house and heard the Farewell broadcast Speech ... The simplicity and sincerity of it were deeply moving, and made me realize, I'm afraid for the first time, something of the King's own suffering throughout ...

It's been a strange year, of much public anxiety and sorrow – the constant war clouds, the tragedy of Ethiopia, the loss of two beloved Kings – and in our little corner goodbye to Cecilia. And yet, *what* calls for Thanksgiving. At least we are not at war, and the Empire has weathered what might have been a wrecking storm. And here we have been given a new priest and new workers (yes, and my new horse too), enough real progress to keep us hopeful, extra special summer visitors, and endless kindness and help from people at Home.

End of the Year 1936

1937

Diary for January, 1937

... Our first real event of the year was the tiny Christmas play I had written for our own Abbey boys and girls to act in Church at Baldonnel ... Certainly [the children] were wonderful, really all eight of them. They forgot nothing, all spoke up perfectly clearly, and each one entered with complete simplicity and directness into his own small part ... And really I never saw a more dignified and convincing Joseph than the tall, young, ruddy, smooth-chinned Canadian, Percy. As for Roy, he exceeded all our hopes ... He is a naturally good actor, but far more impressive than any acting was the real gentleness and purity of his nature, which we know so well in the house, and which shine straight out in the play without any need of acting ...

The next day being St Paul's, Brother Bruno started off to visit the Westergaard family[1] who live up the Halfway River over 70 miles from here ...

Mrs Westergaard lives in that fearfully remote spot with, or rather without, a husband who is away trapping all the winter. She had five children already and another was expected in January; so Jack Bennett's mother[2] (a delightful Newcastle woman) had most pluckily ridden up to her in December to see her through that event. Otherwise there was no one there but Art Jensen,[3] a hired man to do the chores and feed a big herd of cattle. It appeared that Mrs Westergaard had given birth to twin daughters earlier in January and had been very ill indeed. It must have been awful for Mrs Bennett with not only no medical help available, but no medical supplies either and no companion except the hired youth ...

For a time after the babies were born Mrs Westergaard was so weak that it seemed without some kind of restorative she must die. Poor Mrs Bennett in desperation sent Art Jensen up the river to the nearest trapper; and after an interminable absence he came back with – what do you think? Sloane's Liniment![4]

Apparently that did the trick, for when Bruno and Edward[5] arrived about three weeks later they found Mrs W. up and about again and Mrs Bennett ready to come home. The following day Bruno went on up the Halfway, found the only two trappers within reach, and brought them back to be Godfathers (and general congregation) for the family baptism, at which Mrs Westergaard and all her six children were Christened together ...

That finishes January, except for my visit to our dentist[6] – the man you remember who occasionally puts on a movie show in the Community Hall and once nearly caused a riot by producing a Talkie that wouldn't talk.

Hitherto I had avoided him as a *dentist* because his reputation that way is clever but not very clean; and May and Miss Claxton and Mr Flatt had described very vividly how they had stood over him to make him sterilize his instruments and wash his hands.

However, I did go to him last month, because I needed a little treatment and really couldn't waste a whole week and a small fortune going by sleigh to Dawson Creek ...

The first time I went – remembering various warnings – as he approached my mouth I said, 'You haven't forgotten, Doctor, have you to – er – .'

'Ach no – watch me – watch me now – I am mine hands mit strong carbolic soap washing – see – *smell.*'

And he poked his immense wet fingers under my nose.

'Yes, that's better, that's all right, I'm sure.'

'Ach no – not finished – watch me now. I wash mine hands in Lysol – see – SMELL.' (same again)

'Yes, that's fine – now then.'

'Ach NO – not finished – watch me now – I am mine hands in pure alcohol washing – see – SMELL.'

Once started he keeps you under, so to speak, by pouring out volumes of family history with most entrancing recklessness of detail, so that in the end I was quite sorry to go only twice.

'I am very sad today. I am not sleeping or eating – since I have this letter last mail. It is about my wife's father in Saskatchewan. It is saying he should have stolen three horses and must go in the Coop (prison) unless he pay 400 dollars in 30 days. Of course he did not steal the horses. Only he sold a man 15 horses and three were missing – he don't know how – and of course he haven't got 400 dollars. Now my wife's sister say the friends in Saskatchewan are putting on a TEA to help raise some money – and she want ME to put on a TEA in Fort St John. But, Miss Storrs, do you *truly* think a TEA to get my wife's father out of the Coop would GO in Fort St John?'!!!

He seemed to be quite in earnest and dreadfully anxious and I simply couldn't make out whether he was incredibly simple about it all – or quite the opposite – how many clients heard that poignant story, or how many, like me, felt they would rather pay a little extra for the triple hand-washing. Anyway, there has been no TEA so far; but I hope his wife's father is out of the Coop ...

Diary for February, 1937

... [This month I celebrated] my birthday ... I have appointed Roffen my official *Retireometer*, that is to say, when I can no longer mount him from the level or heave the saddle on to his exalted back I shall return to Bournemouth and a Bath Chair. But at present I can still do both – *just*.

One of Roffen's great charms is pulling you up-hill by his tail, I mean, when climbing a bank or a slope too steep to ride. You catch hold of his huge black tail with both hands and give the word, and off you go – up the side of a house if need be. It's the greatest fun, and usually he stops quite politely at the top. Only once he played a practical joke on me by darting off the trail and dragging me a long way in waist-deep snow. You see, I daren't let go of his tail lest he should take a notion to trot home the 50 miles without me ...

The following week was very domestic ... One of those days I rode over to see Mrs Crawford and to take her the good news that Mrs Henderson[7] from up the river would come and work for her till May 1st. On the way across her big field I met Victoria Peace, the buffalo, behaving rather strangely. She is so gentle and quite shy as a rule; but this time she seemed to be charging straight at us with her head down. I was just thinking that it might be as well to step aside and let her have the trail – and Barbary was quite *sure* of it, when the buffalo herself bounded to one side, galloped round us and on again, looking very odd and bewildered, poor thing. Afterwards I learned the explanation from Mrs Crawford. Her cattle are all Herefords, and Victoria Peace doesn't easily make friends with them; but her one dear soul-mate was an old Shorthorn called 'Reddy-cow.' Well, a day or two before that a cattle buyer had been along and bought a bunch of Mrs C.'s steers, and with them that cruel old George[8] went and sold poor old Reddy-cow because she was past milking. The effect on Victoria Peace was extraordinary. Apparently buffaloes have tremendously deep affections. She refused to eat or drink or mix with the Herefords, and spent her time either galloping round and round the fields looking for her friend, or standing by the corral with head down and literally *streaming eyes*.

Isn't that a strange instance of friendship and sorrow? ...

A death happened in February which impressed us all very strangely, although it actually took place in Mexico. Do you remember my mentioning a remarkable Englishman called Mr Geake?[9] He was a retired Naval Commander and a unique sort of man in this country ... He trapped and hunted and prospected for gold; and did all the things you read about in the ideal schoolboy's story book. I only saw him half a dozen times; and he looked exactly like Alan Quartermain or one of those other Rider Haggard heroes,[10] strong and brown with a small black beard and the voice of an English Naval Officer. He wore an open-necked shirt and shorts in the summer, and very little more in the winter, and was always followed by three or four immense dogs ...

The queerest part about him was the way he kept coming and going, appearing and disappearing all over the place and sometimes vanishing altogether for months. Some people really thought he was a secret service agent; but I think he was just a gentleman adventurer.

Anyway, I saw him last fall in the Post Office here and the next I heard of him was a short notice in the *Peace River News*, saying that he had been shot dead in Mexico. A week or two later fuller details came out, so strange and characteristic that I must just tell you the bare facts.

It seems that he and a friend had discovered a bandits' cave somewhere in Mexico, full of gold and treasure, and being the sort of men they were, had determined to rob the robber. So they took a truck (lorry) and drove to the nearest point in the mountains. And there comes an extraordinary thing. The friend who went with him was an ex-Army Officer who had lost his eye-sight and one hand in the War! Well, they got away with a truck load of treasure and went back for another. But this time the bandits were ready for them with an ambush and they were both shot, the blind friend being killed outright. Geake was badly wounded, but succeeded in feigning death till the bandits were gone. Then he crawled to the truck, hauling the body of his friend, and drove 20 or 30 miles to the nearest village. There he found a lawyer, established the identity of both, gave particulars of the murder, made arrangements for burial – and then died.

A strange fine finish to a strange adventurous life. What led him all the way to Mexico to rob robbers nobody knows; certainly not need of money, for he left considerable property to a widowed mother and a clergyman brother in England ...

Diary for March, 1937

March was overshadowed for us all by a great sorrow in the sudden death of our dear friend and comrade Muriel Claxton of the Red Cross. Compared with that event, everything other that happened in the month seems trivial and hardly worth mentioning ...

On Saturday 6th Bruno went across the Pine for his monthly Service at the Gough Memorial where they had begun to arrange a beautiful little Sanctuary in the big attic space upstairs under the rafters ... Before he started I rang up Miss Claxton to ask if they needed anything brought over by him. Certain supplies often run short over there, so we usually do this ... She also mentioned that they were very busy with influenza, and had a pretty bad case just brought in from Moose River 25 miles away. This was the last time I heard her voice in health.

The same afternoon I drove down to Taylor for my monthly visit there ... After [the Service in Church] the absurdest thing happened. I had a Pain – you know, the perfectly undignified kind of pain that children have from green apples! Priscilla and the congregation had gone so I sat peacefully on the Vestry floor and waited for it to go too. Meanwhile to my great embarrassment *both* the Churchwardens came back and found me there. They were very sweet and funny. 'Hullo,' said old Sam Cushway. 'Got the Colic, have you? Wait while I get you the very thing – Essence of Wild Strawberries,' and off he ran, or rather hobbled, being elderly and shaky on his feet. Meanwhile Bert Hadland darted over to the newly built Packwoods' house and came back with a cup of warm water full of partly dissolved ginger powder – awfully potent. Next he announced that he had hitched up Roffen to the cutter for me ... [but] just then Mr Cushway came back with the 'Essence of Wild Strawberries.' Do you know that remedy? It sounds good, doesn't it? Well, it's jet black and tastes perfectly filthy. Old Sam handed me the bottle and said, 'Put it to your lips and drink down to where my thumb is.' I did so; and had a dreadful suspicion that it was liquid Cascara.

Just then there was a shout from the store and my heart failed at the thought that Roffen was gone. Bert rushed off again, and Sam hobbled after him, while I struggled to my feet, strengthened by the wild strawberries.

Thank goodness, Roffen hadn't gone, but bored with waiting and his winter coat and the warm weather, he had lain down and rolled *with the cutter,* and of course broken a shaft!

... The place where he had rolled had been a hitching-place for many

months, and the soft weather had thawed it into a muck-heap. So my beautiful horse looked (and smelt) like a colossal statue modelled in manure,
and you could hardly see the harness at all – a jolly little interlude between
two Sunday Services! But anyway the rage of it entirely cured my colic ...

On Wednesday, March 10th, I rode to town to see Bruno ... In the course
of our conversation he remarked that the patient he had seen in the Outpost across the Pine struck him as very ill indeed. He added, 'I shouldn't
be surprised at any moment to hear that she had died.' Just then a boy
looked in and told him he was wanted in the Post Office on the telephone.
He said, 'You'd better come too; it will probably concern you.' So I went
down with him.

It was Agnes Ayling; and she told us that Mrs Lowe[11] had just died and a
man had ridden off to Moose River[12] to find her son. But she said the
urgent thing was that Miss Claxton had caught the germ, which seemed a
particularly virulent one that mere nursing could not combat without a
doctor. She said she had rung up Dr Kierney, but he couldn't spare the
whole day away from the hospital in town which the condition of the roads
would certainly involve. The illness was still at an early stage and she was fit
to travel, so he told Agnes to send her in somehow and he could look after
her here ...

Within the hour I set off with the best team and most comfortable sleigh
I could collect for the 16 mile drive to the river ... Just before five we reached
the river bank, and a little later Con Thompson arrived with Muriel in a
Bennett waggon[13] ... Her breathing was laboured and she had a bad cough.
But she appeared to be in good spirits and said she had enjoyed the three
changes and the six hours' journey in the open air.

The following day I went to see her twice and found her apparently
better, that is, not coughing so much, and able to sit up and feed herself
quite easily ...

On Friday afternoon I was with her quite a long time, doing small things
for her because the hospital was very full and one or two nurses were ill ...
She told me again of her hopes of getting Home to her family for good
this coming fall; seemed quite confident of recovery, and was counting the
days till the doctor might allow her to move to May Birley's house for convalescence. She ended by telling me a funny little story and then I left her
and promised to come back again next morning ...

Next morning, Saturday, March 13th, at 9.30, we were just finishing our
hour in Chapel and had shortly before prayed for Muriel with other sick
friends, when there was a knock on the door and a boy asked me to go at

once to the hospital ... But when we got there it was already too late; Muriel Claxton had just slipped away.

The Sisters told us she had slept well, and appeared to be still dozing when called in the morning. But they soon discovered it was not natural sleep but a sort of coma. The doctor came at once and tried every means of re-animation. But although the heart was steady to the end, apparently the higher nerve-centres were in some way poisoned and paralysed by the swift disease. For she failed to respond to any form of stimulus, and gently sank into the deep sleep of death.

It was a beautiful close to a most beautiful life, just what she would wish, I am sure. No pain or weakness or infirmity and failing powers – above all no *Fuss*. She always was so completely gentle and unobtrusive in life; and so her way of leaving it was just the same ...

Agnes was wonderful. She had been through a heavy strain already, and this was a fearful blow, for she had learned to love Muriel as indeed no one could fail to do who lived and worked with her. But she was perfectly steady and controlled; and from that moment took her place perfectly both as friend and *acting* next of kin and Red Cross representative. The first matter on which she was quite definite was that Muriel had wished, if she died in Canada, to be buried across the Pine as near to the Outpost as possible ...

On Wednesday the 17th at sundown we brought the coffin into St Martin's and had a short Service there – very quietly just the closest friends only. Thursday was fine but rather cold. The Church looked very joyous with Lady Goodenough's glorious white frontal borrowed from Baldonnel for the occasion, masses of home-made flowers, and in the middle, the small coffin covered with the immense Red Cross flag. All the school children came and a crowd of grown-ups.

... About three o'clock the tiny procession started out to take Muriel across the Pine for the last time. In front was the coffin with its flag and flowers on a rough little Bennett-waggon driven by George Lynn;[14] and behind it rode Mr Brown on Barbary and Agnes on Gill, followed by May Birley on Rama, and myself on Roffen, and lastly Priscilla on Ginger and Rosemary on Tigger.

... We talked very little, but not from a sense of gloom or restraint. I don't think any of us felt like a funeral procession, but much more like a home-going party with Muriel riding amongst us, elusive and unobtrusive as ever, but there all the same ...

Next morning began with a Eucharist ... We had 11 Communicants, a good number considering that everyone was coming to the Funeral Service later on. And indeed they *did* come. Every soul in the district down to the smallest half-breed child seemed to be there. They sat on the ground and the men stood, and even so the Upper Room could hardly contain us all.

We sang the same hymns as yesterday; and Bruno preached: ... 'She has learned to love, widely, tenderly and practically; so she will never be lonely or unemployed. She has learned to Worship, so in God's nearer Presence she will not be ashamed or dumb.'

After that we formed up again for the last procession. It had snowed all night and was still snowing slightly so the sky was grey and the road and fields and trees were white once more – which seemed rather suitable – as someone said, 'typical Claxton weather.'

The Bennett Buggy went first again, then Bruno robed, and we five walking, and then 15 or 20 sleighs each containing one or two complete families; and so we came to the tiny clearing in the bush, with two graves – Mr Simmonds[15] and Mrs Lowe – and the new one just dug in the frosty ground. The men lowered the coffin with reins taken from the leading horses. It was still wrapped in the Red Cross flag and most of the flowers went down with it. After the Commital, we all sang 'Abide with me' and then Bruno gave the blessing.

I have been to numberless funerals, including my own Father's and Mother's, both at Rochester; but none has been more luminous with love, joy and peace, than this one ... And, as Mrs Cuthbert said, 'Whatever memorial we may set up, the greatest memorial must be our lives; for we can never be the same as if she hadn't lived here' ...

After the funeral we all went back to a meal at the Outpost. It was one of those meals that begin very quiet and constrained and end very cheery and high-spirited – partly from reaction but chiefly from the knowledge common to us all that dear Muriel would have *hated* to cause a gloomy party. And those who loved her most seemed the most conscious of her bright pervading spirit ...

Diary for May, 1937
Everything this month seemed to be working to or from the great climax of the Coronation[16] ...

Before the end of April few people were quite sure even of the actual date and *very* few felt that anything need be done about it here. It was one of those subjects which quite suddenly reveal a great cleavage in thought and background ... When it comes to the immaterial symbols of Unity, you *feel* a vast difference in outlook (even if nothing is said) between the Old, the deeply rooted, strongly corporate, essentially British instinct, which makes the Coronation almost as personal to you as your own marriage; and the forward-looking, independent, intensely individual attitude, to which all is remote and shadowy, if not superfluous ...

On May 9th we had special Services of course, and Bruno preached a perfectly magnificent sermon in St Martin's. I'm sure it wasn't wasted on our little handful of people; but couldn't help longing for Montreal Cathedral[17] to be there as well – and maybe even Rochester too ...

I had bought Tommy Hargreaves' old radio (wireless) really for [the Coronation] and no other purpose. We had the usual agonies about whether the batteries were charged and what the reception was going to be like.

... [Tuesday] was the most wonderful night of my life (and the only one in which I had no thought of going to sleep).

About 8.30 [the broadcast] was over; ... and we all went into the Chapel for a very tiny little Prime. We said the Archbishop's Crowning Prayer all together, then sang 'I vow to thee my Country,' then went outside, put up the flag and sang the National Anthem. Then the children went in to breakfast and Priscilla and I went up to town for the Holy Eucharist at St Martin's. It was a glorious opportunity of thanksgiving for the Wonders of the Night ...

End of May and June

... On the 4th we had a great excitement. According to promise I took six of the brattles (boarders)[18] to Rolla to act 'The Bathroom Door'[19] at the Second Annual Musical and Dramatic Festival of the Peace River Block ...

I was amazed at the numbers of children and even grownup competitors collected at Rolla, and at the excellent organization and efficiency of this, only the second festival ever to be held in this part of the world. We really felt that we had crossed the river from the Wild West *straight* into Surrey or Hampshire ...

Our kids did very well, at least I thought so; but the adjudicator was not so struck. He ranked them third, with four marks less than the second place, and criticised them as being 'unsophisticated.' This, I fear, is true, but hardly to be wondered at, since they had never in their lives seen a good play, or even a real good Talkie. Still, it was good for us all to see others better than ourselves; and especially, I think, to see all those people devoting all that time and trouble to 'mere' Culture instead of horses and cows, crops and ploughs, and such like Realities that fill up all our lives.

Next day our [Fort St John] girls won the dancing (coached by a school teacher)[20] so Fort St John did carry home a trophy after all and we were delighted, because of course we had never competed anywhere before ...

Diary for July, 1937

... Priscilla and I had a wind-up Children's Service and Picnic for our Sunday Schools – St Martin's and Fish Creek. Priscilla took the Children's Service, as I had taken Mattins; and directly afterwards we all set out in Braden Herron's truck for the picnic spot high on a point overlooking the Peace. Needless to say the children *adored* the truck drive – all crowded together as we were about 30 of us, with mothers and babies added, a dog or two, cans of food and leaking milk and ice-cream freezers. It was rough enough all the way along the jolly old trail; but when we had to cross Henry McLeod's new breaking – two good sized fields just ploughed very deeply for the first time – I really thought the truck would fly to pieces and everyone would be scattered. Talk of storm at sea! We were hurled from side to side – children and mothers and babies and freezers and milk pails – all banging into each other till it seemed no one could have a tooth left in their head. *And the children simply adored it ...*

When we parted at the Church again, I asked one or two, 'What did you enjoy most today?' and each one said with shining eyes, 'Ooh – the Breaking!'!! ...

Diary for August, 1937

... Monday the 9th, we visited Mrs Bob Beattie,[21] who has four little children, and who is now living at Carbon River, where the Joneses were in old days ... Her husband is usually away on one job or another, hunting or guiding or trapping ... But she never complains or anything, and her face, which is singularly beautiful, seems radiant with the spirit of peace. Of course she was enchanted to have visitors, and after a little talk asked Bruno if he could baptize her baby girl ... So the three little boys were mobilized and the room prepared, and Fern Elizabeth was made a member of Christ ... Then dinner all together, and soon after we came away with real regret. It would do anyone good to stay with Bessie and seems strange that so sweet an influence should have so small a sphere ...

Next day we found the remains of a huge fossilized ichthysaurus in the rock and later met ... three boatloads of Canadian and American schoolboys from the East, conducted by a romantic-looking young man called Count Ignatieff.[22] This person, to my astonishment, penetrated my disguise (pretty complete) and said he remembered me speaking at the

Governor-General's banquet at Pouce Coupé four years ago! After this ro-
mantic encounter we continued on our ways, they down-stream and home-
wards, we upstream and to the unknown. But I shall always regard the
Count as a semi-scalp, whatever Elinor may say ...

Diary from August 22nd – September 9th

I am afraid this story has fallen a little into arrears ... There is no excuse
except what you all know well enough, that I am not a journalist but
only an ordinary Church Worker, a very slow one too. And sometimes life
itself – ideally happy though it is, does take just about all there is of you,
both in time and energy, without writing about it ...

On the 26th we left the Peace and started up the Halfway trail to visit the
three families who live strung out along that river ...

Nels Westergaard is a cattle rancher who traps during the winter over a
line beginning about 100 miles North of their home. His wife is a sweet
fair-haired delicate looking woman of 26 with six children, including the
recent twins ... In spite of their complete isolation, the children were not
the least shy, but on the contrary, most friendly and sweet ... [The little
boys] are as fair as Gloria [the eldest] is dark and the smallest is one of the
sweetest children I have ever seen ... Lastly there were the eight months
twins called Rita and *Didi* (such a good name!). They of course were exactly alike ...

Our next family was the Simpsons, 20 miles further on, and at eight
miles we had to cross the Main Halfway, as this family lives on the right
bank ... The forest was dark and sodden and seemed to be quite endless.
At 6.30 ... we suddenly came out into an open meadow – and there was a
hay stack and there was a HOUSE.

It actually was the Simpsons and such a lovely welcome – Mr Simpson
ran straight out and took the horses as if he had been waiting at the door
for us all his life; and Mrs Simpson (whom we had never seen) pulled off
our soaking clothes, made up the fire and produced a pot of tea – almost
before anyone had said anything. She is North Irish, plump and fair, with a
soft brogue and shy manners, the more shy because she hadn't seen a
white woman for two years (to my eternal shame) and then only two American Dood ladies just passing through.

They had a very good little house indeed, for which everything, including the chairs, beds and all glass, sawn timber for floors, doors, windows,
etc., had been carried out by him 80 miles on pack-horses. They had a
radio and books and a *spare* bed in the living room, which we occupied
thankfully for two luxurious nights. Above all they had five sweet children,

Anna, a lovely refined little girl of eight, Drury, Bobby, Jimmy and Jessie who was born last winter with no woman near to help. I said to Mrs Simpson, 'Aren't you afraid?' And she said, 'Oh no! Bill was with me, I did a big baking and cooked up a lot of meat and potatoes for the children; and then I went to bed and knew everything would be all right' ...

Mr Simpson has a cattle ranch, besides rearing pack-horses. He has, further, a small trading post for the Halfway tribe of Indians, for which he freights with his pack-train 109 miles each way to Fort St John almost every month ...

For the next two days heavy rain gave us a happy excuse for staying on with the Simpsons ... She is expecting another child next March; and he implored me to try and find some nice woman willing to ride back with him after his next (October) visit to town and spend the winter as companion and help to his wife. This I took on as a sacred charge, and on Saturday we left them with very real regret and rode back to the Westergaards.

We spent Sunday the 5th with them and had a delightful time again – Sunday School in the morning, family Prayers at night and games and photographing in between ...

We reached the Abbey at 2.30 [on Tuesday] half an hour before the W.A., stabled the horses, and there found Priscilla with everything ready, and handing out bowls of water to wash all over in the garden, so as not to mess the spotless house! So we did very thankfully, though not without anxious ears cocked for the hoot of Mrs Pickell's car. We were not quite dressed when they came but they didn't mind that, I hope ...

Diary for September, 1937
We found the children back at school, of course, but only six living with us instead of last year's eight. Alf has left school altogether, to do one more year of study (Senior Matric) at home. This school cannot help him there, and he on the other hand, can help his people more, while Roy, the younger brother, is with us. Percy and Phyllis Freer have left school also, for far less adequate reasons ... It's rather sad; for they live on a beautiful but quite isolated farm, 25 miles from Fort St John, where the only intellectual stimulus is provided by cowboy songs and news (chiefly American) on the radio, and the only spiritual stimulus is Bruno's monthly Service at the top of the hill if they go ... Rosaline has gone to live with her step-father near Calgary, and Eileen at Edmonton, where her mother has now got regular work. Of course both of these have excellent schools close at hand ...

So now we have five boys in their own little St Francis House – generally known as the bunk house because they sleep in two tiers of bunks like a ship's cabin.

The boys are: Roy Cuthbert, aged 16; Tony Flatt, aged 15; Michael, his brother, aged 12–13; Johnny Simpson, aged 15 (Baptized and Confirmed last year); Dick Hadland, aged 13, both from Baldonnel and of English or English and Welsh parentage. All but Michael are in High School.

... One new Companion, Hope Onslow,[23] was due about the 18th to have a month with Priscilla before she (Priscilla) went Home with Rosemary on furlough. And the other – Mildred Morse[24] – was expected just before their departure, to fill the gap with Elinor ...

Hope is supposed to be 29, but it's hard to believe it, for she sure is well preserved! She is a bit taller than me, with lovely red hair, and a very lively and direct manner. She comes from the College of the Ascension,[25] which she adores, and of which she is a fine advertisement – if indeed it needs any ...

Diary for October, 1937

September had been a most lovely month ... Certainly this climate when it's not in a real bad mood is far more beautiful than yours at Home. We hardly ever have a *dull* day here. Some days in the summer it pours in torrents; several days in winter are too cold for comfort; but in between all these it is amazingly clear, bright and lovely ...

Hope being safely established with Prisca, ... it seemed the best time for me to go out to Edmonton for my annual Retreat before Priscilla and Rosemary should leave us for England ...

The following week was full of thought and preparations for the departure of Priscilla and Rosemary. We gave them immense lists of things to do, and far bigger lists of people to see ...

Finally on Monday the 25th, Priscilla emerged from her shirt, overalls and sheepskin like a bursting crysalis [*sic*] and flashed forth in a long green dress and coat – a very beautiful dragonfly – and we started together in the Mail-truck. I went with her as far as Taylor, where my place was taken by Rosemary – also looking quite a stranger to me!

And there, if you please, arrived two days before and already apparently quite at home, [was] our newest Companion of all – *Mildred Morse* ...

She is quite small – such a nice change – somebody I can look down upon at last! She is dark and rosy and most cheerful and adaptable. She had never ridden a horse in her life till the day before; but we hoisted her up on to Rosemary's enormous Tigger, and she trotted with me the ten miles home to the Abbey without turning a hair.

There she met Hope and the boys and Bruno who was spending his usual Monday night with us; and the next morning we started our real life together at the little Altar of the Holy Cross ...

Diary for December, 1937

November ended with the close interweaving of pathos and gaiety which so often makes up the pattern of this life; the night of Friday the 26th being divided for me between stage-managing Hope and two boys in their noble farce called 'The Sausage'[26] and slipping across to the Church House to make a big wreath of artificial flowers for Jean Hanson's[27] funeral next morning.

'The Sausage' was the contribution from this house to a W.A. Concert – an absurd little play in which the main point is an unlucky rash wish which causes an immense sausage to stick magically tight to the end of Hope's nose! The theme was hardly classical; and we found the magic rather hard to work. But Hope and Roy were quite delightful together; and they brought the house down all right; so I felt that one of my two remaining brown silk stockings had not been stuffed and fried in vain ...

Did I tell you that we have at last got a real Messenger Uniform for Services? Well, we have anyway. I chose it with Bishop Burgett when I was at Edmonton and it's very nice – just a rather voluminous dull blue cassock light enough to carry about and wear over everything, and a veil to match. It certainly is much nicer than the previous black cap and gown called by the Companions 'John Knox'[28] ...

I got home for supper, realizing suddenly that it was the last chance to write Home for Christmas, because Elinor and I were going to the Hope next day. So we both set to work and wrote steadily till five a.m ... As we had to be up at 6.30 as usual I was in two minds about undressing for bed, but in the end I did, down to the very ground, and was thankful I had. You have to have a couple of days with the minimum of washing when you ride to the Hope, so it's just as well to start fresh ...

On Friday the 3rd we had dinner with that jolly Bohemian couple – Mr and Mrs Joe Zelenke – only they were not at all jolly at the time, both being far from well. She is that woman I told you about, who used to be a professional pastry cook in Prague, and now dresses and works like a man beside her husband on their beautiful but terribly strenuous farm ... Overwork had strained his back, and her teeth were troubling her badly, so they were in a rather sad way. After much discussion made more difficult by the *very* peculiar English they both talk, I persuaded them to accept a little help from the Samaritan fund; and they promised to come out to Fort St John to see a doctor and a dentist ...

The ride home from the Hope was the slowest I have ever made, only 65 miles, but it took from Thursday afternoon to Sunday morning and from dark to dark each day ...

Christmas Day was cold and brilliant ... Hope and I came home to prepare a Bachelors' Supper to which we had invited six so-called lonely men. Hope had never drawn and trussed a turkey before; and of course I hadn't, so we had a great time trying to make him look restful! ...

About five o'clock two of our guests turned up, i.e., our two next door neighbours, Mr Holland and Mr Mowick.[29] But the other four apparently took fright and never came at all. We waited till 6.30 and then proceeded to demolish the turkey without them. Mr Holland is very highly educated, and loves to talk rather advanced political philosophy. Dear old Mowick is a nearly stone deaf Norwegian, also a great talker and politician of a simpler kind. He couldn't hear a word of Holland's but kept throwing in helpful comments in very broken English, such as, 'I hear *that* Hitler has just unheaded forty men. I say let England and France get around and unhead him both together' ...

All through the day Hope was splendid. I know what a first Christmas here is like. You can't help being a bit Homesick. But she showed no sign of it at all, cooked the dinner splendidly and was the life and soul of the party afterwards ...

On the 30th [Bruno] had supper for us all – Elinor and Mildred included – and on New Year's Eve we had a Midnight Service for the first time. But alas! There was a big dance on, so we four welcomed the New Year by ourselves. It was rather disappointing; but I'm sure next year there will be more. It was a new idea and such take slowly everywhere, not only in Fort St John.

1938–9

Diary for January, 1938

... Hope and I stayed over [at Charlie Lake], she for a well earned rest, I for a spot of visiting ... [with] poor Jenny Nicholson (née Solorenko) whom I knew to be in terrible trouble ... Only a few days before this, poor Jenny heard the awful news that her father, always a violent man and especially when drunk, had murdered her mother after a Christmas party and then committed suicide ... I heard she would like to see me. So I went to supper, and found her in her one room shack with two tiny babies; she herself looking scarcely more than a baby still, but white and shy and terribly forlorn.

Next morning while it was still dark, Hope and I started for home in the little Mail caboose (covered sleigh) which, as they often do, had a small stove in it. After so much fresh snow the trail was very heavy and it took us five hours to get to Fort St John ...

Diary for April and May, 1938

... I secured about 30 cords of firewood and set to work to get it sawn up and split in time to dry out during the spring and summer months. This is quite a big job. First the complete tree-trunks are hauled and piled at a convenient place. Then you have to engage a wandering wood-saw which is hauled down on a sleigh with three or four men described as the 'Outfit.' These and the biggest of the schoolboys work together in a fine rhythm, heaving the long logs into position and cutting them into stated lengths – say 27 inches for our heater and 17 for our cooking stove ...

After that splitting can be done by the boys (and ourselves when time allows). It generally takes several weeks; and while two people are splitting a third works hard at 'cording,' i.e., piling the split logs in neat walls four feet high and eight wide all along the outside of the house fence.

By this means you get as much fuel as possible dried out well for the following winter. It is a laborious and cumbrous process, taking a lot of time and space and no little cash; but the result for both cooking and heating is delightful; and I wouldn't change it for all the coal or gas or electric fires in the world ...

For most of the next day [Holy Saturday] we decorated St Martin's for Easter, using the usual spruce boughs and artificial flowers. Only this year we were enriched by six of the loveliest sprays of big Madonna lilies sent out from England. We put these on each side of the sanctuary in the big earthenware jars (from Peter Jones!)[1] and they looked so marvellously natural that Bruno's boy Jack came in on Monday morning and watered them, and STILL didn't find out his mistake ...

[After the evening Service] I crept upstairs like a mouse and there was *Priscilla* back from England and waiting up for me. She looked awfully well; and we longed to stay up and talk all night, but instead we went to bed almost at once, which was very disciplined you will agree. She seemed quite happy to be back; and we agreed that she should take over the housekeeping again as soon as possible, and set Hope free to go for a Retreat and holiday via Edmonton to Victoria ...

During the latter part of May your Samaritan fund was, I think, the means of practically saving two lives. One was ... an ex-soldier who has suffered from acute gastric ulcers for ten years, could get no assistance and was gradually becoming a complete wreck. We sent him out to Edmonton on the Fund. He had a big and critical operation performed free by the Specialist. The Fund paid his hospital bill and brought him back, while your Trust Fund supplied seed oats for a neighbour to sow his crop for him. He is wonderfully better, and full of hope, and beginning to work again.

The other was a little girl of 13 in my Sunday School who was suffering from acute ophthalmic goitre, with frightful nerve and heart symptoms. Nothing could be done for her at Fort St John; so I visited her mother, a woman separated from her husband and in wretched circumstances, and offered to send the child to Edmonton if she would give permission for an operation to be performed if necessary. The mother thankfully agreed, and it was arranged at once that Leila should go out with Agnes and Hope when they started together for their holiday on May 24th. Leila went to Edmonton, and was apparently the youngest patient the surgeon had ever treated in so serious a condition of this complaint. The operation was completely successful, and Leila is rapidly returning to perfectly normal health ...

But the Samaritan Fund is BROKE

July

... Our diet in the holidays consists almost entirely of milk products because, you see, when the boys are away, Maple still produces two large pails of milk daily which has to be consumed somehow. Luckily Priscilla is a mine of resource this way; and I must say I never knew that home-grown milk could assume so many forms. During that same week a very nice couple of American dudes (total strangers, of course, who were 'looking over the country') rode up just in time to enjoy a meal of home-made bread, butter, cheese, buttermilk, sour curds and – milk! We were half inclined to apologize, but they thought it *wonderful* – so 'cute' and 'rustic,' that we were a little afraid they might go home and send along a stream of friends. But evidently they haven't got home yet ...

This year [at Camp] we drove straight to the opposite side of the lake, about two miles away, where a man has settled with a 'kicker' boat (outboard motor) and he brought us all – complete to the last gramophone record – right across to Galilee for one dollar. Later in the week he also took us for a trip to the North end of the lake (about ten miles off) and we visited the only two houses on the shore.

The first was an obvious trapper's cabin, but Bill the boatman didn't know who lived there. 'Let's land and ask him who he is,' someone said – so we did. We found a pleasant and obviously educated Swedish bachelor, dressed exclusively in a pair of trousers, but beautifully clean, and delighted to see us. He said his home had never seen such a crowd of ladies – which I can well believe. Then after we had admired his cabin with its furs and horns and snow shoes, and his hopeful patch of vegetables outside, Hope and he had a shooting match with his .22 rifle, to the great admiration of all the rest of us.

After that he asked if he might come with us to visit the people across the lake. We agreed willingly; and after five minutes alone in the cabin, he joined us wearing a blue suit and grey cap. This quick change from a rather fine bronzed semi-Tarzan to a little suburban gentleman almost took our breath away! ...

Prisca [meanwhile] was having a campaign of Purification of the Abbey (apparently rendered necessary by our squalid habits and general neglect during her leave in England), but it was varied for her by a spot of Sunday duty while Bruno was at Hudson's Hope and the rest of us were in Camp. On one Sunday she took the Services at all three Churches, and made her way from one to the other leading Maple the cow who was travelling to her annual country holiday on a farm at Taylor Flats. This new combination of sacred and secular duties was worthy of Priscilla ...

But Prisca brought sad news and that was that dear old John McLeod had died. You remember, that fine old half-breed neighbour of ours who was so devout. Well, two days before Camp broke up his sons sent for me (Bruno being on his way down from the Hope). Prisca went instead and spent all the time she could sitting in his little cabin. He had been ailing for some time, but this was clearly the end. She said he lay in a kind of coma while his three grown-up sons sat round day and night and allowed no one else to touch him. Occasionally he recognized them and seemed glad to have her [Priscilla] there. Shortly before she had to come away he made a great effort to sing one of the bright little mission hymns he used to teach his grandchildren. But after a line or two his strength failed, and he explained, 'I can't sing any more now; but soon I shall sing for all eternity.'

After that he didn't speak any more; but his face grew more and more serene and beautiful and late that night he died.

I was dreadfully sad not to have seen him again, but thankful that Prisca had been with him ...

Meanwhile Bruno had brought back from his latest visit to Hudson's Hope, Mrs Joe Zelenka, that nice Bohemian woman with whom, as you remember, we have fairly often spent a night on the trail. She had long been suffering from acute digestive trouble, but we simply couldn't persuade her to come in and see a doctor. At length Bruno induced her to come along with him in a buggy, and warned Joe that he might have to carry on alone for a fortnight. Unlike true Canadians, Joe is terribly hen-coddled; and actually viewed the prospect of so much baking and cooking for himself with some dismay; but he was very good about it and fully realized that something had to be done for his wife's health.

Bruno brought her to us, and as she was terrified of a doctor, I drove her up next day, saw her into the hospital and stood by for the first interview. The verdict was that her teeth were poisoning her whole system and must all come out at once. She was awfully good about this, lost them all, and two days after came back to wait for transportation home.

Then the trouble began. I had planned for her to wait till Thursday the 28th, when my companions were all going up the river on a trip with King Gething, and would gladly take her home. But Mrs Z. suddenly got restive and said Joe would starve and she must go *at once* which was really impossible.

On Sunday I had to take the Service ... and preached about Mary Magdalene.[2] Mrs Z. came and followed the Service with difficulty, as she still has very little English. Afterwards she got restless again; so we tried to pacify her with hopes of a truck which was said to be coming up from Dawson Creek to the Halfway. All the afternoon I played her hymns on the Church harmonium and sang them till I was hoarse, while Hope scoured the town and telephoned here and there trying to get news of the rescue truck ...

At six o'clock we persuaded her to have supper, and then urged her to wait another night, but in vain. She grew agitated and insisted that she must walk. It was a blazing hot evening and she was still weak after losing all her teeth, but we could not detain her any longer. However, we tried to make her promise to stay the night at Somans, a house six miles on her way, and we hoped the truck would catch her up next morning.

But alas, that night she seems to have become temporarily deranged, was found next morning wandering in the bush and quite distraught. She was brought back to hospital under restraint.

The doctor thought it was all due to results of the blood poisoning, and decided that home surroundings would give her the best chance. So after a few days, Joe came and fetched her home. We heard no more, but could only hope against hope that the poor thing would soon be better ...

On Friday the 29th, Bruno and I shared the most unpleasant experience either of us have so far met in this parish. We had occasion to attend a meeting across the Pine got up in connection with the Gough Memorial Outpost and the newly built CHURCH, which is mainly a memorial to Miss Claxton. Bruno drove me over and we went quite unsuspectingly to an emergency meeting which had been called in one of the schools over there. No sooner did the meeting begin than it became apparent that it had been packed and manipulated by a group of two or three families that hate the Church. No one else had been warned that anything was afoot, so, with characteristic inertia, especially at this busy time of the year, few of our many loyal friends were there; and those who came were as much taken aback as we were by the sudden and ferocious attack made upon us.

We were charged with all kinds of sharp practice, unfair influence, etc., all patently absurd insinuations and quite easily refuted. Only the general atmosphere was so bad that reason and truth and courtesy were quite at a discount. Bruno kept his temper splendidly, and more or less kept mine for me too. It all led nowhere; but it was a painful blow to us to find that even a small group could entertain and work to disseminate such amazing and unworthy suspicions.

We drove home next morning feeling sadly perplexed; but really I suppose any servant of God should be ready to expect far more misunderstanding and hostility than that. Bruno says there will have to be another meeting when the Bishop comes next month, in order to give everyone a second chance to come to speak and hear the truth ...

Diary for August, 1938

August opened as quiet as a mouse, everybody away except Priscilla and me; but it soon speeded up and became very lively indeed round two important visitors – first Geoffrey Guiton[3] and then the Bishop ...

Meanwhile, between Sundays and Confirmation classes, Bruno was across the Pine, working with a handful of volunteers on the new Church there in a strenuous effort to have it ready for Consecration by the Bishop before the end of the month. He also had to supervise at intervals the building of another little Church at Hudson's Hope. Both these Churches were most generously financed by parishes in Montreal, after which they were to be named respectively St Matthias[4] and St Peter.[5]

St Matthias, the larger and more ambitious of the two, was to be furnished and adorned entirely in memory of Muriel Claxton; and the furniture was all being made in Fort St John by our one really good carpenter, Harry Downey.[6] The Church building was in the hands of one local paid supervisor, aided by volunteers. St Peter's, a much smaller and simpler Church, was contracted for by a Hudson's Hope man who built it single-handed, except for the help of young Hugh Mortimer,[7] who acted as a green but strong and most willing apprentice ...

In the middle of all this our first visitors arrived – the Rev. Geoffrey Guiton and another student called Norton Deane.[8] Mr Guiton was, so to speak, the founder of this parish. He came in 1930 (my first summer here) and also in '31 ... Soon after that Geoffrey Guiton volunteered for the Canadian Mission at Kangra in North India. He has been there five years as Headmaster of the big boys' school at Palampur; this was his first furlough and he wanted to spend ten days by the Peace.

It was very nice to see him again, eager, restless, boyish as ever, strung on wires, confident, capable, a bit dogmatic, and yet underneath gentle, generous-hearted and *most* considerate ...

... I think they enjoyed their visit, and we certainly did. Geoffrey doesn't know the meaning of repose and I don't think he can live very long; but such lives are like bright hot birchwood fires compared with the smouldering glow of green poplar. He broke right across our cold and cautious North Western outlook with vivid flashes of a warmer, subtler, anyway quite a different way of following the same Way.

After that I had one and a half days to clean and moss-chink the Chapel thoroughly, and on Wednesday the 24th the Bishop came.

The next ten days contained the climax of our year, namely the Consecration of the two Churches ...

The Red Cross Meeting which we had rather dreaded, turned out much better than its deplorable precursor last month. I won't bother you with all the miserable business that made this meeting necessary. It is too involved and petty. What matters here is that the Bishop handled it with great firmness and dignity. Even the two or three noisily hostile families gave him a respectful hearing, and the general atmosphere was entirely loyal and friendly. Agnes has resigned from the Red Cross, as she wishes to be unhampered in more definite work for the Church; and for the time being the atmosphere of the Outpost is to be completely secularized under the new Red Cross Committee at Vancouver. But Bruno and I are still to be accorded the privilege of free lodging there and I am sure that with patience and toleration it will all come right in the end ...

The Service [of Consecration of St Matthias] was at eight o'clock, the waning daylight augmented by a dozen or more little silvery stable lanterns, relics of the now dismantled hospital Chapel. All the faithful came and the Bishop consecrated every part of the Church ... Then he unveiled the simple brass tablet and dedicated it with all the furnishings of the Church.

'In affectionate and grateful memory of
Elsie Muriel Claxton, O.B.E., R.N.
First Red Cross Nurse of the Gough Memorial
Outpost who devoted the last years of her life to
the service of this Community.
By love serve one another.'

... St Peter's [at Hudson's Hope] has the sweetest exterior of all the Churches. It is small and rugged with a lovely little Spire; and has the charm of a village Church translated into logs. Within it is very plain and roughly finished (or rather unfinished) ... Yet it is a real House of God, and capable with love and care of becoming very beautiful ...

After dinner [next day] Priscilla and I started for home ... We bathed and had supper at Red River, visited the Zelenkas and found her better and more cheerful than we had expected ...

September, 1938 – March, 1939

Dear Friends of the Peace,

I am at length sending you some account of our life during the closing months of last year.

And if you feel that it can have no possible interest for you now, being such an old story, and almost smelling of decay, I can only apologise most humbly ... But I shall send it all the same because I am told that there is in England a small eccentric minority which still enjoys reading the lives of the Pharaohs! ...

On Tuesday the 13th Bruno and I paid our last visit to the Montney before his approaching holiday. We went in his buggy and drove across the Indian Reserve, discussing the Epistle to the Romans SO briskly that we lost the trail, and went at least an hour out of our way. But finally we reached the Williamsons at their brand new little stopping-house called *The Welcome Inn*, and certainly found a warm welcome there ...

We had ... a very pleasant evening with the Williamsons, only overshadowed by terrible wireless reports about Germany and Czechoslovakia.[9] Next morning came further news of Hitler's aggressive speech, and we drove home across the Reserve in such deep perplexity that I must confess we lost the trail again! ...

Sunday ... was Harvest Thanksgiving, and on Monday the 19th Bruno departed in the Mail for Montreal. He had been summoned back after two years' absence to have a short holiday and do a lot of lecturing and preaching for the Fellowship of the West. He was to be away till December 3rd, leaving me for over ten weeks to act as his deputy. It was an anxious time to be without him, but orders were orders; we had been praying almost continuously since the troubles began, and at the actual time of his departure it seemed as if Chamberlain's first flight to Germany might save the peace[10] ...

All the week the European news had been getting steadily more ominous, and that Sunday morning (September 25th) War seemed to be inevitable. Before Church I cleaned the barn, fed, watered and harnessed the horses, and in so doing met two or three men and begged them to come and pray for peace. 'What's the good?' said Jim Hill. 'It's too late now; nothing can save it but a miracle.' 'Well, but it's prayer that works miracles. Come and try.' Jim came. And so did a good few others. It was supposed to be Harvest Thanksgiving; but for once we were hardly concerned with crops. I read and spoke upon the story of Hezekiah laying the letter before the Lord,[11] and the rest of the Service was nearly all Intercession ...

Afterwards I drove home as quickly as possible and wrote letters to Ronald and Pet, Mabel and Adeline, sending all my love, and saying I would come Home and take my share if, and as soon as, circumstances should permit.

Agnes was still staying with us waiting to go to her new work in Edmonton diocese; so the following morning (Monday the 26th) I was delighted to have her companionship for the monthly journey to Hudson's Hope. We waited in Fort St John till after one to hear a broadcast of Hitler's horrible harangue, then started off, very sick at heart ...

We visited everyone on the trail, prayed with some, and reached the Hope at eleven that night. Mr Ferguson,[12] who has a good radio, told us he had listened to Chamberlain's speech and there was no hope of peace. But just as I was getting into bed at midnight, I heard a new voice, and running downstairs, was in time for Roosevelt's[13] last message to the rulers of Europe. At first it sounded all fantastically unreal, just part of a broadcast programme based on some story by Wells.[14] But gradually as I listened, the log-built room itself became unreal, and faded into column after column of tanks and guns streaming to every frontier amid the roaring of countless battle planes ... I felt I must leave everything at once and go Home while there was yet time.

But with the President's last sentences, urging the rulers to try once more the way of negotiation, the logs came back again and with them a new hope of solidarity in a melting world – .

'Perhaps after all this is the turning point,' said Agnes as I got back into bed ... About 11 [next morning] Mr Gaylor,[15] the telegraph operator, ran out and told me that Hitler had invited a new Conference to Munich[16] ...

Nevertheless, when we got home on Friday night and heard the full terms, we were still relieved, but *not* proud; and our deep thankfulness was tempered by sore perplexity.

All through this time I want to say that the spirit and attitude of our people up and down the trail was most loyal and sympathetic. They took a tremendous interest in the problem produced by aggressive dictatorships, and nearly all expressed readiness to back England whole-heartedly if it came to War. I know of several young men who were expecting to join the forces at once. And Mr Flatt and Tony had all plans made to start for the Old Country together.

October and November
... [On Saturday the 22nd] we were all at dinner together ... when there was a knock at the door and in walked Roland Cuthbert and Mr Akister. There was the usual rush for more knives and forks and food; but it was clear that this was no ordinary visit; so drawing Mr Akister aside, I learned from him the sorrowful news that his wife had died last night. He had come to ask whether I would take the funeral next morning instead of the ordinary Service, and of course I readily agreed ...

Mrs Akister looked very happy lying there in state in the little Church.

The sun shone in upon the improvised pall, which was turned down like a bedspread, upon the strangely assorted leaves and flowers, upon her grey hair, and the sweet friendly face, from which all wrinkles had been smoothed away by the serene hand of death.

... I remembered her unfailing welcome and hospitality to all of us, and the loyal devotion which hardly ever missed a Church Service, often walking five miles each way through soaking mud or deep snow. I recalled my last visit to her a few weeks ago when she was so ill, and we had whispered the 23rd Psalm together. 'I will fear no evil; for Thou art with me. Thy rod and Thy staff, they comfort me.' ...

On Sunday I took Chapel Mattins for the last time [before I left for Home on my long-awaited furlough]; then Bruno called for me and I drove round to all three Services as a Lady of Leisure. It was snowing nearly all day, but there were good numbers to welcome Bruno. I had a farewell Eucharist at the Good Shepherd with Elinor and Hope, and lots of Good-byes everywhere all day.

... I packed for most of the night and on Monday ... Bruno, Priscilla and Mildred brought us down to the Mail-truck. We piled into the back on the sacks, and watched them waving and dwindling as we drove away.

Priscilla is left in charge and all will be well, I know. Elinor comes Home when I go back in June – unless we are at War, which God forbid ...

And so I came Home.
But I've got two Homes now
Which is very puzzling.

POSTSCRIPT

When Monica Storrs returned to England in 1938 it is doubtful whether she realized just how much the next few months were to alter her life. Even in the isolation of Fort St John she kept abreast as much as possible with world events, and had been deeply touched by the appeals of Bishop George Bell of Chichester[1] on behalf of German Jews. When the Church of England Committee for Non-Aryan Christians[2] was organized to rescue children of European Jewish Christians, Storrs offered to be a guarantor and foster parent for two of the refugees. She requested two boys, about ten years of age, having heard that boys of this age were hardest to place, and planned to bring them with her when she returned to Canada early in 1939. In March 1939, therefore, Hugh (Horst) Schramm[3] and David (Arwed) Lewinski,[4] selected in Berlin by Quaker representatives on behalf of the Church of England Committee, arrived in Harwich on a Kindertransport.[5] They were met by Storrs and Adeline Harmer.

Hugh, twelve years old, was the son of an Aryan father and a Jewish mother, upon whom a divorce was forced after the Nuremberg Laws of 1935 declared marriage between Jews and non-Jews to be treason to the state. David Lewinski's parents were both Jewish, although his father was a member of the German Evangelical Church, as were the Schramms. Both David and Hugh had been baptized.

The boys expected to leave for Canada almost immediately, but this was not to be. Much to Storrs's consternation, the Canadian government would not grant the children visas, because, she was told, they were not legally adopted and Storrs, as a single woman, under British law, could not adopt them. Storrs used the term 'adopt' loosely, however, because neither Hugh nor David was eligible for adoption. 'Guardian' is a more accurate designation of her role, yet, under the circumstances, legal relationship was hardly a reason for the delay. Was it because the boys were Jewish refugees that no visas were forthcoming? Canada's immigration laws were being interpreted very narrowly indeed at this time, and Jews, even Jewish refugee children, were not welcome.[6] It seems likely that Storrs suspected this might be the cause, for after 'two months of negotiation,' she wrote to Robert Symons that she was going 'straight to Ottawa for another attempt at close quarters to obtain their [Hugh and David's] admittance. If this fails, I shall be very anxious for the soul of Canada, which can close its doors to such harmless immigrants.'[7]

Reluctantly, Storrs placed the boys with a friend in London who had a son slightly older than Hugh and David. As a result of this unexpected delay the children experienced the added trauma of the London blitz and consequent evacuation into the countryside.

Storrs, meanwhile, returned to Canada to do battle with the obdurate bureaucracy, as she had threatened. She personally met with the governor-general and the minister responsible for immigration, as well as with other officials. Her brother, Sir Ronald Storrs, wrote letters to the highest levels of government, as did Church of England leaders and Monica's friends. Finally, in 1940, Storrs received word that Hugh and David would be allowed to enter Canada with a group of evacuated British schoolchildren. In October of that year, she met them at last in Edmonton and took them to the Abbey to begin a new life – a new life not only for them but certainly also for the fifty-two-year-old church worker.

The boys adapted well to their new home and community, to Storrs and the various 'aunties' who worked with her, and even to her unusual lifestyle, for she continued as much as possible to be busy about her parish duties. When Hugh was of high-school age, Storrs sent him to St John's College School in Winnipeg, at that time a private Anglican school. David, two years younger, was able to complete his matriculation in Fort St John, not long before Storrs retired to England. Both boys were confirmed as Anglicans after they left Storrs's home; both maintain that she did not ever pressure them to conform to her religious practices and persuasions – no mean feat for one as dedicated to her church as was Monica Storrs. Hugh and David have lived productive, successful, and useful lives; both acknowledge that but for her, they too likely would have died in the death camps of the Third Reich, as did most members of their families.

With the onset of the war Storrs ceased writing her diaries, feeling they were of no importance when compared to the dangers her family and friends were experiencing in England. She did, however, occasionally write long letters to the Fellowship of the Maple Leaf, excerpts of which were published in the Fellowship's newsletters.[8] These are letters filled with the exploits of Hugh and David, the building of the Alaska Highway, and the expansion and changes in Fort St John, and with details of her own ever-extending ministry.

In 1946 she returned to England, where she was received in private audience by the Queen (now the Queen Mother).[9]

Storrs hoped, during these months at home, to find someone to replace her when she retired. She wrote, 'Now I'll tell you the sort of person I hope for my successor. The ideal would be a young, middle-aged, strong, rather plain (!) War Widow or consecrated Spinster with a small personal income. England used to be packed with just such. And now the war is over there ought to be more, at least one, ready for a call such as this. Ideally she should have two or three younger companions, as I did up to 1940. There would still be plenty of horseback work, but I am sure the thing needed here now is a car.'

Later that same year Storrs did, in fact, return to Canada with two workers, Mary Duncan Jones[10] and Patricia Tottenham,[11] and even received a car, 'Bluebird,' purchased by British supporters.

The main thrust of her work during these last few years, in addition to the visitation and parish duties, was the use of the Abbey as a hostel for high-school girls. She also welcomed one last Companion of the Peace, Bernice Hunten,[12] a Canadian from Montreal.

Monica Storrs retired in 1950, leaving Mary and Tom Humphries in charge of the Abbey, and Queenie Calvert,[13] formerly with the Caravan Mission, at Taylor. In England Storrs and her old friend Adeline Harmer purchased a log house situated in a beautiful wood of chestnuts, birches, and Scotch pine, near Liss, Hampshire, which they named 'Peacewood.' Here they warmly welcomed anyone connected with the Peace, whether known or unknown to them personally.

Storrs visited Canada twice in the next years, in 1958 and 1963. Her health was beginning to fail, and in 1965 she twice was hospitalized. Her eyesight was also deteriorating. Adeline Harmer wrote to David Lewinski,' [S]he could neither read nor see what she had written, though she could still see the general shapes of things and beauty generally and colour, and rejoiced in every aspect of the house and garden and the world in which we live.'[14]

In late 1967, and in spite of her poor health, Storrs insisted on attending a retreat and conference of the Village Evangelists.[15] While there, she collapsed. A few weeks later she suffered a stroke, and on 14 December, she died quietly without ever regaining consciousness. As Adeline Harmer wrote to Hugh Schramm, 'It was a very wonderful way to end this life.'[16]

Yet Monica Storrs had also lived her life 'in a very wonderful way,' for in spite of her faults and idiosyncrasies, she fulfilled her desire to 'make God and his world more wonderful' to those around her. Robert Symons summed it up: 'I know better than many, how utterly she felt failure, ... but I also know, better than she ever did, what changes she did finally bring about.'[17]

Requiescat in pace

NOTES

Introduction

Letters or copies of letters, and tapes of interviews, unless otherwise noted, are in the possession of Mary Kinnear or Vera Fast.

1 Monica Storrs to R.D. Symons, n.d.
2 *Dictionary of National Biography 1951–1960*, 7th supplement (New York: Oxford University Press, 1971), 931.
3 W.L. Morton, ed., *God's Galloping Girl: The Peace River Diaries of Monica Storrs 1929–1931* (Vancouver: University of British Columbia Press, 1979), xxxii.
4 Adeline Harmer to R.D. Symons, n.d.
5 Dorothy Warr to R.D. Symons, 27 February 1970.
6 Interview, Vera Fast with Dorothy Warr, May 1992.
7 *The Story of St Christopher's College, Blackheath 1909–1930, with insert 1930–38* (n.d., n.p.).
8 Interview, Mary Kinnear with Vida Archibald, 22 July 1991. Archibald attended St Christopher's 1928–31 and went to Canada after working as a Sunday School [S.S.] organizer for the Episcopal church in Scotland. Her experience after the Second World War exemplified the diversification of many church workers: 'In the summers I went up to join the Bishop's Messengers under Marguerita Fowler ... I would run Vacation Bible Schools for the children and might take the place of a Messenger who was on holiday ... In the autumn I went to Winnipeg to teach Sunday School and work at St John's College in the library.'
9 Notebooks of Frances Wilmot, Laurence Wilmot Collection, Winnipeg.
10 Vera Fast, *Missionary on Wheels: Eva Hasell and the Sunday School Caravan Mission* (Toronto: Anglican Book Centre, 1979), 22, 25, 27.

11 Ibid., 26–7, 32.

12 Ibid., 44, 39.

13 Morton, ed., *God's Galloping Girl*, xxxix.

14 Marilyn Barber, 'The Fellowship of the Maple Leaf Teachers, ' in Barry Ferguson, ed., *The Anglican Church and the World of Western Canada 1820–1970* (Regina: Canadian Prairies Research Centre, 1991), 154.

15 Ibid., 157, 159, 164.

16 Meredith Hill, 'The Women Workers of the Diocese of Athabasca, 1930– 1970,' *Journal of the Canadian Church Historical Society* 28:2 (1986), 66.

17 Grace Hallenby, Anglican Women's Training College: A Background Document (Toronto, 1989).

18 Alyson Barnett-Cowan, 'The Bishop's Messengers: Harbingers of the Ordination of Women,' *Journal of the Canadian Church Historical Society* 28:2 (1986), 77.

19 Interview, Vera Fast with Hope Symons, September 1976.

20 Marguerita Fowler, *The Story of St Faith's* (London: Society for the Propagation of the Gospel, 1950).

21 Barnett-Cowan, 'The Bishop's Messengers,' 81.

22 Brian Heeney, *The Women's Movement in the Church of England* (Oxford: Clarendon Press, 1988), 5, 6.

23 Brian Heeney, 'The Beginnings of Church Feminism: Women and the Councils of the Church of England 1897–1919,' in Gail Malmgreen, ed., *Religion in the Lives of English Women, 1760–1930* (London: Croom Helm, 1986), 267.

24 Sheila Fletcher, *Maude Royden: A Life* (Oxford: Blackwell, 1989).

25 Jacqueline Field-Bibb, *Women toward Priesthood: Ministerial Politics and Feminist Praxis* (Cambridge: Cambridge University Press, 1991), appendix C.

26 Heeney, 'Beginnings of Church Feminism,' 261.

27 Catherine Prelinger, 'The Female Diaconate in the Anglican Church: What Kind of Ministry for Women?' in Malmgreen, ed., *Religion in the Lives of English Women*, 184.

28 Monica Storrs Journal, April 1932.

29 Interview, Vera Fast with Hope Symons, September 1976.

30 Storrs Journal, March 1933.

31 Interview, Vera Fast with Hope Symons, September 1976.

32 Ibid.

33 Storrs Journal, April 1932.

34 Interview, Vera Fast with Hope Symons, September 1976

35 *Alaska Highway News*, 26 June 1958.

36 Ibid., 17 January 1968.

37 Albert Memmi, *The Colonizer and the Colonized* (New York: Orion Press, 1965), 79.

38 Storrs Journal, September 1934.

39 Ibid., September 1932.

40 Duncan Cran to R.D.Symons, 23 January 1970.

41 Dorothy Warr to R.D.Symons, 27 February 1970.

42 *Victoria Times*, 22 January 1936.

43 Ibid.

44 Vera Fast, *Missionary on Wheels*, 77.

45 Interview, Vera Fast with Hope Symons, September 1976.

46 Storrs to Fay Thomson, Easter 1940.

47 Interview, Vera Fast with Muriel Secretan, September 1980

48 *Montreal Gazette*, 31 August 1971.

49 Interview, Vera Fast with Jean Ingram, October 1980.

50 Interviews, Vera Fast with Eleanor Postans and with C. de Sausmarez, October 1980.

51 Interviews, Vera Fast with Betty Selness, October 1980, and with Hope Symons, 1979.

52 Adeline Harmer to R.D. Symons, 14 February 1970.

53 Interview, Vera Fast with Kate Webber Earle, May 1992.

54 Interview, Vera Fast with Hope Symons, September 1976.

55 Interview, Vera Fast with Monica White, November 1980.

56 Lillian Faderman, *Surpassing the Love of Men* (New York: William Morrow and Co., 1981), 311.

57 Interview, Vera Fast with Claire Adams, October 1980.

58 Canada, Department of the Interior, *Description of Surveyed Townships in the Peace River District in the Provinces of Alberta and British Columbia*, 2nd ed., 1913.

59 Storrs Journal, August 1937 (unpublished).

60 Census of Canada, 1931, II, table 33, 492.

61 Ibid. This included Dawson Creek and Pouce Coupé, towns visited by Storrs only on occasion.

62 Gerald Friesen, *The Canadian Prairies: A History* (Toronto: University of Toronto Press, 1984), 383. See also James Gray, *The Winter Years: The Depression on the Prairies* (Toronto: McClelland & Stewart), 1966; Michael Horn, ed., *The Dirty Thirties: Canadians in the Great Depression* (Toronto: Copp Clark, 1972); and A.E. Safarian, *The Canadian Economy in the Great Depression* (Toronto: McClelland & Stewart, 1970).

63 Friesen, *Canadian Prairies*, 388.

64 Ibid., 395.

65 *Census of Canada*, 1931, II, table 41, 532–3.

66 Province of British Columbia, Department of Education, Peace River Directory, 1934; W.A. Plenderleith, 'An Experiment in the Reorganisation and the Administration of a Rural Inspectoral Unit in British Columbia,' Ph.D. thesis, University of Toronto, 1937; John Calam, ed., *Alex Lord's British Columbia: Recollections of a Rural School Inspector 1915–1936* (Vancouver: University of British Columbia Press, 1991).

67 Province of British Columbia, Department of Education, Annual reports of the public schools, 1931–9. Note that teachers' salaries dropped as the Depression deepened.

68 *Census of Canada*, 1931, II, table 62, 844.

69 *Census of Canada*, 1941 (II, 807) lists three marriages in the area under the age of 15, 379 between 15 and 17, 718 between 20 and 24, then tapers off sharply.

70 Elections British Columbia, *Electoral History of British Columbia 1871–1986*, 173–201.

71 E.g., Storrs Journal, October 1932.

72 Clive M. Panta, the first MLA for the Peace River electoral district was a member of the Non-Partisan Independent Group, Conservative party candidates who followed W.J. Bowser's leadership. Elections British Columbia, *Electoral History of British Columbia 1871–1986*, 362, 396.

73 Canada, Report of the Chief Electoral Officer, 1935, 476.

74 Morton, ed., *God's Galloping Girl*, xliv.

75 Pat Barr, *The Memsahibs* (London: Secker and Warburg, 1976); Helen Callaway, *Gender, Culture and Empire: European Women in Colonial Nigeria* (Urbana: University of Chicago Press, 1987); Antonette Burton, *Burdens of History: British Feminists, Indian Women and Imperial Culture 1865–1915* (Chapel Hill: University of North Carolina Press, 1994); Antoinette Burton, 'The Feminist Quest for Identity: British Imperial Suffragism and "Global Sisterhood," 1900–1915,' *Journal of Women's History* 3:2 (1991), 46–81; Philip Carrington, *The Anglican Church in Canada: A History* (Toronto: Collins, 1963); Nupur Chaudhuri and Margaret Strobel, *Western Women and Imperialism: Complicity and Resistance* (Bloomington: Indiana University Press, 1992); Barry Ferguson, ed., *The Anglican Church and the World of Western Canada 1820–1970* (Regina: Canadian Plains Research Centre, 1991); Kumari Jayawardena, *The White Woman's Other Burden: Western Women and South Asia during British Rule* (New York: Routledge, 1995); Alyson Barnett-Cowan, 'The Bishop's Messengers,' *Journal of the Canadian Church Historical Society* 28:2 (1986); Claudia Knapman, *White Women in Fiji 1835–1930* (Sydney: Allen and Unwin, 1986); Margaret Macmillan, *Women of the Raj* (New York: Thames and Hudson, 1988); Anne McClintock, *Imperial Leather: Race, Gender and*

Sexuality in the Colonial Contest (New York: Routledge, 1995); Sara Mills, *Discourses of Difference: An Analysis of Women's Travel Writing and Colonialism* (London: Routledge, 1991); Brian Stanley, *The Bible and the Flag: Protestant Missions and British Imperialism in the 19th and 20th Centuries* (Leicester: Apollos, 1990); Margaret Strobel, *European Women and the Second British Empire* (Bloomington: Indiana University Press, 1991); Marianna Valverde, '"When the Mother of the Race Is Free": Race, Reproduction, and Sexuality in First-Wave Feminism,' in Franca Iacovetta and Mariana Valverde, eds, *Gender Conflicts* (Toronto: University of Toronto Press, 1992), 3–26; Margaret Whitehead, 'Women Were Made for Such Things: Women Missionaries in British Columbia 1850s–1940s,' *Atlantis* 14:1 (1988), 141–50.

76 Ruth Compton Brouwer, *New Women for God: Canadian Presbyterian Women and India Missions 1876–1914* (Toronto: University of Toronto Press, 1990); Rosemary Gagan, *A Sensitive Independence: Canadian Methodist Women Missionaries in Canada and the Orient 1881–1925* (Montreal and Kingston: McGill-Queen's University Press, 1992); Myra Rutherdale, 'Revisiting Colonization through Gender: Anglican Missionary Women in the Pacific North-West and the Arctic, 1860–1945,' paper presented to the Canadian Historical Association, 1994; Myra Rutherdale, 'Appropriation of Social Landscape,' paper presented to the Canadian Historical Association, 1995.

77 See Bella Brodski and Celeste Schenck, eds, *Life/Times: Theorizing Women's Autobiography* (Ithaca and London: Cornell University Press, 1988); Helen M. Buss, *Mapping Our Selves: Canadian Women's Autobiography in English* (Montreal and Kingston: McGill-Queen's University Press, 1993); and Carolyn G. Heilbrun, *Writing a Woman's Life* (New York: Norton, 1988).

78 Morton, ed., *God's Galloping Girl*, xxxvi.

79 Storrs to Willard Ireland, 6 October 1959.

80 Morton, ed., *God's Galloping Girl*, 222.

81 Ibid., xxxii.

82 Mary Percy Jackson, *Suitable for the Wilds: Letters from Northern Alberta, 1929–1931*, intro. by Janice Dickin McGinnis (Toronto: University of Toronto Press, 1995), 17–18.

83 Edward Bennett to R.D. Symons, 19 April 1970.

84 Bradford Angier, *Wilderness Neighbors* (New York: Stein and Day, 1979).

85 Morton, ed., *God's Galloping Girl*, xii.

86 Storrs to R.D. Symons, 28 February 1967.

87 See, e.g., J. Burgon Bickersteth, *The Land of Open Doors* (London: Wells Gardner, Darton & Co., 1914). For an exception to the trend see S.A. Archer, ed., *Heroine of the North: Memoirs of Charlotte Selina Bompas 1830–1917* (London: Society for Promoting Christian Knowledge, 1929).

88 Eva Hasell, *Across the Prairies in a Motor Caravan* (London: Society for Promoting Christian Knowledge, 1922); Hasell, *Through Western Canada in a Caravan* (London: Society for the Propagation of the Gospel in Foreign Parts, 1927); Hasell, *Canyons, Cans and Caravans* (London: Society for Promoting Christian Knowledge, 1930).

89 Jo Ann McNamara, *Sisters in Arms: Catholic Nuns through Two Millennia* (Cambridge, Mass.: Harvard University Press, 1996), 6.

90 Morton, ed., *God's Galloping Girl*, xxiii.

1931

1 Adeline Harmer, daughter of Bishop and Mrs John Reginald Harmer, came to assist Storrs for six months in 1931 and again for a short term in 1932. Muriel Haslam was recruited by Eva Hassel of the Anglican Sunday School Caravan Mission for the Fort St John area while Monica was absent on furlough. See W.L. Morton, ed., *God's Galloping Girl* (Vancouver: 1979), 181ff. Cecilia Goodenough (1905–), worked with Monica from 1931 to 1936. She was, in Monica's words, 'a very brilliant student from Oxford [History Honours], a fine needle-worker, a good cook and horsewoman, a tremendously keen Christian, and most loyal companion.' At the time of this writing, she lives in retirement in London.

2 Probably refers to her schoolboy boarders, who at this time were Erving Foster and Harvey Childerton.

3 Possibly the Albert Kelly family, whose son 'Georgie' is mentioned in these diaries. They moved out of the district to settle on a new homestead in what Monica called the 'East Montnay circuit.'

4 Monica's name for the Rev. George Hedley Wolfendale (1899–1944), born in England, son of a physician. He served and was wounded in the First World War, then attended the Montreal Diocesan Theological College (MDTC), was a member of the Fellowship of the West, and was ordained priest by Bishop Rix of Caledonia in Fort St John in August 1931, the first resident priest of the parish. In September 1934 he returned to Montreal. R.D. Symons, a long-time friend and game warden at Fort St John, says, 'Typically, Monica omitted to mention that it was she who largely made it possible for [Mr Wolfendale] to be appointed; she paid half his stipend from her own small resources.' Wolfendale enlisted in 1939 as a private in the Canadian army, but in 1941 was appointed chaplain. He was awarded the O.B.E. in 1944, the year he died of wounds while a prisoner of war.

5 The austerity of St Francis of Assisi and the faith of Elijah, who was fed by ravens during a time of great famine (1 Kings 17:4–6) seems to be the intent of this reference.

6 The school, built in 1931, at one time had 35 pupils, 30 of them Alexanders. Cora Ventress, Marguerite Davies, and Edith Kyllo, *The Peacemakers of the North Peace* (Fort St John, 1973), 233.

7 The six Alexander brothers were Jim, Sam, Bert, Bob, Will, and Ed; their sister Irene was married to Jim Pratt (ibid., 234ff.).

8 Called 'Herby's Flat' after Donald Herbert and Charlotte Taylor, who came to the area in 1912, the name gradually evolved into Taylor's Flat (or Flats), and finally into Taylor. While Monica uses both Taylor's and Taylor Flats, for the sake of consistency Taylor Flats or Taylor has been used throughout in this volume. For more information about the Taylors see Ventress, Davies, and Kyllo, *Peacemakers*, 30f.

9 So named by Jack Abbott, a settler, after the Irish county from which he came (ibid., 214). When Monica first arrived in the area it was known as East Fort St John, and here she financed the building of St John's Church Hall in memory of her father, the Rev. John Storrs. The hall could be used for either church services (one end was consecrated for this purpose) or community meetings. The building is now a private residence, but its outward appearance remains unchanged.

10 Robin and Miles, horses belonging to Monica.

11 The William Lea family arrived in the area in 1929, with Mrs Lea the first woman in the district. Their children were Jimmy and Muriel; a baby girl was born later.

12 Monica refers to Pouce Coupé, named after an Indian Chief, as the 'County Town' of the Peace River Block. It contained the provincial administrative centre, a police post, and a land office.

13 Edith May Birley, her sister Nina, and brother Kenneth were born in Brisbane, Australia, but moved to the Isle of Man when still children. May, a graduate nurse, served in the First World War and received the Croix de Guerre for outstanding service. After the war she bought land in Fort St John adjacent to that of her brother. When Monica arrived in 1929, she lived with May and Nina. Kenneth, a former North West Mounted Policeman, came to the Peace as an employee of Revillon Frères, a fur-trading company. In 1914 he began farming. Nina, an avid gardener, died in 1959. Although May suffered a stroke that left her partially paralysed, she lived until 1965. Monica wrote a 'Tribute' to her in the *Alaska Highway News*, 21 April 1966, in which she relates that when May wrote to her, she always began her letters, 'Dear You.' For more information see Ventress, Davies, and Kyllo, *Peacemakers*, 154–7.

14 Tommy Hargreaves owned and operated the garage in Fort St John, drove the first taxi, and also owned the 'Empty Belly' ranch at Rose Prairie.

15 Pineview school, whose first teacher, Jessie Rutherford, later married Art MacLean and taught at Fort St John.

16 This farming area, called Montney, comprises the communities of Stoddard Creek, Blueberry, and Murdale. According to local history, a small band of Indians, whose chief's name was 'Montegue' or 'Montaganais,' were camped here when the settlers arrived. Because the settlers could not pronounce his name, it was shortened to Montney (Ventress, Davies, and Kyllo, *Peacemakers*, 247–8). Monica uses various spellings in the diaries, but for the sake of clarity the present spelling of Montney has been used throughout.

17 Belle Jarvis came to the area in 1930; her home, larger than most, was the centre for many gatherings.

18 Hubert Orr came to North Pine with Belle Jarvis. His shack was across the fence from her home and he did the heavy farm work for her in exchange for board and laundry.

19 Probably refers to Mr Sinclair, who began holding services in 1929; Mr Lester, a student minister, arrived in 1930, then Mr Hilliard and Mr Toll. The latter started to build a manse at Montney in 1932. (Ventress, Davies, and Kyllo, *Peacemakers*, 255.)

20 Joe and Minnie Robbins and their children, George, Lenore, Hazel, Pearl, Lloyd, and William (Willie) arrived in 1928. Mrs Robbins was apparently a skilled cabinetmaker as well as an excellent gardener (ibid., 285).

21 Refers to the Earl Wilson family, with children Jim, David, Hazel, Bert, and Jessie and the men who drove their cattle (ibid., 287).

22 Sunday School by Post, a cornerstone of Anglican work in the Peace River, was first begun by a Mrs Gwynne of Grenfell, Saskatchewan, who originated the concept of sending Sunday School lessons, pictures, and other material by post to families in outlying areas. The idea was later developed by Bishop George Exton Lloyd and Miss Bolton, and enthusiastically embraced both by Eva Hasell and her Caravan Mission and by Monica Storrs.

23 Helen Price, mentioned frequently in Monica's earlier diaries, came from a prominent and wealthy Quebec family. She spent several years as a vanner for Eva Hasell.

24 Fred and Janet Williamson were married in England while Fred was overseas. They came to the North Pine in 1929, with their daughter, Freda Elizabeth. Fred also served as mail-carrier for many years.

25 The North Pine District covers the valley of Indian Creek and 'the slope leading down to the Beaton, or as it is better known locally, the North Pine River' (Ventress, Davies, and Kyllo, *Peacemakers*, 298).

26 The Anglican church in Fort St John, St Martin-in-the-Fields, was built in 1931 and consecrated by Bishop Rix. Funds for building the church were provided 'by two sisters from St Martin-in-the-Fields, London' (Mary Naylor, *The Fellowship of the West 1928–1978* [Montreal: Published by the Bishop of the

Anglican Diocese of Montreal, 1984], 48). See also *The North Peace River Parish, Diocese of Caledonia* (Fort St John, 1954).

27 Crystal Springs school opened in 1931, after children had been taught in a local settler's cabin for a year. The first teacher was Dorothy Tilton, who boarded with the Alex Bells.

28 Monica formed the first Guide Company north of the Peace, and was very dedicated to Guiding. As W.L. Morton points out, Guides 'were not necessarily dependent on, or centred in the church, and were certainly not denominational. They did, however, with their discipline and observances, join readily with church work in Sunday School and informed services and became, in effect, auxiliary to Sunday Schools and genuine church work (Morton, ed., *God's Galloping Girl*, xxvi).

29 Harry and Edith Waite, who was an English war bride, arrived in the Montney in 1930. Their children were Jim, Harold, Clifford, Ralph, Joyce, Connie, and Mary.

30 Probably the Alex Turner family, which arrived in 1930

31 An area of London.

32 Hold-up or Holdup, is now known as Murdale. Thelma Paynter was the first teacher there.

33 Mr and Mrs Fred Callison settled at the Holdup in 1928. Their children were John, Lynch, Norma, Elijah (called Lash), Dennis, Daisy, Molly, Pat, and Doris.

34 Benjamin Simpson (not William, as in Morton, ed., *God's Galloping Girl*, 291, n.47) also served as lay-reader at Monica's services. His lay reader's licence was issued in August 1929. Parish correspondence, Diocese of Caledonia Archives (D of C), Prince Rupert, B.C.

35 'How the Story Grew,' by O.W. Gleason, published as a pamphlet play by Eldridge Entertainment House, n.d.

36 Nebuchadnezzar's image, of which Monica seems rather fond, had feet 'part iron, part clay' in contrast to the splendour of its upper body. See Daniel 2: 31–4.

37 James and Irene McKnight with their son, Ernest, arrived at Taylor in 1920 and ca. 1927 built a 'stopping place' for travellers, which was advertised as 'Taylor's Landing Hostelry – Accommodation for Man and Beast at all hours and at all seasons' (Ventress, Davies, and Kyllo, *Peacemakers*, 47).

38 St Christopher (ca. 250), patron saint of travellers, is said to have carried people over a bridgeless river.

39 Delirium tremens, that form of delirium coupled with terrifying delusions to which heavy drinkers are liable (*Concise Oxford Dictionary*).

40 Phyllis Moon, teacher of the Peace View school, which opened in 1931,

frequently spent her holidays at the Abbey. As a Ranger, she had attained the highest level of Guiding, the order being Brownies, Guides, and Rangers.

41 Albert and Elizabeth Spence arrived in the Cecil Lake area in 1930. Their children were Jean, Marjorie, Marion, and Lorna, Albert (Bert), Sheila, and Gordon (Ventress, Davies, and Kyllo, *Peacemakers*, 373ff.).

42 Cesare (not Caesar) Copes came to Cecil Lake in 1928 and did custom-threshing as well as farming.

43 Probably Herluf Rasmussen, known locally as Olaf.

44 Anton and Lillian Framst and their children, Muriel, Doreen, and Eli, arrived in the Cecil Lake area in 1931. The Cecil Lake school, with Mrs Framst as teacher, opened the same year.

45 Fred, a son of R.H.A. Neilson, was brother to Violet, Joyce, and Gordon. Fred later became a schoolmaster in Edmonton.

46 Harriet Alexander, whose children were Evelyn, Earl, and Sam, Jr.

1932

1 Cannot identify 'Jim.' Douglas Whatmough is mentioned by Mary Naylor, *The Fellowship of the West*, 48, as Brother Wolf's first helper.

2 Daniel 3: 6ff.

3 Alice Hunter, daughter of Mr and Mrs Lester Hunter, who managed the hotel for a short period of time.

4 Thelma Howe, daughter of Gilbert and Sadie Howe, and granddaughter to the Mrs Millar with whom Monica stayed on certain weeknights during her first year in Fort St John.

5 Bert Bowes, a partner with Braden Herron in the garage then owned by Tommy Hargreaves. Vera Bowes was a sister to Braden. See Marguerite Davies and Cora Ventress, *Fort St John Pioneer Profiles* (Fort St John Centennial Committee: 1971), 36.

6 Mr G.M. Neal who taught Division I, while Miss F.L. Richards taught Division 2 of the Fort St John School (B.C. Public Scools Report).

7 The Victoria League, now known as the Victoria League for Commonwealth Friendship, was organized in 1901 to promote closer union between different parts of the then British Empire.

8 The Imperial Order Daughters of the Empire, a patriotic and philanthropic organization, was founded in Montreal in 1900 by Mrs Clark Murray.

9 The Fellowship of the West was organized in 1929 by three Montreal priests, Geoffrey Guiton, Elton Scott, and R.K. Naylor, who had been deeply moved by reports of the desperate need for clergy in the Peace River Block. The primary purpose of the Fellowship was 'to supply Church ministrations where the need seemed greatest,' and the primary method employed was 'for a

priest and a layman to go in pairs during the summer months to the dioceses of Athabaska and Caledonia (later also Edmonton)' to minister in pioneer settlements. For a detailed description see Naylor, *The Fellowship of the West*; also Morton, ed., *God's Galloping Girl*, xxvii f.

10 The Nicolas Solorenko family was one of the first to settle in the Cecil Lake area; they left the Peace in 1935.

11 The Binnels' children were Dolores, Mary, and Lloyd.

12 The hymn book was published by the Community of the Resurrection, a Church of England order, whose Mother House was the House of the Resurrection, in Mirfield, West Yorkshire. The hymns were known as 'popular' hymns, easy to sing and more appealing to the generally unchurched.

13 Dorothy Maud, called Messenger Maud because of her work as a Bishop's Messenger, was also active in the Girls' Diocesan Association; Monica also belonged to both groups.

14 The United Church of Canada was formally initiated on 10 June 1925, a union of all Canada's Methodist congregations, most of the Congregationalists, and approximately two-thirds of the Presbyterians.

15 The Book of Common Prayer was first authorized in 1662.

16 The Sunrise school was built in 1931, with Miss E. Murray as teacher. After the building was destroyed by fire, classes were resumed in the Henry Gullickson home.

17 John Brown's parents, the George Browns and their five daughters, came from Kingston, Ontario, to take up land adjoining that of John and Caroline Brown. See Ventress, Davies, and Kyllo, *Peacemakers*, 186–7.

18 Letitia Petter, school teacher at Fort St John, boarded with May Birley when Storrs first came there in 1929, and Petter and Storrs became firm friends. Petter married Braden Herron in 1935; she died tragically in an plane crash a few years later.

19 Muriel Claxton took charge of the Red Cross Outpost at Grandhaven, near Fort St John, when the previous nurse, Miss Roberts, married and moved to Rose Prairie. In 1935 Miss Claxton became head of the Gough Memorial Hospital. The building of this hospital and Miss Claxton's death are chronicled in some detail later in these diaries.

20 The Providence Hospital, built in 1931, at the instigation of Father Luc Beuglet, O.M.I., was staffed by the Sisters of Charity of the Order of Providence. The first nursing sisters were Sisters Alfred of the Cross, Catherine de Bologne, and Miss Laura Murphy, R.N., later to become Sr Marcella. See Ventress, Davies, and Kyllo, *Peacemakers*, 400f.

21 Charlie Lake, just north of Fort St John at the junction of the Moberly and Peace rivers, was used extensively to provide ice blocks for drinking water (even the hospital depended on this source), for floating logs to a small saw

mill owned by Ollie Southwick, and for recreation and camping. The annual boy scout and girl guide camps were held here. May Birley and later Monica herself also owned cottages on the lake.

22 William Colpitts married Annie Cushway; their children were Ken, Marjorie, Louise, and Charles.

23 The policeman was Constable Peter B. Smith (*Wrigley's B.C. Directory*, vol. 42, 1932, 264).

24 George Teather, a bachelor, was a close friend to the Framst family, and worked in partnership with Mr Framst. Some years after the latter's death Mrs Framst and Teather married.

25 Mr and Mrs M. Slyman began their store-cum-trading post in 1929. Although Mrs Slyman was a Roman Catholic, she was very friendly to Monica and is frequently mentioned in the diaries.

26 Frank Nasser appears to have been a partner in the Slyman's business; however, he did not stay long in the area.

27 The Smiths, with children George, Sharon, Florence, and Irene.

28 Flora and R. Leo Pickell came to Fort St John in 1923. Their sons were Cecil, William (Bill), and Owen. For more information about this prominent family see Davies and Ventress, *Fort St John Pioneer Profiles*, 18.

29 The Provincial Industrial School for Boys at Coquitlan was organized in 1904. In 1933 it had 192 boys on its rolls, ranging in age from 11 to 19 years. Very comprehensive Principal's Annual Reports list everything from nationality and reason for apprehension to daily menus. See British Columbia Sessional Papers, Coquitlan Industrial School for Boys, Principal's Annual Reports, Provincial Archives of British Columbia.

30 Rose Prairie, formerly known as Whisky Jack Creek, lies 18 miles north of Fort St John; it was first settled in 1928.

31 Mr and Mrs Alex Thompson with baby son Bertram (Buddy) arrived in the area in 1928, she being the first white woman and Buddy the first white child. Other children born to the family include Gerald, Mona, Yvonne, Gunder, and Joan; another son died in infancy (Ventress, Davies, and Kyllo, *Peacemakers*, 282–3).

32 The story of Jacob and Esau is found in Genesis 25:24f.

33 The Flemish painters, David (the Elder) 1582–1649 and his son, David (the Younger) 1610–90.

34 A quarterly review of religion, theology, and philosophy.

35 The annual boat race between the universities of Oxford and Cambridge epitomizes the fierce rivalry between the schools. Putney to Mortlake mark the points along the Thames River between which the boats race.

36 Monica crossed land belonging to several bands: Fort St John Reserve 172,

Doig River, Blueberry, Rose Prairie, and Halfway. This reference is likely to the Halfway band.

37 The Phil. Nicely family, with two daughters and a son.

38 Warren and Ida Titus both loved music, she an accomplished pianist and he playing the violin. They opened their store and trading post in 1931, then later moved to Fort St John to open 'Titus Rooms and Mercantile' (Davies and Ventress, *Fort St John*, 39).

39 Although it has not been possible to further identify Mrs Murphy, a Mr Murphy was 'handyman' in Fort St John, while Sister Marcellina was born Laura Murphy. Since this is the only family by that name in the district, Mr Murphy appears to have immigrated, as his wife hoped he would.

40 Repudiation of the Oath of Loyalty to the British Crown occurred in Ireland on 3 May 1933.

41 *Wrigley's B.C. Directory* lists 'Rev. M.E. Burch (Presbyterian)' as a resident of Fort St John in 1932.

42 Tertia, the Third One.

43 Fish or Little Stoddard Creek, north of Fort St John, was at one time head-quarters of the Hudson's Bay Company (HBC) and a focal point for incoming settlers.

44 The John Middleton family later left the Peace River; the children included Bill, Margaret, George, Lucy, Walter, and Gordon.

45 Probably Miss Margaret McIntyre, who taught in several schools in the Block, including Charlie Lake; *Wrigley's Victoria Directory*, 1932, lists the Queen Alexandra Solarium, with Dr C. Wace as medical officer.

46 Foster and Maude Morrow came to the Blueberry in 1929.

47 A reference to St Paul's description of his trials, which included the beasts of Ephesus (1 Cor. 15:32).

48 John and Betty Ardill came to the Peace in 1919, on the same boat as May Birley. Mrs Ardill was a warbride from Holland; their children were also named John and Betty. See Ventress, Davies, and Kyllo, *Peacemakers*, 75–80; also letter of J.R. Ardill to Bishop, 3 Jan. 1929 (Diocese of Caledonia Archives).

49 No further information has been found yet on these men and their sisters.

50 A dear friend of Monica's, and daughter of Archdeacon Henry Maxwell Spooner of Maidstone and Canon of Canterbury.

51 Although Margaret and Ronald Harris sent letters to the Fellowship of the Maple Leaf and also to the Bishop of Caledonia related to their Canadian visit, information about them personally has not been found.

52 Rt. Rev. George Alexander Rix (1865–1945), consecrated bishop in 1928,

annually made the long and arduous journey from Prince Rupert to the Peace River Block.

53 The story of Jonah is found in Jonah 1:3–15.

54 Iva and Iowne Sandry, who appear to have left the Peace not long after Monica's encounter with them.

55 Daughter of the Neil Stevenson family.

56 The Otto Hoffstroms homesteaded at Taylor in the late 1920s, setting up a sawmill on the south side of the river.

57 Monica describes Rolla as 'a perfectly awful little place consisting of two hotels, and two or three stores and a garage and a school, and a United Church plumped down quite naked, so to speak, on a treeless waste of prairie' (Morton, ed., *God's Galloping Girl,* 112).

58 Alfred E. Taylor, *Faith of a Moralist* (London, 1930), the Gifford Lectures, 1926–8.

59 Maud Monahan, *Life and Letters of Janet Erskine Stuart* (London, 1924). The *Week-End Book,* edited by V. Mendel and F. Meynell (published in London), was an anthology of poems, songs, and games.

60 Neil Gething arrived in the Peace River area in 1901, prospecting for minerals and coal. He found coal and began tunnelling in 1919. In 1922 his family moved to Hudson's Hope to provide the children with an education, only to find there was no school and local trappers were opposed to having one. Against all odds, Mrs Gething raised $500 locally and the government built the school. The Gething children were Lloyd, Vesta, Larry, Lillian, Wes, and Quentin. See Ventress, Davies, and Kyllo, *Peacemakers,* for more information about the Gething family and their enterprises.

61 No further information has been found to date on either Jim McNamee or 'Racehorse Ed.'

62 Mr and Mrs James (Jim) Beattie moved to 20-Mile (or Gold Bar) in 1919; their children were Louise, Mary, Clarisse, Bob, Olive, Ruth, and twins Jim and Bill (Ventress, Davies, and Kyllo, *Peacemakers,* H42–3). Jim Sr freighted, farmed, trapped, and was a Justice of the Peace, rancher, and sawmill operator.

63 Madge and Charlie Jones moved to Carbon River in 1919. They made arrangements with the Vancouver Public Libraries to receive discarded books and thus started the 'Gold Bar Library' in their home. The Joneses moved to Victoria, and when Charlie died, Madge returned to England (ibid., H36).

64 Although old-timers in the Fort St John area seemed to remember these interesting brothers, no one could definitely identify them, nor is there reference to them in any local histories or in the Fort St John archives.

65 Louise, Dennis, and Marvellee Murphy were neighbours to Joe and Larnie Barkley and their daughter, Clara.

66 The Henry Kehler family was one of the first to settle in Peace View in 1930; they were not ethnic Russians, however, but Russians of German descent.

67 Hudson or Hudson's Hope. Monica used both names but for the sake of clarity, Hudson's Hope, the official usage of the B.C. government, will be used here. Ventress, Davies, and Kyllo, *Peacemakers*, H3ff. contains a most interesting historical account of the area.

68 Canon Thomas D. Proctor, L.Th., was Rural Dean and Superintendent of the Peace River District 1929–43, and canon of St Andrew's Cathedral, Prince Rupert.

69 Arius (ca. 250–336), Alexandrian priest and heresiarch, caused great controversy because of his unorthodox views of Christ's divinity, which were condemned by the Council of Antioch (see *New Catholic Encyclopedia*, vol. 1).

70 St Athanasius (ca. 295–373) was deeply involved in the Arian disputes; he was exiled and exonerated several times for both religious and political reasons, but finally was completely victorious (ibid., vol. 1). 'Contra Mundum,' literally 'Against the World.'

71 Mr and Mrs Rodgers (Rogers) came to the Peace in 1930 with their hired man, Bill Mann, whom Mrs Rogers later married. She lost both her husband and a baby who drowned. See Morton, ed., *God's Galloping Girl*, 174.

72 Luke 10:38–42.

73 Both the 1662 and 1928 versions of the Book of Common Prayer were authorized by the Church of England.

74 A Dr Buggins practised in Fort St John, although his main office was at Dawson Creek.

75 Probably the Edwin Tuckers, who had a store and meat-cutting business in Murdale (see Ventress, Davies, and Kyllo, *Peacemakers*, 256).

76 Areas of London.

77 Harry Downey, who often did carpentering for the Abbey.

78 Miss Horne and her driver, Miss Selby; no Miss 'M.'

79 It was customary for the bishop's wife to assume a leading role in the Women's Auxilliary of the Anglican Church. After her harrowing experience it is rather interesting to read Bishop Rix's comment to Canon Proctor in 1933: 'Mrs Rix regrets that she will not be able to accompany me this year. She had such an entertaining experience last year that it is very tempting to make the effort to go again' (Parish correspondence, Peace River Block, D. of C. Archives).

80 The Dr W.A. Brown family with their five children came to Fort St John from
   Toronto in 1930. Monica refers to them as 'the charming Brown family'
   (Morton, ed., *God's Galloping Girl*, 176).

81 Esther Armstrong and her son DeLoris or Loris.

82 Unidentified; earliest burial records, which could have identified the mother,
   were destroyed in a church fire.

83 Esther (Tess) Wolfendale, who, after Bro. Wolf's death, remarried and now
   lives in Ontario. Canon Proctor wrote to Bishop Rix in 1933, 'Mrs Wolfendale
   ... is a tremendous help in the North and has made a different man of
   Wolfendale, his weak points are her strong points and it makes a splendid
   combination' (Parish correspondence, Peace R. Block, D. of C.A.).

84 Alex and Elizabeth Bell and their family arrived at the Montney in 1929.

85 In her diary of 19 September 1931, Monica calls the Phillips family 'very
   superior' people from Vancouver (Morton, ed., *God's Galloping Girl*, 263).
   Their sons were Harry and John.

86 Arthur and Beatrice Hadland, with sons Austin, Richard, and Roger, came to
   the Peace in 1928, together with Bert (H.G.) and Jennie Hadland, whose
   children were Edith, Diana, and Philip.

87 The Charles Ohland family with sons Robert, Harvey, and Roy were also
   pioneers in the Baldonnel area.

88 George Kirkpatrick settled near Taylor; Jack and his family were among
   Baldonnel's first settlers.

89 Mr Soman and his wife Mable were interested in music; Mrs Soman played the
   piano and her husband the banjo and violin. Mabel Soman was also known as
   a good cook.

90 W.R. McLeod is listed as school inspector, resident in Pouce Coupé, in
   Wrigley's B.C. Directory, 1932.

91 Both Gumbo Slim and the S. family are unidentified.

92 The Cutbank was later renamed Kiskatinaw.

93 Howard Feenie and his wife served meals to travellers, while Howard also did
   some freighting in addition to assisting Herbie Taylor on the ferry.

94 Charles and Beatrice Akister opened a store at Cecil Lake; they had an only
   daughter, Nancy.

95 Monies received in England for Monica's work were put into trust funds to be
   used as required; later these trusts were re-named the 'Samaritan Fund.'

96 As late as 1931 males outnumbered females 185 to 100 in the Peace River
   Block. See C.A. Dawson and R.W. Murchie, *Settlement of the Peace River Country*
   (Millwood, N.Y.: Kraus Reprint Co., 1974), 62.

97 The Beaver were an Athapascan tribe living in the Peace River area from the
   mountains in the west to the Peace River Falls about 40 miles downstream

from Fort Vermilion. They were a nomadic tribe with no permanent dwellings. See P.E. Goddard, 'The Beaver Indians,' *Anthropological Papers of the American Museum of Natural History* 10 (1916).

98 Frank Reid (Kansas Pete) took nine months to drive with team and wagon to the Peace River from Kansas. He lost the sight of one eye when a professional ball player, and not long after Monica's visit was forced to go to a home for the blind in Kamloops, B.C. (Ventress, Davies, and Kyllo, *Peacemakers*, 113).

99 The Clarence Morrison family with their six children; Kansas Pete was known for his love of children and the story is told that before he left for Kamloops, he gathered the district's children and bought each one a small bag of sweets (ibid., 113).

100 The two parishes in which Monica had lived with her family: St Peter's Church, Eaton Square, in London and Rochester Cathedral.

101 Refers to the furious ride described by Robert Browning in his poem 'How They Brought the Good News from Ghent to Aix,' written 1833–68.

1933

1 Reference to martyrs for the faith, Hebrews 11:37.

2 Leslie Hunter, son of Leslie Hunter, Sr.

3 Anthony (Tony) Flatt, son of Tommy and Madeline Irene Flatt, was born in Egypt, where his father served first in the army and then with a bank. They came to the Peace in 1924 because of Mrs Flatt's health. The other children in the family were Michael, Hilary, and Philomena Churchill. Tony finished his education in Fort St John, joined the army in 1940, married, and then worked in various branches of the government. He and his wife live in retirement in Edmonton (interview Vera Fast with Tony Flatt, June 1992).

4 Racing officials consulted by the editor suspect this is an error in transcription and should read: Point to Point, a common, self-explanatory racing term.

5 Henry McLeod carried freight to Fort Nelson and sometimes as far as Aklavik; the work paid approximately one dollar a day. Ventress, Davies, and Kyllo, *Peacemakers*, 91–2.

6 The Costello family settled near the Jarvis family at Cecil Lake.

7 The Indian agent in 1933 was Joe Galibois.

8 J.H. Cummins is listed as game warden in 1932; Jack Williams was his successor (*Wrigley's B.C. Directory*).

9 The story of Joseph and his brothers, the children of Jacob (Israel), is found in Genesis 42–3.

10 There are ten promises in the Guide Law, which include, among others, to be trustworthy, loyal, obedient, and pure in thought, word, and deed.

11 Robert Ogilvie arrived in the area in 1913 from Scotland and later returned to bring back his bride, Mary. There were four children: Jim, Kathleen, Eunice, and Margaret. See Ventress, Davies, and Kyllo, *Peacemakers* for more information.

12 Probably refers to the Simon Bakstad family.

13 The George Kemp family, with children Dorothy and Stanley. Mrs Kemp was especially loved in the district for her great hospitality, e.g., when she took in the nine members of the Albert Spence family, plus their two men (Ventress, Davies, and Kyllo, *Peacemakers*, 374).

14 The government agent at Pouce Coupé was M.S. Morrell; the subagent in Fort St John was Leo Pickell.

15 One of Jesus' miracles: Mark 6.

16 Sir Walter Scott (1771–1832), great Scottish novelist and poet; Stanley Weyman (1855–1928), novelist and biographer.

17 Monica several times uses the terms 'Roundheads' or 'Cavaliers' to describe local men, presumably because their large hats reminded her of the followers of Cromwell or Charles I.

18 Farmers' Institutes were first organized in British Columbia as early as 1897. Those in the Peace River Block were called the District 'J' Institutes. See 'District "J" History,' by John Close, Dawson Creek *News*, 18 August 1965. The Fort St John Horticultural Club, organized in 1923, resolved in July 1931 that 'this Agricultural Association organize a Farmers' Institute' with J.W. Abbot of Baldonnel as first president (Ventress, Davies, and Kyllo, *Peacemakers*, 182–3).

19 The Herron family arrived in the Fish Creek area in the early 1930s. Braden was known as a skilled mechanic; he also owned a trucking business in addition to his partnership in the Bowes-Herron Garage. See Davies, and Ventress, *Fort St John Pioneer Profiles*, 35–6.

20 Another reference from Genesis 42–4 to the story of Joseph and his brothers, especially to Benjamin and Manasseh.

21 The Beaver Indians signed Treaty Number 8 in 1899.

22 Wilfrid Reid (Wop) May, 1896–1952, a WWI flying ace with a Distinguished Flying Cross, became a bush pilot after demobilization. See Vancouver *Province*, 23 Nov. 1977; also Iris C. Allan, *Wop May, Bush Pilot* (Toronto, 1966).

23 F.H. Leacy, ed., *Historical Statistics of Canada* (Ottawa: 1983), shows that the Indian and Inuit population increased between 1881 and 1931 from 23,037 to 128,890.

24 The image in Daniel 2:32 had a head of 'fine gold.'

25 Philip and Emily Tompkins came to the Peace in 1919; their seven children were Eric, Brian, Alice, Art, Jim, Margaret, and Bill. 'Attachie' was their farm location.

26 Likely one of the Clarke brothers.

27 The Henry McLeod family lived by the old Hudson's Bay Company (HBC) fort.

28 Frank Beaton came to the Peace country as Factor for the HBC in 1883. He married Emma Shaw; their children were James, Mary (Mrs Ken Birley), Kenneth, George, Thomas, Margaret (Mrs Carl Mikkelson), John, Angus, Frank, Fred, Duncan, and Bill (Ventress, Davies, and Kyllo, *Peacemakers*, 13ff.).

29 There is no Bishop Hines in Canada listed in *Crockford's* for this period. The reference is almost certainly to John Hines of the Church Missionary Society, ordained priest in 1880, who served as missionary in the North West Territories 1875–88, and as Rural Dean at Cumberland House 1890–1905. See *Crockford's Clerical Directory 1900, 1910, 1920.*

30 William and Eileen Simpson and their family are mentioned frequently in the letters Monica wrote later.

31 Fred Cassie (Cassey) came north to freight in 1918.

32 W.E. Lutyens, *Notes for Meditations for Daily Use* (London, 1933); H.G. Wells, *A Short History of the World* (London, 1919).

33 John Cramer became a surveyor as well as an amateur photographer of note.

34 The son of Arthur and Mary Hadland, Roger eventually became a school teacher.

35 Mrs Brisbin (Brisbane) became housekeeper at the Gough Memorial Hospital in 1934.

36 Isabel (Isa) McArthur (1900–79) came to Naicam, Saskatchewan, in 1931, and volunteered to work as a Companion 1933–4. She returned to Scotland to practise chiropody with her father in Edinburgh, then retired to Cambridge, where she died.

37 Katherine (Kitty) Arnold, the daughter of the Conrad Arnolds, was a secretary and Sunday School teacher and very musical. She served as a Companion 1933–4 and on her return to Britain helped the Fellowship of the Maple Leaf (FML), working closely with Dr Andrews, its secretary. In 1937 she married Vernon Forbes, vice-principal of a college in Paipur, India. In 1940 they moved to Rhodes University, Grahamstown, South Africa. They raised four children before retiring to Capetown, where Kitty died.

38 Katherine (Kate) Webber (1912–) was born to the Alexander Webbers, a Nottingham surgeon and his wife. She attended Westfield College (now part of the University of London) taking a degree in Classics. Fresh from university

but anxious to do mission work, she contacted the FML and was immediately sent to the Peace River, where she served 1933–4. On her return, she taught in several private schools, until she married the Rev. Charles Earle in 1937. After a very active parish ministry and raising three children, the Earles now live in retirement in Hertfordshire.

39 The Fellowship of the Maple Leaf was organized in England in 1917; while Monica personally did not receive any aid, many of her fellow Companions were supported wholly or in part by the FML, which also supplied a modest operating grant for their work in Fort St John.

40 From Pouce Coupé Canon Proctor wrote to Bishop Rix: 'Glad to say that we have been able to get Miss Storrs down as far as Pouce Coupé Hospital for a rest before leaving for England tomorrow' (Parish correspondence, Peace River Block, 2 Nov. 1933, Diocese of Caledonia Archives). Her condition was serious indeed to merit such arrangements

1934

1 With resumption of the diaries on her return to Canada in 1934, Monica abandoned the practice of using only initials instead of names. Caroline Brown was the wife of John Brown, mentioned earlier in the diaries.

2 Gwendolen Hampshire (1876–1961), came from a Devon farm family. She attended St Christopher's College 1933–4, and came to assist Monica chiefly with housekeeping and cooking, 1935–6, although she was also experienced in artistic book-binding. She then worked at Ashmont in the Diocese of Edmonton until ca. 1941, when she returned to England to serve in the Diocese of Southwark until her retirement.

3 Nathan Noseworthy was serving in St Clement's parish, Montreal, when he agreed to be Wolfendale's successor at Fort St John for two years, together with his wife, Jean.

4 The log church of St Andrew at Sunset Prairie was built in 1930 with funds raised by Eva Hasell of the Caravan Mission; it was the first Anglican church in the Peace.

5 The Bedaux expedition, organized by Charles Bedaux, originated in Edmonton. It included two new limousines, five Citroën tractors, and some 150 horses (largely purchased in Fort St John), which were loaded with tins of gasoline and other supplies. Bedaux brought along his valet, his wife Mme Bedaux and her friend Mme Chiesa, a maid, surveyors, and a host of other personnel. The purpose ostensibly was for exploration and mapping, but it was widely thought to be publicity for Citroën. By October, the expedition had turned back, 200 miles short of its destination. See Ventress, Davies, and Kyllo, *Peacemakers*, 405–7; file in the University of Alberta Archives; file in

the Provincial Archives of Alberta; Edmonton newspapers July and October 1934.

6 St Christopher's College, Blackheath, London, was opened in 1909 as a training college for women interested in Anglican church work. It initially offered courses in Bible, prayer book, Church history, psychology, and teaching methods; its charge was 'to explore and experiment and do all in its power to raise religious education to the level attained by the best secular teachers' (Founder's memoir, St Christopher's *College Terminal Magazine*, 1953). The school also sought to 'balance the spiritual with the material [secular].' Because most of Monica's Companions attended St Christopher's, its influence on her work is significant.

7 Tommy was the only child of Fred and Martha Kingsley; Fred operated a barbershop at Fish Creek.

8 Douglas Birley, son of Mary and Kenneth Birley. May and Nina Birley had a tennis court on their property.

9 Edith was the daughter of John and Louise Hodgson. Other siblings included Myrtle, Margaret, Earl, and Grace. Joseph Charles (Scotty) Stewart often helped Monica with work at the Abbey. She describes him as 'dark and good-looking, a tremendous worker, cheerful and lively and withall devout' (unpublished segment of August 1935 diary).

10 H.G. (Bert) Hadland was a warden of St John's, Baldonnel, and a community leader.

11 The chapel, completely restored, is now on the grounds of the Fort St John–North Peace Museum.

12 Rev. Mr Gordon Peddie, who succeeded Mr Burch.

13 The chapter on love.

14 Although mentioned in *Peacemakers* there is no further information on this family.

15 This is the first mention of a shepherd's pipe; Peter Storrs, Monica's nephew, believes it may have been a gift from her brother, Sir Ronald Storrs.

16 Joyce stayed with the McArthur family from the fall of 1934 to May 1936.

17 Rosaline Beck, whose mother married a Mr Chancellor, left the Peace River for Edmonton during the next year.

18 No Claytons are named in local histories for this period, although a Walter Clayton, barrister, is listed in the Pouce Coupé section of *Wrigley's B.C. Directory*, vol. 42, 1932.

19 The Julius Kisselbachs took up land near the Indian Reserve in 1930, but moved into Fort St John shortly thereafter. He was a carpenter as well as janitor for St Martin's.

20 The Nor'Pioneer Women's Institute, organized in 1933 by the Cecil Lake women, met in each other's homes once a month

21 The Rev. P.J. Andrews, 1884–1974, educated in Saskatchewan and ordained priest in 1916, joined the Fellowship of the Maple Leaf in 1920 at the behest of Bishop George Exton Lloyd, and from 1921–54 served as its secretary. See *The Canadian Churchman*, 21 Oct. 1915, 12 Jan. 1922, Sept. 1974 (thanks to M. Barber).

22 Prebendary Gough chaired the FML Board in 1933.

23 The daughter of Ed and Edith Alexander, Alma with her brother Howard brought the fire under control and rescued her sister Margaret and brothers Everett and Kenneth.

24 'Whoever has two coats must share with anyone who has none' (Luke 3:11).

25 'Pet' was Petronella Moor (1896–1978), Monica's younger sister, married to Dr Frewin Moor, who lived near Canterbury.

26 Audrey Martley (1904–83), daughter of the Rev. Canon H.L. Martley of Chichester and his wife, attended St Christopher's College 1931–2 and left for Canada a short time thereafter. She was primarily a Caravan Mission worker but assisted Monica 1934–5.

27 The Anglican Sunday School Caravan Mission was organized by Eva Hasell in 1920 to reach children who were too far away from a church to attend Sunday School. The work was initially carried on mostly by British women who paid their own expenses and worked in pairs (a driver and a teacher) to each self-contained van.

28 Peter Smith, who farmed in the Cecil Lake area, later helped build St Matthias Church.

29 Likely the Rev. W. Simpson, who was educated at Edinburgh.

30 Aline and Betty, Bob and Dan, were the children of Ross and Margaret Darnall (not Darnell), who arrived in the area in 1928.

1935

1 A Vestal Virgin was a priestess who had charge of the sacred fire in the temple of Vesta. Storrs named everything – every broom, pot or even potholder. Tony, therefore, is carrying 'Wolf,' a firepot containing live coals from the kitchen stove.

2 The sons of Mrs Thompson, who was affectionately known as 'Granny,' were Conrad, Newton, Walter, and Oliver; there was one daughter, Mabel.

3 Philip, son of the H.G. Hadlands, died at the age of 11.

4 The Levites, a priestly order, served in the temple.

5 The Claire Stokkes returned from Fort Nelson to open a hotel and store in Fort St John. Mrs Stokke's mother was Mrs W. Waide; the Waides and Stokkes came to the Peace together in 1919 (Ventress, Davies, and Kyllo, *Peacemakers*).

6 Jennie married Alexander Nicolson at St Martin's Church.

7 Roy Taylor, a big man, made local news when he was seriously injured and a small ski-equipped plane, landing in front of the hospital to fly him to Edmonton, was unable to take off. Monica describes the incident later in the diaries, as do Ventress, Davies, and Kyllo, *Peacemakers*, 145. Abbie Taylor was Roy's wife.

8 Mrs Kerkhoff also served as organist at St Martin's.

9 Monica's mother, Lucy Anna Cust, came from Ellesmere in Shropshire. She was a cousin to the Earl Brownlow, after whose death her brother Adelbert became the fifth Baron Brownlow. Mrs Storrs died in 1923 after a long illness.

10 King George V and Queen Mary.

11 Father Jungbluth or Youngblood, as he was called.

12 Priscilla Oldacres (1905–48), daughter of Mr and Mrs Frederick Oldacres of Surrey, ran her own clinic for dogs in Byfleet, Surrey. She served as a Companion 1935–40, when she married the Rev. (later Bishop) Russell Brown at St Martin's church; they moved to Sherbrooke, Quebec, where she died very suddenly, leaving three small children. Priscilla had a way with animals. When Monica asked her about it, 'she explained to me that this was done by the use of certain words that no animal could disobey – only they were so terrible that I must never ever hear them' (Fort St John Museum file).

13 Ella and Emery Watson and their children, including Jimmy who won the dog race, and grandfather Henry Banghart came to Bear Flat in 1931. Mr Banghart, in his eighties, rode on a bed fixed to the hayrack, over which a tent was draped. They left for land near Gibbons, Alberta, in 1935, returning to the Peace again a few years later (Ventress, Davies, and Kyllo, *Peacemakers*, 73).

14 As medical officer for the natives in the Fort St John area, Dr Brown not only attended treaty days to examine those who were ill, but also toured the reserves once a year.

15 Catherine Newby became Principal of St Christopher's College in 1932 and retired in 1943. She died in 1958. Monica Hardcastle, her successor, commented on her 'vivid mind, vital personality and almost impish humour' (Oct. 1958 college newsletter).

16 It is interesting to speculate whether these were the same three women Monica mentions in her diary of February 1930 who 'are touring North West Canada on their legs' (Morton, ed., *God's Galloping Girl*, 62). Mary Percy Jackson, a pioneer doctor in northern Alberta, also met 'three mad Englishwomen' on skis that same year (ibid., 293n67).

17 Emily Crawford, an intelligent, strong-willed woman, owned and operated the XY Farm, which featured registered Hereford cattle. She also wrote articles promoting the Peace River country and its agricultural potential.

18 Sylvia W. Steward, a graduate of St Christopher's, had worked in Alberta, in a boys' hostel among other places; she then moved to Ashmont to work with Sybil Grove. In 1936 Sylvia was joined by Marion Kettleworth (now Dame Marion) as well as by Gwen Hampshire (Bishop Sovereign's correspondence, Provincial Archives of Alberta).

19 Rosemary Geraldine Owen (1908–87), daughter of Col. and Mrs Charles R.B. Owen of Llangarren, Wales, trained at St Christopher's College (1932, 1933–5); she also received an 'inter-Diocesan Certificate of Recognition' for her work with women. She served as a Companion of the Peace 1935–7; on her return to Britain she was told by doctors that she would be unable to resume work in the North, and therefore took up work in the Diocese of Chester. When her health broke down in 1943 she changed her line of work completely. She received the 'Certificate for Plain Cookery' from Edinburgh College of Domestic Science and worked in that capacity in the Bishop's Palace and other places. She retained her great sense of service to others until the time of her death. Interview, Vera Fast with Miss Patricia Owen, 1992.

20 In the federal election of 14 October 1935, the incumbent Conservatives suffered a disastrous defeat at the hands of the Liberal party, although the C.C.F. and the Reconstruction party also gained some seats.

21 A reference to the story of the Good Samaritan who took the wounded traveller to the inn and looked after him (Luke 10:33–5).

22 Gradually the Companions became more formal in the attire worn to services: from corduroy breeches and beige top to black cap and gown, to the blue smock with red cord and smocking to wear over breeches, and a veil (interview with Sr Dorothy Warr, 1992). However, Mary Humphries comments that by 1947 no formalities in dress during services were observed.

1936

1 Travel through Canada between Britain and Australia was routine at this time.

2 Mrs Bill Bedier, whose baby, Bruce, was the first child born at the Outpost Hospital. The story Monica relates later in the diaries about Bill's accident is also found in Ventress, Davies, and Kyllo, *Peacemakers*, 368.

3 Tom Boichuck (not Boychuck) was the first mail carrier to Cecil Lake.

4 Naaman the leper was commander of the armies of King Aram; he was completely cured when he followed the directions of the prophet Elisha (2 Kings 5).

5 Harold Sexton became Bishop of the Province of British Columbia in 1936. The Empress Hotel (not Empire) was completed in 1908 by the Canadian Pacific Railway.

6 Sir Richard Stewart Lake came to Canada in 1883 and married Dorothy

Schreiber of Ottawa in 1910 He served as lieutenant-governor of Saskatch-ewan 1915–21, was active on a national level with the Red Cross, and retired to Victoria.

7 The Prince of Wales Fairbridge Farm School, in existence 1935–61, 'was part of a philanthropic scheme aimed at strengthening the British Empire and improving the condition of underprivileged British children. [It] was con-ceived by Kingsley Fairbridge, a South African–born reformer.' The Prince of Wales led an appeal for funds for the Canadian farm school (hence the name), and 1100 acres were purchased at Cowichan Station, near Duncan, B.C. See original ms, 'The Prince of Wales Fairbridge Farm School,' Provin-cial Archives of British Columbia.

8 Deaconess Margaret Robinson came from Putney and trained at the Rochester and Southwark Diocesan Theological College for Women. She attended St Christopher's 1912–13, and was ordained deaconess in Winches-ter. She worked in both Vancouver and Victoria before retiring to England, where she died suddenly within a week of her arrival in April 1961.

9 The Rt Rev. Arthur Edward Burgett (1869–1942) was born in India and educated at Cambridge and Oxford. He served as Bishop of Edmonton 1932–40, when he resigned because of ill health. He is buried in Jasper Park, at his request.

10 William Aberhart (1878–1943), called 'Bible Bill' by his detractors, was a Baptist minister and high school teacher when he founded the Calgary Prophetic Bible Institute in 1929. He became Social Credit premier of Alberta in 1935 and remained in office until his death.

11 The evangelistic team of Dwight L. Moody, who preached, and Ira Sankey, who directed the music, was an American phenomenon. One of the best-loved of Sankey's books was *Sacred Songs and Solos* (London and Edinburgh,: n.d.), a copy of which survives in the Fort St John Museum.

12 Sir Henry Walford, eminent organist, educator, and composer, held a position at St George's Chapel, Windsor, among other achievements. Harvey Grace was an organist and writer on music, and editor of the *Musical Times.*

13 Agnes Ayling trained as a nurse and also at St Brigid's House (College), which opened in the Highbury area of London in 1923, for the training of young women for work overseas. She came to assist at Cecil Lake and served there 1936–8, when she left for Drayton Valley, Alberta. In 1944 Agnes married the Rev. Mr A. Hunt and returned to the parish ministry in England. She now lives in retirement in Hertfordshire.

14 Hitler broke the Treaty of Locarno by sending troops into the demilitarized Rhineland, whereupon war seemed imminent, yet Storrs seems even more upset about Italy's invasion of Ethiopia (Abyssinia).

15 Hockey, dances, and theatre groups appear to have been the main sources of

entertainment during the 1930s in the Peace River Block. Some plays were performed locally first and then repeated in places like Rolla.

16 R.G. Sprinkling taught at Fort St John together with Miss Rutherford and Miss Petter.

17 Donald was the son of Victor and Kathleen Peck. They moved into the Hudson's Hope area in 1923, with their four sons, Vernon, Donald, Keith, and Bruce. Mrs Peck was a trained nurse, while Mr Peck farmed and trapped.

18 Stanley Baldwin, prime minister of Great Britain, and 1st Earl Baldwin of Bewdley; Archbishop Cosmo Gordon Lang, 1st Baron of Lambeth, and Archbishop of Canterbury in 1936.

19 To Troop the Colours 'is to perform that portion of the ceremonial known as Mounting the Guard in which the Colours are received' (*Oxford English Dictionary*, vol. 18).

20 The Ceremony of the Keys takes place every evening at 10 p.m., when the Tower's three main gates are locked for the night, and an exchange of sentries takes place. See R.J. Minney, *The Tower of London* (London: Prentice-Hall, 1970).

21 *Sphere* is a London illustrated news magazine.

22 Mrs Selinka (Zelinke), a former pastry cook in Europe.

23 'The Iron Ann,' by Arthur Grahame and Adelaide St Clare, published by Stevenson Augusta as a Children's Classic in Dramatic Form (n.p., n.d.).

24 Mabel Causton, approximately ten years Monica's senior, was a close friend who actively assisted in the distribution of her diaries and the collection of funds for her mission. During the war, Monica and her sister worked weekends in canteens and a munitions factory in Woolwich, where she met the other Causton and Miss Stubbington.

25 The site was discovered by Capt. George Vancouver in 1791; the city was incorporated in 1886.

26 The store was moved by Mr McQueen from Dawson City for $600. It later became the Central Department Store. Carl and Anne Donnis, who opened a store in Taylor in the early 1920s, had six sons and three daughters. See Ventress, Davies, and Kyllo, *Peacemakers*, 15.

27 Russell Featherstone Brown (1900–88), served the North Peace parish 1936–40. He married Patricia Oldacres at St Martin's in 1940 with Canon Proctor officiating. Mr Brown was consecrated Bishop of Quebec in 1960; after his retirement in 1972 he volunteered with CUSO as a teacher in Papua New Guinea until 1975. Bishop Brown was very enthusiastic about getting Storrs's diaries into print.

28 Percy and Phyllis Freer were the children of George and Edith Freer. The family were Methodist but had no difficulty with Monica's Anglican ways.

29 Daughter of the Mrs Brisbin who looked after Monica during an illness before her return to England in 1933.

30 Reference to the civil war then raging in Spain.

31 Caedmon, the 7th-century shepherd-poet and monk who was known to prefer his cattle to performing at entertainments.

32 Jack Bennett, son of Tom and Mary Louise Bennett, served in the navy during the Second World War and was awarded the Military Medal. Monica speaks highly of him, commenting that although he sat with the men and boys in back of the church, he alone would kneel for prayers (unpublished segment of diary).

33 Elinor Wordsworth Higginbotham (1904–90), was the daughter of George Higginbotham, a mechanical engineer of Cheadle, Cheshire, and a great great granddaughter of the poet William Wordsworth. She trained as a gardener at the Studleigh Agricultural College, attended St Christopher's 1935–6, and served as a Companion 1936–9. She returned again (1947–9) to work at Cecil Lake. Elinor loved music and sang in the Wells Cathedral Choir for many years after she returned to England to care for her aging parents. She also supplied much information for both this volume of Monica's diaries and for *God's Galloping Girl.*

34 Dr Garnet Kearney arrived in Fort St John in 1935 and stayed some 25 years.

35 The schoolteacher who boarded with the Tompkins.

36 Clinton Parsons, whose children were Guy, Alice, Ray, and Lee; Ray has been mentioned previously in Monica's diaries.

37 Cecilia returned to Oxford to read Theology for two terms, then, in 1938, became Warden of the Talbot Settlement in Bromley, Kent, a position that involved visiting, 'all kinds of social work, particularly on the side of children's moral welfare work' (St Christopher's College newsletter). She also lectured at the College and was active in the Fellowship of the Maple Leaf. In 1992 she was living in retirement in London.

38 Mrs Wilfrid Sowden, whose daughter, Dorothy, is mentioned frequently in Storrs's diaries.

39 The abdication crisis of Edward VIII climaxed on 10 December when he signed the instrument of abdication, after a reign of 10 months and 22 days.

40 The ethnic origin of the settlers in the Peace River at this time was 50.2 per cent British.

41 Mrs Wallis Warfield Simpson was to become the Duchess of Windsor. A morganatic marriage was considered, whereby Mrs Simpson would become the King's legal wife but not be crowned Queen; however, this was deemed unacceptable.

1937

1 Nels and Rosetta Westergaard came to the Peace in 1928; Nels was both trapper and rancher. Their children were Gloria, Matt, Lyle, Deedie, Rita, Sidney, Stanley, and Elmer. Mrs Westergaard remembered one two-year period when she did not see another white woman (Ventress, Davies, and Kyllo, *Peacemakers*, 99).

2 Mary Louise Bennett was repeatedly praised in interviews with former Companions for her kindness and serenity. Jack Bennett also remembered this trip his mother made: 'First time in her life on a saddle horse and made the 75 mile trip over rough country in two days' (ibid., 61).

3 The Jensens farmed at Cecil Lake.

4 A widely distributed patent medicine for rheumatism and all aches and pains.

5 Edward was the elder son of the Tom Bennetts, who, like Jack, frequently assisted 'Bruno.' When he expressed an interest in entering the ministry, the priest tutored him extensively and Edward entered MDTC, was ordained, and later served the Episcopal Church in the U.S.A. for many years (ibid., 62; Naylor, *The Fellowship of the West*, 109).

6 Dr V.B. Szibgy was born in Budapest, Hungary. He left Fort St John in 1952 for Fort Nelson; the Fort St John Museum contains memorabilia related to his practice.

7 Mrs Andrew Henderson, listed in *Wrigley's B.C. Directory*, 1932.

8 George Bouffioux, trapper, farmer, and rancher, was in partnership with Emily Crawford; local history credits him and not Mrs Crawford with obtaining Victoria Peace, the buffalo, from the Dominion Government for breeding purposes (see Ventress, Davies, and Kyllo, *Peacemakers*, 162).

9 Commander Edward Reginald Mayo Geake of Pouce Coupé and Major John Hartley of Vancouver, prospector and engineer, were killed by bandits on 6 Nov. 1937, at Coamp, Duranga Province, Mexico. Commander Geake, who left an estate of $300,000, some of it bequeathed to local residents, had been a member of the Bedeaux expedition that Monica describes. See the Dawson Creek paper for Friday, 12 Feb. 1937.

10 Allan Quartermain was the hero of approximately 40 boys' adventure stories, written by Rider Haggard between 1885 and 1927.

11 Mrs Lowe came to Moose River in 1920 with her son, Allan, as Jim Good's housekeeper. She apparently brought a piano with her in the covered wagon (Ventress, Davies, and Kyllo, *Peacemakers*, 377).

12 Moose River was later renamed Alces River.

13 A Bennett wagon, more commonly a Bennett buggy, consisted of a car body

without its engine, drawn by horses. It was named after the depression-era prime minister, R.B. Bennett.

14 George was the eldest of the six sons of the Arthur Lynne family of Cecil Lake.

15 Dewey Simmonds died a year after opening a store in the area; his widow, J.B. or Ma, carried on the business.

16 The coronation of King George VI and Queen Elizabeth on 12 May at Westminster Abbey. Approximately 1,000,000 people lined the streets to see the procession.

17 Actually Christ Church Cathedral in Montreal.

18 Monica uses the term, which means 'to rush noisily,' quite frequently in these latter diaries.

19 'The Bathroom Door,' by Gertrude E. Jennings (New York: n.d.).

20 The teacher probably was Miss E.M. Magee, who taught the lower grades at Fort St John at this time.

21 Bob Beattie, a brother to Jim Beattie, served with the British army in India. In 1927 he married Bessie; their three sons, Donald, Robert, and Gerry, were later joined by daughters Fern and Bertha, then Arnold and Cecil.

22 Count Vladimir (Jim) Ignatieff, Ph.D., and his brothers Nicholas, Alexis, George (well-known Canadian diplomat), and Leonide were sons of Count Paul Ignatieff who left Russia in 1919. Vladimir and Nicholas operated a ranch near Dunvegan and frequently took parties of students on camping expeditions (see typed 'Memoir' in University of Alberta Archives).

23 Hope Onslow (1908–89), daughter of Maj. and Mrs G.A. Onslow, Shropshire, trained at the College of the Ascension 1936–7, and served as a Companion 1937–44, in spite of being terrified of horses! She married the local game warden, Robert Symons, in 1945 and together they moved into a remote area of the Peace to the Hope Springs Ranch; later they retired to Silton, Saskatchewan. They had one daughter, Marigold, who was Monica's godchild. Hope contributed some of her memories of Monica to Morton, ed., *God's Galloping Girl*, xxxiii f., and was also most helpful in providing information used in these pages.

24 Mildred Morse received her training through the Church Missionary Society. She was the daughter of the Rev. and Mrs Stanley R. Morse of Worthing, Sussex, and served as a Companion 1937–44, then returned to Europe for social-service work with the British Army of Occupation. In 1945 she married a Major Polkinhorn. Mildred was not particularly interested in the visiting aspect of her work, but took such great delight in the little house, Bethlehem, in Taylor where she was situated, that co-workers called her 'house-proud.'

25 The College of the Ascension opened in 1923, as one of a group of Selly Oak

colleges outside Birmingham. It was a Church of England training centre for women, supported by the Society for the Propagation of the Gospel for its overseas missionaries; its diploma was also recognized by the Inter-Diocesan Board for Women's Work. See Margaret D. Western, *The Story of the College of the Ascension* (London: SPG, rev., 1954).

26 R. Gow, 'The Sausage,' (New York: Samuel French, n.d.).

27 Jean Hanson, wife of Herman Hanson, died at the age of 20 (St Martin's church register, Diocese of Caledonia archives).

28 Somewhat satirically named for the Scottish Presbyterian reformer, known for his stern and unbending ways.

29 Alwin Holland attended McGill University; he taught school in lower B.C., then visited New Zealand and Australia before enlisting in the First World War. Upon his release from a prisoner-of-war camp, he came to the Peace in 1919 to take up land, some of which he later sold to Monica. He also taught school in most of the North Peace schools, wrote his surveyor's examinations, and started a Presbyterian mission. See Ventress, Davies, and Kyllo, *Peace-makers*, 399.

Ivor Mowick, also Movick or Moik, is mentioned frequently by Monica, but little information is available about him.

1938–9

1 A London department store, in fashionable Sloan Square.

2 Mary Magdalene, 'from whom seven devils had gone out,' appears often in the gospel narrative, including the resurrection story.

3 The Rev. Geoffrey Guiton (1892–1947), one of the founders of the Fellowship of the West, served in the Fort St John area, where Storrs met him, during the summers of 1930 and 1931. In 1932 he became Headmaster of the Harriet Buchanan High School for Boys at Palampur, India. He spent many of his holidays on expeditions to Tibet, gathering information that eventually won him election to the Royal Geographic Society of London. He died suddenly in India (see Naylor, *Fellowship of the West*, 162–7).

4 The building of St Matthias was largely financed by the Young People of St Matthias Church, Westmount, Quebec. Its builder was Newton Thompson (ibid., 73).

5 St Peter's Church building was partially financed by St Peter's, Town of Mount Royal, Quebec, on land donated by the HBC. Local labour supplied the unusually fine logs; Hugh Murray, builder (ibid.).

6 Harry Downey of Cecil Lake also built Burch Presbyterian Church in Fort St John.

7 The Rev. Hugh Mortimer, educated at Bishop's University, served as rector of a Montreal church before going to Fort St John. Here he stayed from 1944–9, not only ministering to the six-point parish but also active in community affairs, both cultural and social. He returned to parish work in Montreal, then enlisted as a naval chaplain in 1952. He and his wife retired to Victoria (interview, Vera Fast with Hugh Mortimer, June 1992).

8 Deane, from the Town of Mount Royal, assisted Guiton during most of the latter's tour of the Fellowship of the West's posts in the Peace River Block.

9 The proposed annexation of Czechoslovakia's Sudeten territory by Germany.

10 Sir Neville Chamberlain, prime minister of Great Britain, flew to Germany on 14 September 1938 to make a personal plea to Chancellor Adolf Hitler to avert war.

11 Hezekiah, King of Judah, received a message from the King of Assyria, threatening destruction. He took the letter 'and spread it before the Lord' (2 Kings 19:14ff.).

12 Bob Ferguson and his wife Maude, built the new, beautiful log hotel in Hudson's Hope, ca. 1930.

13 F.D. Roosevelt, president of the United States, made a personal plea for peace; the front page of the *New York Times*, 29 September, read 'Roosevelt Plea a Factor.'

14 Orson Welles, one of cinema's greatest producers, shocked the nation with his terrifying radio drama 'War of the Worlds,' based on a story by H.G. Wells.

15 Fred Gaylor operated the telegraph at Hudson's Hope until 1942, when he was transferred to Fort St John.

16 Munich only deferred the war when the allies agreed to the annexation of Sudetenland to Germany.

Postscript

1 George K.A. Bell, 1883–1958, Bishop of Chichester 1929–57. See Ronald C.D. Jasper, *George Bell: Bishop of Chichester* (London, 1967).

2 The Committee was organized in 1937, but owed its existence to prior Anglican relief organizations; it sought guarantors from among Church of England adherents to ensure that none of the refugees would become dependent on the state. All casework in Germany was left to the Society of Friends, with the Committee paying the salary of one worker. The George Bell Papers, vols 27–35, Lambeth Palace Library, London, hold most of the information still extant on this Committee and its work.

3 Horst (Hugh) Gunter Schramm, born Berlin, 26 January 1927, to Helmut and Hildegard Schramm. Helmut Schramm is believed to have been killed on

the Russian front; his wife escaped to Shanghai, China, with her youngest son. She and Hugh were later reunited when she was admitted to the United States after the war.

4 Arwed (David) Lewinski, born Frankfurt am Main, 3 January 1929, the only child of Walther and Kathe Sandman Lewinski. Although there is no documentation, Mrs Lewinski seems to have died in a transport on her way to the concentration camp; her husband survived Auschwitz. David and his wife, Nora, flew to Germany in 1953 to be reunited with his father.

5 Trains, boats and, in a few instances, planes transporting Jewish refugee children to Britain from Europe.

6 In spite of urging by the British Government, Canada did not then open its doors to Jewish refugees. 19 February 1939: '... the Canadian government is not yet admitting Jewish refugees.' Irving Abella and Harold Troper, *None Is Too Many: Canada and the Jews of Europe 1933–1948* (Toronto: Lester Publishing Ltd, 1991), 53, 70, 101f.

7 Morton, ed., *God's Galloping Girl*, xlii.

8 The original letters were destroyed when the headquarters of the FML were bombed during the Blitz.

9 Humorously described by Monica in an article published in the *Alaska Highway News*, August 1947.

10 Mary Duncan Jones, daughter of the Very Rev. Arthur S. Duncan Jones, served on Miss Hasell's vans for two summers, then returned to Canada because she 'loved it right from the start.' She attended St Christopher's and became engaged to Thomas Humphries before leaving to become one of Monica's Companions. The Humphries were married at Hudson's Hope in 1948, and served the mission both there and at the Abbey. Mary still lives an active life in retirement at Fort St John (interview, Vera Fast with Mary Humphries, June 1994).

11 Very little is known of Patricia Tottenham, except that she came to Fort St John with Storrs and Mary Duncan Jones in 1947, but left for Montreal after several months. It seems likely that a personality conflict developed between her and Monica.

12 Bernice Hunten, daughter of the Asherton Huntens of Johnville, Quebec, visited Monica at Fort St John and decided to stay as a Companion. She served in the area 1948–50, and wished to remain after Monica's retirement, but the Bishop felt Fort St John was overstaffed and would not provide a grant for her room and board, much to Monica's dismay (Clergy files, 2 Nov. 1950, Diocese of Caledonia Archives). Hunten, therefore, went to assist at the Indian Boarding School at Prince Albert, Saskatchewan.

13 Ethel Queenie Calvert was the daughter of Mr and Mrs Rhodes Calvert, a

solicitor practising in Headingley, Leeds. A very independent woman, Queenie came to Canada with the Caravan Mission, but repeatedly ran into problems with either Miss Hasell or local church authorities. She thoroughly respected Monica, however, and worked as a Companion in 1944, returned to take charge of Taylor in 1950, and finally became responsible for closing the Mission in 1952. She also assisted Agnes Ayling at Drayton Valley as housekeeper for some months. Queenie died at her home in Surrey in 1971.

14 Harmer to David and Nora Lewinski, 27 Dec. 1967.

15 Monica loved the work of the Village Evangelists, an organization co-founded in 1948 by her friend Evelyn Gedge, with its aim 'the evangelization of the England of our day.' See Archbishop Geoffrey Fisher Papers, vol. 24, 41ff., Lambeth Palace Library, for detailed reports and correspondence related to its work and founding.

16 Adeline Harmer to Hugh Schramm, 27 Dec. 1967.

17 Quoted in Morton, ed., *God's Galloping Girl*, xlix.

PHOTO CREDITS

Index

Abbey, the, 3, 14–15, 17, 23–4, 27, 157, 171, 190, 200–1
Adams, Claire, 17
Akister, Charles, Bernice, 92, 135, 196–7
Alaska Highway, 25–6
Alberta, 6–7, 105
Alexander, Alma, 135, 224n23
Alexander, Mrs Sam, 45
Alexander clan, 31–2, 209n7
Allen, Robin, and sisters, 71, 152
Andrews, Rev. P.J., 135, 149, 167, 224n21
Anglican church. *See* Church of England
Anglican Women's Training College, 8
Archbishops' Western Canada Fund, 5
Archibald, Vida, 203n8
Ardill, John and Betty, 71, 160, 215n48
Ardill, Johnny, 160
Armstrong, Esther, 87
Armstrong, Loris, 87
Arnold, Katherine (Kitty), 120, 221n37
Athabasca, diocese of (Anglican), 7

Ayling, Agnes, 158–9, 164, 178–9, 189, 194–6, 227n13

Bakstad, Simon family, 105–6
Baldonnel, 31–2, 38–9, 41, 45, 50, 57, 81, 169, 185, 209n9
Barkley, Joe, Larnie, and Clara, 79
Bear Flat, 165
Beaton, Frank and Emma, 113–14, 221n28
Beattie, Jim and Elizabeth, and family, 77–9, 115, 117, 131, 216n62
Beattie, Robert and Elizabeth (Bessie), and family, 182, 231n21
Beaver tribe, 18, 93, 101, 218n97
Beck, Rosaline, 132–3, 163–6, 184
Bedeaux Expedition, 125, 222n5
Bedier, Bill, and family, 155–6
Bell, Alex and Elizabeth, 87
Bell, George K.A. (bishop of Chichester), 199
Bell, Mildred, 88
Bennett, Edward, 25, 174, 230n5
Bennett, Jack, 166, 189, 229n32
Bennett, Mary Louise (Mrs Tom), 173, 230n2
Bethlehem, 129, 157, 171

Binnell family, 51, 213n5
Birch (Burch), Rev., 69
Birley, Kenneth, 14, 18, 46, 48, 89,
  153, 169, 209n13
Birley, May, 24, 32, 46, 48, 62, 88–9,
  94, 103, 105, 108, 121, 127, 155–6,
  167, 171, 178–9, 189, 209n13
Birley, Nina, 121, 209n13
Bishop's Messengers, 7–8, 17, 203n8
Blueberry River, 59, 70, 83
Boichuck (Boychuck), Tom, 156
Bosanquet, Aylmer, 5
Bouffioux, George, 175, 230n8
Bowes, Bert, 49, 109–10, 130
Brandon, diocese of (Anglican), 8
Brisbin (Brisbane), Mrs, housekeeper,
  120
Brisbin, Eileen, 165, 184
British Columbia, 3, 6–7, 17
Brown, Johnny, 53, 123, 213n17
Brown, Rev. (later Bishop) Russell, 11,
  164, 166, 173–4, 177–81, 185–6,
  189–92, 193–5, 197, 228n27
Brown, Dr W.A., 103, 111, 120–1, 144,
  147–9, 168, 218n80
Brown, Mrs W.A., 86
Buggins, dentist, 84
Burgett, Arthur E. (bishop of Edmon-
  ton), 18, 157, 186, 227n9

Cache Creek, 96, 117
Caledonia, diocese of (Anglican), 11,
  14, 18, 212n9
Callison, Fred, and family, 37–8, 65,
  211n33
Calvert, Ethel Queenie, 201, 234n13
Carbon River, 76, 78, 131, 182
Carlisle, diocese of (Anglican), 5
Cassie (Cassey), Fred, 116
Causton, Mabel, 26, 162–4, 167–9,
  195, 228n24

Causton, Violet, 162, 164, 167–9
Cecil Lake, 43
Chancellor, Mrs, 166
Charlie Lake, 57, 90, 93, 94, 97–8,
  137, 144–5, 213n21
Cheverton family, 55
Cheverton, Harvey, 42, 51, 54–7, 61–2,
  64–5, 129, 136
Church of England, 3–4, 6, 8–10,
  12–13, 18, 20, 45, 68, 86, 101–2,
  111, 166, 200
Church of England Committee for
  Non-Aryan Christians, 199, 233n2
Clarke, Nona, 5
Claxton, Muriel, 56, 83–4, 90, 93, 97,
  102, 114, 126–7, 135, 141, 156, 158,
  177–80, 192–4
Clayton family, 132–3
College of the Ascension, 185, 231n25
Colpitts, William, and family, 57, 89,
  214n22
Companions of the Peace, 3, 4, 6, 8,
  10–11, 15–17, 20, 22–3, 27, 42, 95,
  123, 139, 158–9, 167, 171, 185
Copes, Cesare, 43, 212n42
Costello family, 99
Cramer, John, 117
Cran, Duncan, 13
Crawford, Emily, 134, 150, 175,
  225n17
Cree Indians, 18, 101, 113–14, 157
Crystal Springs School, 35, 211n27
Cushway, Sam, 177
Cust, Lucy (Mrs John Storrs), 3, 145,
  225n9
Cutbank, later Kiskatinaw, 91
Cuthbert, Alfred, 150, 154, 165, 184
Cuthbert family, 150, 180
Cuthbert, Peggy, 132–3, 150
Cuthbert, Robert, 196
Cuthbert, Roy, 165, 173, 184–6

Darnell (Darnall), Aline, 138
Darnell, Betty, 139
Dawson Creek, 20, 39, 49, 65, 74, 87, 90–2, 106–7, 109, 118–19, 124, 129, 148, 166–7, 171, 174, 191
Deane, Norton, 193
Deep Creek, 132
Donis, John, 164
Downey, Harry, 193
Drift Pile, 101

Earle, Kate. See Webber, Katherine
East Montney Circuit, 62
Edmonton, 6, 15, 65, 119, 123, 134, 144, 146–9, 157, 162, 184–6, 189, 200
Erinlea, 145

Farmers' Institute, 108, 220n18
Feenie, Howard, 91, 218n93
Fellowship of the Maple Leaf, 6–7, 15, 22, 25–6, 120, 135, 167, 201, 222n39
Fellowship of the West, 23, 49, 195, 212n9
Ferguson, Robert, 196
Fish Creek, 69, 129, 134, 144, 182, 215n43
Flatt, Anthony (Tony), 96–7, 103, 108, 132–4, 140, 142, 150, 154, 165, 171, 185, 219n3
Flatt, Michael, 165, 185
Flatt, Tommy, Madeline, and family, 96, 153, 219n3
Fort Dunvegan, 18
Fort McLeod, 18
Fort Nelson, 93, 98, 143
Fort Resolution, 123
Fort St John, 3, 12, 18, 20, 23, 31, 35, 38–9, 51, 54–6, 58, 60, 65, 69–70, 84–6, 89, 94, 99–100, 106–9, 111, 117, 122, 125, 131, 134, 136, 141,
143, 146, 152, 156, 164, 166, 174–5, 182, 187–9, 196, 199, 201
Fort Vermillion, 18
Foster, Erving, 42
Foster family, 88
Fowler, Marguerita, 8, 10–11, 16–17, 203
Framst, Anton, Lillian, and family, 43, 58–9, 212n44
Freer, Percy, 165, 173, 184
Freer, Phyllis, 165, 184

Galibois, Joe (Indian Agent), 101, 110–11
Galilee, camp, 190–1
Gaylor, Fred, 196
Geake, Edward, 176, 230n9
Gedge, Evelyn, 10, 15, 26
Gething, King, 191
Gething, Neil, 76, 216n60
Girl Guides, 13, 27, 35, 43, 48–9, 69–70, 73–5, 90, 93, 98, 100, 104, 124, 144, 211n28, 220n10
God's Galloping Girl, 23, 26
Goodenough, Cecilia, 10, 12, 15–16, 22–3, 25, 31–2, 35–41, 43–50, 52–3, 56, 58–9, 61, 64–7, 69–82, 84–6, 90, 92, 95, 100, 105, 108, 111–12, 114–17, 120–1, 123–5, 128, 130–1, 134–5, 150–2, 154, 157, 159–60, 169, 171–2, 208n1, 229n37
Goodenough, Lady, 43, 45, 179
Goodenough, Admiral Sir William, 49
Good Shepherd Church, Taylor, 81–2, 88, 124, 129, 151, 197
Gough Memorial Outpost, 135, 141, 146, 155, 158, 164, 177–8, 180, 192, 194
Grande Prairie, 87, 149
Groate, Ed, 91
Guardians of the Peace, 120–2

Guiton, Rev. Geoffrey, 193, 232n3
Gumbo Slim, 91
Gundy Ranch, 107–9

Hadland, Arthur, Bernice, and family,
    89, 120, 218n86
Hadland, Dick, 185
Hadland, H.G. (Bert), 128, 177
Hadland, Philip, 141
Hadland, Roger, 120
Halfway River, 83, 85, 112, 115,
    117–18, 150, 160, 173, 183–4,
    191
Hampshire, Gwen, 123, 125–6, 128,
    133, 140, 143, 147, 149–52, 222n2
Hanson, Jean, 186
Hargreaves, Tommy, 32, 49, 135, 181
Harmer, Adeline, 4, 15–17, 22–3, 31,
    36, 87, 92, 95, 98, 195, 199, 201–2,
    208n1
Harris, Margaret and Ronald, 71–2
Hasell, Frances Hatton Eva, 4–6, 8,
    10–11, 14–17, 23, 25–6
Haslam, Muriel, 23, 32, 34, 43–5, 48,
    53, 57, 60–4, 66–9, 208n1
Henderson, Mrs Andrew, 175
Herron, Braden, 182, 220n19
Herron, M.W., 110
Higgenbotham, Elinor, 25–6, 167,
    183, 187, 197, 229n33
Hill, Jim, 195
Hines, Rev. John, 113–14, 221n29
Hodgson, Edith, 223n9
Hoffstrom, Mrs, 74–5
Hoffstrom, Otto, 74–5, 80, 129
Holdup, 37–8, 52, 59, 66, 211n32
Holland, Alwin, 187, 232n29
Holt, Miss (teacher), 168
Holy Cross Chapel, 57, 69, 128–9, 142,
    159, 164, 181, 185, 197, 223n11

Howe, Thelma, 48, 212n3
Hudson's Bay Company, 18
Hudson's Hope, 18, 25, 76, 80, 82, 85,
    100, 102, 110–11, 117–18, 130, 150–
    2, 159–60, 170, 190–4, 196
Humpheries, Mrs Tom. See Jones,
    Mary Duncan
Hunten, Bernice, 201, 234n12
Hunter, Alice, 48, 212n3
Hunter, Leslie, 96

Ignatieff, Count Vladimir (Jim),
    182–3, 231n22
Imperial Order Daughters of the
    Empire, 49, 60, 212n8
Indian Creek (later North Pine), 33,
    63–4, 73–4, 98, 102
Ingram, Jean, 16

Jarvis, Belle, 33, 64, 210n17
Jones, Charlie, 78–9, 182, 216n63
Jones, Madge, 78–9, 115
Jones, Mary Duncan, 201, 234n10

Kansas Pete. See Frank Reid
Kearney, Dr Garnet, 168
Kehler, Lillian and Willie, 82
Kelly, Mrs Albert, and family, 31, 63–4,
    208n3
Kemp, Dorothy, 137–8
Kemp, George, and family, 106,
    145–6, 220n13
Kemp, Stanley, 138, 146
Kierney, Dr, 178
Kindertransport, 199
Kingsley, Fred, Martha, and family,
    126–7
Kinney family, 100
Kirkhoff, Mrs, 139, 145
Kirkpatrick, George, and family, 89

Kisselbach, Julius, and family, 134, 148–50

Lake, Sir Richard and Lady, 157, 226n6
Lea family, 32–3, 147–9
Lewinski, David, 199–201, 234n4
Lowe, Mrs, 178, 180, 230n11
Lynn, George, 179

McArthur, Isabel (Isa), 16, 120, 132, 221n36
McKnight, James, Irene, and family, 40, 121, 211n37
McLeod, Henry, and family, 98, 113, 157
McLeod, John, 157–8, 190–1
McLeod, W.R., 90
McNamee, Jim, 77
Mann, Mrs Bill, 83–4, 217n71
Martley, Audrey, 137, 140, 142, 145, 170, 224n26
Maud, Dorothy (Messenger), 51, 213n13
May, Wilfrid Reid (Wop), 110, 112, 220n22
Middleton, Mrs, and family, 69, 124–7, 129, 161, 163
Mirfield Mission Hymnbook, 51, 116, 213n12
Montney district, 46–7, 65, 68–9, 87, 91, 147, 195, 210n16
Montreal, 134, 153, 193, 195, 201
Moon, Phyllis, 45, 60–1
Moor, Petronella (née Storrs), 3, 22, 136, 195
Moose River, 177–8
Morrison, Clarence, and family, 94
Morrow, Frank, Myrtle, and family, 70–1

Morse, Mildred, 185, 187, 197, 231n24
Mortimer, Rev. Hugh, 193, 233n7
Morton, W.L., 23, 211n28
Mothers' Union, 43
Mowick, Ivor, 114, 187
Murphy, Dennis, Louise, and family, 79–80
Murphy, Mrs, 68, 215n39

Nasser, Frank, 59
Neal, G.M., 49, 212n6
Newby, Catherine, 149, 151, 225n15
Nicely family, 67
Nielson, Fred, 44, 51, 54–5, 66, 96–8, 103–4, 119–20, 140, 142, 146, 150–1, 154, 212n45
Nielson, Gordon, 96
Neilson, Joyce, 119–20, 132
Nielson, R.H., 74, 104, 119
Nor'Pioneer Women's Institute, 135, 223n20
North Pine District, 51, 210n25
Noseworthy, Jean, 124, 134–5, 159, 161, 165
Noseworthy, Rev. Nathan, 124, 134–5, 138–9, 148, 154, 158–9, 164–5, 222n3

Ogilvie, James, 105, 220n11
Ohland, Charles, and family, 120, 218n87
Oldacres, Priscilla (later Mrs Russell Brown), 145–6, 149, 151, 153–4, 157, 169, 177, 179, 181–2, 184–5, 189–91, 193–4, 197, 225n12
Onslow, Hope, 8, 11–12, 15, 185–91, 197, 231n23
Orr, Hubert, 33, 210n18
Owen, Rosemary, 150–2, 157, 159–62, 169, 179, 185, 226n19

Packwood family, 177
Parsons, Clinton, 168, 229n36
Peace River, 3, 6, 10, 18–19, 22, 80,
    106–7, 112, 121, 183
Peace River Block, 6, 13–14, 17–18,
    20–1, 23, 27, 69, 181
Peace View, 31–2, 42, 45, 51, 82, 146
Peacewood, 17, 201
Peck, Donald, 159–60, 228n17
Peck, Vernon, 160
Peddie, Rev. Gordon, 130
Petter, Letitia, 213n18
Phillips family, 88, 98, 101, 218n85
Pickell, Leo, 61, 100, 107, 109, 134,
    172, 184, 214n28
Pickell, Flora, 160
Pine River, 35, 43, 58, 88, 98, 101,
    106–9, 138, 146, 150, 178, 193
Pine View School, 32, 209n15
Polenenko family, 131–2
Pouce Coupé, 6, 15, 32, 39, 90, 112,
    183, 209n12
Presbyterian church, 12, 20, 69, 86, 145
Price, Helen, 34, 210n23
Prince of Wales Fairbridge Farm
    School, 65, 157, 227n7
Proctor, Canon Thomas, 82–3, 85–6,
    124, 130, 217n70
Proctor, Mrs, 83
Providence Hospital, 53, 56, 118, 120,
    191, 144, 146, 161, 167–8, 213n20
Provincial Industrial School for Boys,
    62, 65, 214n29

Racehorse Ed, 77
Red Cross, 60, 93, 135, 177, 180, 194
Reid, Frank, 97, 219nn98–9
Rix, George (bishop of Caledonia),
    72, 80, 82–4, 118–19, 129–30, 164,
    192–4, 215n52

Rix, Mrs, 82–6, 217n79
Robbins, 33, 210n20
Robinson, Deaconess Margaret, 157,
    227n8
Rolla, 75, 109, 181, 216n57
Roman Catholics, 20, 34, 59, 80, 111,
    145, 159
Rose Prairie, 62, 68, 214n30
Royden, Maude, 9, 10–11

St Brigid's College, 158
St Christopher's College, 4–6, 8–9,
    15–16, 126, 137, 150–1, 223n6
St Faith's House, 8, 10
St Francis House, 184
St John's Church Hall, Baldonnel,
    23, 38, 44–5, 49, 51, 74, 81–2, 88,
    128–9, 209n9
St John's College, 203
St John's College School, 200
St Martin-in-the-Fields, 13, 23, 44–5,
    82, 94, 116, 129, 134–5, 138, 145,
    148, 154, 179, 181–2, 189, 210n26
St Matthias Church, 193–4, 232n4
St Peter's Church, 193–4, 232n5
Sandry, Iowne and Iva, 73, 98, 100,
    104
Saskatchewan, 5, 8, 99, 119–20, 174
Sayle, Iris Eugenie Friend, 5, 6, 8, 14
Schramm, Hugh, 199–202, 233n3
Selinka (Zelenke), Joe, and family,
    160, 186, 191–2, 194
Simmonds, Dewey, 180
Simpson, Benjamin, 38, 66, 97,
    211n34
Simpson, Johnny, 185
Simpson, William, Eileen, and family,
    115, 183–4
Simpson, Rev. W., 138, 145
Sisters of Charity of the Order of

Providence, 56, 118, 120–1, 179, 213n20

Slyman, Mrs M., 59, 214n25

Smith family, 60, 70, 83–4

Smith, Irene, 70, 83

Smith, Pete, 38

Smith, Peter B. (policeman), 61–2, 65, 101, 107–9, 138

Solorenko family, 50, 106, 137, 142–4

Solorenko, Jenny (later Nicholson), 142, 144, 225n6

Solorenko, Nellie, 50, 143–4, 188

Soman, family, 90, 145, 218n89

Sowden, Mrs, 170–1

Spence, Albert, Elizabeth, and family, 43, 50, 108–9, 119, 212n41

Spence, Jean, 119–20, 133, 150

Spence, Marjorie, 50

Spooner, Ruth, 71, 75–6, 79–80

Sprinkling, R.G., 159

Squaw Creek, 93, 101

Stevenson, Dorothy, 74

Stewart, Edith, 128

Stewart, Sylvia, 150–1, 226n18

Stokke, Claire, and family, 143–4, 224n5

Storrs, Christopher (bishop of Grafton, New South Wales), 3–4, 24, 155–8

Storrs, Mrs John. See Cust, Lucy

Storrs, Monica Melanie, 3–4, 6–8, 10–26, 199–202

Storrs, Sir Ronald, 3, 13, 96, 195, 200

Stubbington, Christina, 162, 164

Sunday School, 5, 11, 16, 23, 32–3, 35, 57–8, 67, 69, 75, 77, 97, 145, 189, 203

Sunday School by Post, 7, 34, 53, 70, 77, 210n22

Sunrise School, 52, 213n16

Sunset Prairie, 124–5

Symons, Hope. See Onslow, Hope

Symons, Robert, 6, 13, 22–5, 200, 202

Szibgy, Dr V.B., 174

Taylor (Flats), 16, 31–2, 74–5, 81, 85, 113, 129, 177, 185, 190, 201, 209n8

Taylor, Herbie, 91–2

Taylor, Roy, and family, 144, 149, 225n7

Tea Creek, 132, 165

Teather, George, 58–9, 107, 214n24

Ticehurst, Winnifred, 5

Thomas, Ed, 162

Thompson, Bertram (Buddy), 62, 214n31

Thompson, Conrad, 178

Thompson, Mrs, 62, 141, 224n2

Titus, Warren and Ida, 67, 94, 215n38

Tomlinson, Cyril, and family, 67

Tompkins, Philip, Emily, and family, 112, 167–9, 221n25

Tottenham, Patricia, 201

Transpine, 43, 106, 108

Tucker, Edwin, 84

Turner family, 36–7, 52

United Church of Canada, 12, 20, 33, 51, 69, 86, 88, 213n14

Vancouver, 21, 147, 157, 163, 194

Victoria, 70, 107, 135, 155–7, 189

Victoria League, 49, 212n7

Village Evangelists, 10, 201, 235n15

Waite, Harry, Edith, and family, 36, 211n29

Warr, Dorothy, 4, 13

Watson, Donald, 146

Watson, Emery, Ella, and family, 146, 225n13

Webber, Kate (later Mrs Earle), 16, 26, 120, 221n38
Westergaard, Nels, and family, 183, 230n1
Westergaard, Rosetta, 173–4, 183
Western Canada Sunday School Caravan Mission, 4–5, 7, 85, 137, 201, 224n27
Williamson, Janet, and family, 34, 98, 100–2, 104, 118, 195, 210n24
Wilson, Earle, 33–4, 210n21

Winnipeg, 5, 60, 203
Wolfendale, Esther (Tess), 87, 93, 118–19, 121, 128, 130, 218n83
Wolfendale, Rev. George, 11, 23, 31, 35, 39–41, 44–9, 51, 53–4, 66, 68–9, 75–6, 80, 83, 85–7, 94, 96, 102, 111, 118–19, 121, 124, 127–8, 130, 139, 152, 208n4
Womens' Auxiliary, 7, 31, 39, 85, 88, 145, 161, 184, 186
Women's Institute, 135, 137